Becoming

An Anthropological Approach to Understandings
of the Person in Java

Becoming

An Anthropological Approach to Understandings of the Person in Java

Konstantinos Retsikas

ANTHEM PRESS
LONDON · NEW YORK · DELHI

Anthem Press
An imprint of Wimbledon Publishing Company
www.anthempress.com

This edition first published in UK and USA 2014
by ANTHEM PRESS
75–76 Blackfriars Road, London SE1 8HA, UK
or PO Box 9779, London SW19 7ZG, UK
and
244 Madison Ave. #116, New York, NY 10016, USA

First published in hardback by Anthem Press in 2012

British Library Cataloguing-in-Publication Data
A catalogue record for this book is available from the British Library.

Library of Congress Cataloging-in-Publication Data
The Library of Congress has catalogued the hardcover edition as follows:
Retsikas, Konstantinos.
Becoming : an anthropological approach to understandings of the
person in Java / Konstantinos Retsikas.
p. cm.
Includes bibliographical references and index.
ISBN 978-0-85728-529-4 (hardback : alk. paper)
1. Ethnology–Indonesia–Java. 2. Ethnospychology–Indonesia–Java.
3. Personalism–Social aspects–Indonesia–Java. 4.
Kinship–Indonesia–Java. 5. Java (Indonesia)–Social life and
customs. I. Title.
GN635.I65R47 2012
305.8009598'2–dc23
2012021807

ISBN-13: 978 1 78308 310 7 (Pbk)
ISBN-10: 1 78308 310 7 (Pbk)

This title is also available as an ebook.

For M.

CONTENTS

LIST OF MAPS AND FIGURES

ACKNOWLEDGEMENTS

The research for this book was supported by a generous grant from the Greek State Scholarship Foundation (IKY) and the Firth Award of the Association of Social Anthropologists of the Commonwealth. The Royal Anthropological Institute and the University of Sussex have provided further financial backing through the Leach Fellowship, as well as encouragement for turning what started out as a thesis into a book. Finally, the project has greatly benefited from a two-term sabbatical leave kindly granted by the School of Oriental and African Studies (SOAS).

I wish to thank a number of individual people as well. At the University of Edinburgh, Janet Carsten, Dimitri Tsintjilonis, and Yael Navaro-Yashin were a great source of inspiration and unwavering support. Andrew Beatty, Leo Howe, and Terry King have generously given me the benefit of their expertise at various occasions. At SOAS, Magnus Marsden, Gabriele vom Bruck, Caroline Osella, and Trevor Marchand have helped me sharpen my arguments and supported me with their friendship.

Fieldwork was carried out under the auspices of the Indonesian Institute of Sciences (LIPI) and Universitas Airlangga in Surabaya. The late Pak Nyoman Naya Sujana, then dean of the faculty of social sciences, was extremely helpful in expediting permits. During my brief stay in Surabaya, Ari Sufiati, Desianto Budi Utomo and the family of the late Zainal Abidin were unfailingly hospitable. My thanks are also due to Sri Kustiati of Universitas Jember for lending me her unpublished dictionary of Madurese language.

This book owes a great deal to the people of Alas Niser and Probolinggo. My debt to them is as great as my affection for them. Since I refer to the fieldwork site by a pseudonym, I take the liberty here to refer to some of my companions by their real names: the family of the late Kyai Marzoeqie for their kindness; the families of Pak Suparman, Pak Bakir, Pak Bushit, Ibu Holida and of the late Haji Mashuri for being such good neighbours; the family of the late Pak Mahmur Yunus, in particular Mohammad Hanafi, for their abiding friendship and hospitality; Kyai Haz, Kyai Herianto, Kyai Hoirul Maruf, Mas Rushdi, Pak Putro, Pak Danang, Pak Noer, Pak Guco, Pak

Sugeng, Ibu Halima, Ibu Salmah for dispensing their knowledge and wisdom; Pak Priyono, Pak Mukhlis and the late Pak Pinto for enriching my stay with their art. Special thanks are also due to the students of the Islamic boarding school for teaching me about Islam. I would also like to thank A'lek Anna Triwiyastuti, Mas Mohammad Yusuf, Mas Hamzah and Mas Untung who were fine guides to local life's many facets.

Thanks are due to the publishers and editors of the following journals for allowing me to use parts of already published materials. Certain sections of Chapter 1 have previously appeared in an article entitled 'Being and Place: Movement, Ancestors, and Personhood in East Java, Indonesia' in *Journal of the Royal Anthropological Institute* 13, no. 4 (2007): 969–86. Part of the material discussed in Chapter 2 has been also considered in 'The Power of the Senses: Ethnicity, History, and Embodiment in East Java, Indonesia' in *Indonesia and the Malay World* 35, no. 102 (2007): 183–210; while Chapter 6 is based on reworkings of 'The Sorcery of Gender: Sex, Death, and Difference in East Java, Indonesia' in *South East Asia Research* 18, no. 3 (2010): 471–502.

PROLEGOMENON

Subjects as motion

> [T]he best images and parables should speak of time and becoming:
> they should be a eulogy and a justification of all transitoriness.
> (Nietzsche 1969, 111)

> It pertains to the essence of becoming to move and pull in both
> directions at once. Good sense affirms that in all things there is a
> determinable sense of direction; but paradox is the affirmation of both
> senses or directions at the same time.
> (Deleuze 2001, 3)

Guntur was a 25-year-old single man I befriended in the late 1990s in the town of Probolinggo, a beautiful and serene coastal small town in the province of East Java. As was the case with most town residents, Guntur was a fluent speaker of both the Javanese and Madurese languages. He had acquired these languages from his father, a retired civil servant who had come to Probolinggo from Surakarta in Central Java some thirty years before to take up a post in the local branch of the Department of Agriculture, and from his mother, a Madurese vegetable seller originally from the market town of Pamekasan in the adjacent island of Madura.

Guntur's parents' life stories are typical of many of the town's inhabitants. Their biographies as well those of many others are marked by migration, the movement away from their places of origin, commonly located in other parts of Java and in Madura, and centre on a conjunction, a coming together that is best conveyed in the emphasis people place on finding a job and a spouse, having children and prospering in the small town of Probolinggo.

At home, Guntur's Javanese side was actively cultivated by his father, an avid exegete of Javanese 'custom'. He schooled all of his four children in Javanese language, teaching them its low- and middle-level speech levels, and passed on to them his enthusiasm for puppet-theatre performances (*wayang kulit*, Ind.). Despite being unable to follow the high-level speech employed in such performances, Guntur, who was a student of economics in the local university, used to spend his Saturday evenings in the company of university friends watching televised puppet-theatre performances together and talking about them with much enthusiasm. I would often join this company and get drawn into the adventures of the characters discussed, especially those of Arjuna that held so much fascination for my interlocutors. The friends' approach to puppet theatre, its characters, and performances is indicative of wider engagements with the art form carried out by locals and anthropologists of Java alike. According to such engagements, *wayang kulit* exemplifies all that the category of 'Java' is about. This 'Java' Guntur and his friends would often describe as being bound with the quality of *halus* (Ind.), a dispositional and affective capacity for acting with eloquence, refinement, humility and circumspection towards others with which the Javanese are held to be endowed.

At the same time, Guntur had a discernible Madurese side to him which his relationship with his mother supported and sustained. Despite speaking Javanese to his father at home, he, his mother and siblings would converse in Madurese, deploying the lower speech level deemed appropriate for such intimate relations, it being only one they commanded. In addition, Guntur would often use low Madurese with some of his neighbours – while engaging with others in Javanese – as well as with the traders, both male and female, in Probolinggo's central market where his mother was making a living as a vegetable seller and where he acted as her trusted assistant. The employment of low Madurese in the market context as the instantiation of Guntur's Madurese side was accompanied by his movement and speech acquiring a certain assertiveness, forcefulness and even combativeness that turned his dealings with the other traders into an event with visible losers and winners. Bargaining hard over prices, a common practice in which Guntur excelled, was accompanied by humour and joking, often crass, obtuse and filled with sexual innuendo, which traders enjoyed participating in often at the expense of one another. Gundur's habitual style in the market involved the deployment of a series of distinct dispositions and affects which are locally qualified as *kasar* (Ind.); that is, coarse, unrefined, boastful and fierce. Such affects and manners of orientation are closely associated across Java with the category of 'Madura' and with the people that inhabit this arid island located just off the eastern coast of Java and across a narrow strait.

Condensed in these recollections of Guntur as an actor embedded in relationships and moving transversally across varied contexts and situations is the key theme this book addresses: namely what are we as anthropologists, social scientists or humanities scholars to make of people like Guntur who, rather than being endowed with a given, singular identity, are differentially actualized and constituted as a result of the relationships in which they participate? Somewhat differently put, the central question this book raises and seeks to answer is how are we to conceive of individuals such as Guntur who, despite their obvious givenness due to being veritably produced out of specific relationships such as those of filiation, friendship and trading, move (and are moved) in opposite directions, avoiding mere repetition and affirming difference?

Guntur's capacity for actualizing both the categories of 'Java' and 'Madura' in the modes of his behaviour and with regards to specific relations pose considerable challenges to our thinking of the person as an individual endowed with an identity. The becoming-Javanese and becoming-Madurese that Guntur participates in are marked by an indifference towards the assertion and achievement of 'identity' and instead foreground personhood as entangled in a process of endless *transformation*. The subject these becomings enunciate is thus transitive and more akin to a verb rather than a noun, closer to the unfolding of a process than to the manifestation of an essence. This is so for Guntur's person is motivated neither by choice nor by interest. Both choice and interest involve the positing of the subject as determined in advance and with *a priori* knowledge of who he/she is. For such a subject, social relations are assumed to be exterior and of secondary importance as it is taken to correspond, first and foremost, to pure, disembodied consciousness. In contrast, Guntur is a self-differing person in the sense that the process he is involves movement in opposite directions with his becoming-refined implicating his becoming-coarse. Such a person I call *diaphoron*, for it is constituted on the grounds of an irreducible difference that animates and motivates it. The *diaphoron* person is devoid of unity either dialectically or transcendentally achieved for it is always in motion and already a becoming. As becoming it differs constantly from itself.

Guntur is *halus* now, *kasar* before; Javanese tomorrow; Madurese yesterday. To the extent that we differ constantly from ourselves, difference assumes a positive form of relationality that cannot be negatively defined as the lack of self-similarity without letting difference's ontological and sociological potential slip like water through our hands. This potential is more productively taken hold of and realized when we take difference as guiding the relationship articulated between becomings. For Guntur, the becoming-refined and becoming-coarse can indeed be grasped as exclusive alternatives – Guntur is either Javanese or Madurese, this person is either man or a woman, this woman is either a wife or a sister. However, this is a conceptualization imposed on us by thinking in terms of individuals as singular and of identities as given. The end result is for identity to be seen as original and difference as derivative; for relationships to become exterior and secondary, while self-identical individuals are taken as primary. But if we are to do justice to ethnographic encounters and the surprises they entail, which constantly throw us off balance in the field, if we are to situate ourselves in precisely those moments of surprise and wonder and seek to recover and seize on feeling off-balance for the purpose of anthropological analysis, then ethnographic descriptions can be neither straightforward nor retain an aura of persuasiveness rooted in the evocation of the familiar and the common.

What this book aims to achieve is to do justice to my ethnographic encounters with Guntur and the people of Probolinggo that unfolded during 18 months of fieldwork from October 1998 to March 2000, as well as during subsequent visits to the area, the more recent in the summer of 2010. Such an endeavour demands that Western metaphysics are bracketed and the positing of the individual as an autonomous, self-identical, indivisible and naturally given entity is interrogated as a figure that has been produced (and is still being produced) by at least two centuries of religious disenchantment, labour alienation, democratic representation, and biomedical organicism. There is no reason, however, to repeat here the uncomfortable and counterintuitive lessons Nietzsche's (1967, 1969) and Foucault's (1973, 1979) genealogical readings of Western science, philosophy, and morality have taught us.[1] There is equally no reason for going over the significant contributions of Mauss (1985) and Dumont (1986), which have shown us from a different perspective and with unparalleled insight the culturally peculiar and historically contingent status of the self-identical and self-interested individual in the record of human diversity. The Industrial Revolution, the capitalist definition of goods as commodities and of markets as a separate domain of social action, taken together with the ideals of the European Enlightenment have had a profound influence on the way we understand the person. Conceived as an individual, this way of understanding the person corresponds to a key presupposition that critical

---

1 In *On the Genealogy of Morals*, Nietzsche laments the fateful accidents that grammar introduces to thought: 'only owing to the seduction of language (and of the fundamental errors of reason that are petrified in it) which conceives and misconceives all effects as conditioned by something that causes effects, by a "subject", can it appear otherwise' (1967, 45). The overcoming of language necessitates for Nietzsche a strategy that is best exemplified in his concept of eternal recurrence. If the putative givenness of the subject is rooted in the misrecognition of an effect of forces as the ultimate cause, then, he asserts, the willing affirmation and enthusiastic embracing of the subject as an effect opens up and activates a new figure. This new figure that Nietzsche calls the over-man is not so much a negation of the human as we know it but a reconceptualization of it as a becoming, an effected 'entity' that is capable of acting only on condition of this very affirmation. Both Foucault's conception of the subject as discursively produced and to anticipate what follows, Deleuze's emphasis on becoming form further elaborations of Nietzsche's critical insights. For a short summary of the convergences and divergences of the work of these philosophers, see Colebrook (1999).

scholarship has elicited as foundational to Western metaphysics. This and other unnatural givens, such as the culture–nature, subject–object, modern–traditional, individual–society distinctions, require no further explication as to their pervasiveness in the West (Latour 1993; M. Strathern 1988; Viveiros de Castro 1998). What requires rehearsing, however, is 'becoming' and its own modality of producing the given. Lest I am accused of drawing too rigid a distinction between the West and Java, let me try to loosen it with an amusing example that will throw further light into the relation that becoming privileges.

Lewis Carroll's (2006) heroine, Alice, follows a white rabbit down a rabbit hole and finds herself in Wonderland, a place in which nothing is as it seems. Here not only are animals capable of language and suckling babies turn out to be pigs – these ideas are, after all, well known to anthropologists working in Southeast Asia as well as beyond – but the magic contained in cakes, potions and mushrooms allows Alice for the first time to experience and undergo profound transformations with her size shooting up and down 'like a telescope', shrinking to ten inches short and growing into the dimensions of a full-blown house, and vice versa.

Alice is Gilles Deleuze's favourite heroine, too. In *The Logic of Sense* (2001), Deleuze uses Carroll's books as an opening to his exploration of the makings and un-makings of sense and non-sense. What Alice's adventures amount to, according to the French philosopher, is the foregrounding of becoming as an unlimited, infinite process that the virtual place called Wonderland privileges, calling for the liberation of difference from its subordination to identity as prior and given. This is how Deleuze 'reads' Alice:

> All these reversals as they appear in infinite identity have one consequence: the contesting of Alice's personal identity and the loss of her proper name. The loss of the proper name is the adventure which is repeated throughout Alice adventures. For the proper or singular name is guaranteed by the permanence of *savoir*. The latter is embodied in general names designating pauses and rests, in substantives and adjectives, ... But when substantives and adjectives begin to dissolve, when names ... are carried away by the verbs of pure becoming and slide into the language of events, all identity disappears from the self, the world, and God. (2001, 5; italics in the original)

In Wonderland, Alice's identity/size is subject to fluctuation and reversal; she is becoming smaller than she is now and is bound to become larger later. She is certainly not larger and smaller at the same time; her becoming is a differential relation that unfolds through her moving and pulling in two directions at once with her size eluding both stability and the present. Alice is precisely a *diaphoron* person, a self-differing person as she does not grow without shrinking and does not shrink without growing. Her size in any given moment does not correspond to a prior or original identity, rather is only a pause and a rest; such pauses and rests are derivative of the transitive process that her unending becoming amounts to.

What Carroll and Deleuze invite us to ponder is Alice-as-becoming. Such becoming is the person, a person that constantly differs from itself. At the same time, they insist on seeing Alice's proper name, i.e. her identity, as a secondary principle produced by the unfolding of difference. In this regard, Alice's becoming is best conceived as a *relation between reciprocally presupposed differentials*. Let me explain: in this scheme, 'small' is not the opposite of 'large' and 'large' does not amount to the negation of 'small'; difference is not conceived as a relation between two terms each of which is endowed with a prior identity. Rather, difference is the ontological ground of unlimited becoming and the means by which the empirical diversity of sizes, forms and identities is given.[2] The inversion of the order of priority of difference and identity effected in this way is complemented by Deleuze's reworking of what appear to be oppositional terms and contradictory phenomena into immanent dimensions of becoming; that is, equally necessary and mutually implicated aspects of a single process with one term 'always concealed by the other, yet continuously coming to the aid of, or subsisting under, the other' (2001, 4). Alice's operation 'like a telescope' offers no better image of the dynamic co-implication of small and large as her larger size subsists under and inheres in her smaller frame, and vice versa.

As the unfolding of a process, becoming is, for Deleuze, synonymous with two operations: as well as constantly working towards the disaggregation, or deterritorialization if you prefer, of any given form Alice takes, causing

---

2 Becoming is a difference-driven process 'by which the given is given' (Deleuze 1994, 222). The given, Deleuze tells us in *Difference and Repetition* (1994) must be understood as a secondary operation under which difference is pressed into temporary forms and multiplicity is translated into singularity. His philosophy thus rests on a consideration of the morphogenetic processes that create individuated forms out of differential multiplicities. These processes, which are both unstable and reversible, are discussed on the basis of a tripartite ontological scheme that posits three closely interrelated planes: the virtual, the intensive, and the extensive. By means of the mediation of the intensive, the multiplicities that organize the virtual become actualized in the extensive as the distinctive and singular forms we take for granted. At the same time, however, a reverse process is always in operation which acts to disaggregate and detotalize what is already given before a new cycle of formation/production takes hold. The political implications of these notions are worked out in the two volumes of the Capitalism and Schizophrenia project, *Anti-Oedipus* (1977) and *A Thousand Plateaus* (2004), that Gilles Deleuze co-wrote with Félix Guattari.

her to be swept and carried away, reeling her into different shapes, it also passes through all of these shapes while connecting them disjunctively, i.e. through affirming their difference. Becoming is therefore nothing more, and nothing less, than a specific kind of relation, a particular mode of relating differentials; it is, in other words, 'a positive principle of relationality, meaning both disjunction and connection … rather than a merely negative want of similarity' (Viveiros de Castro 2009, 245.) Small and large are thus not only reciprocally presupposed as immanent dimensions of a process but are also intrinsically connected to each other through their processual unfolding. The relation becoming privileges therefore amounts to a disjunctive synthesis or a pairing of two terms with each term providing the context and the ground of the other. As such, becoming is not to be conflated with the Hegelian dialectic that operates by synthesizing two opposing terms into a higher or superior unity, itself accomplished by the positing of a third term which manages to contain and thus overcome the earlier opposition. Indeed, Deleuze (1994) explicitly denounces the dialectic as subordinating difference to identity, process to stasis, and becoming to being. Alice by contrast forces us to take her self-differing seriously and without recourse to a superior unity invites us to see difference at the very heart of being as infinite becoming.

In a way, all that the current book is about is already here: the becoming-Javanese and becoming-Madurese of Guntur are running in parallel with the becoming-smaller and the becoming-larger of Alice. In both cases, the person is a becoming and thus differentially actualized in accordance to the contexts and relationships in which it is embedded. Immanent in these actualizations are two sides, each of which subsists under and inheres in the other even as one side is concealed and hidden from view in favour of the other which in the course of events comes to be revealed and made known. The categories 'Javanese' and 'Madurese', 'small' and 'large', thus do not amount to exclusive alternatives but to mutually implicated lines of movement, the trajectories traced by the person as it unfolds and is unfolded. This person I refer to as the *diaphoron* person.

The *diaphoron* person is elusive due to the multiplicity of the shapes it assumes, yet its presence is both definite and distinctive. Its transitive temperament, due mainly to the never-ending processes of transformation it participates in as an effect is coupled with it being veritably agentive. Both *this* and *that*, the *diaphoron* person resists the assignation of cross-contextual and atemporal identity, for it is an assemblage made of differentiated parts. Such parts are often coded in Java as differential dispositions, affects and capacities. Made up of and moving towards both Java and Madura, the past and the future, the feminine and the masculine, the higher and the lower, the human and the non-human, alternately and successively, the person I wish to designate *as such* is conditioned by a fundamental, irreducible difference – i.e. made up by an internal alterity – which, as we shall see shortly, furnishes the very grounds of its sociality.

In this book, the *diaphoron* person is a figure of thought through which I am attempting to explore the uncommon conditions of possibility of the person. In this thought experiment, the figure of the *diaphoron* person is emergent, evolving out of my involvement in long-term fieldwork in the East Javanese town of Probolinggo and of my wonder and constant bafflement regarding the events, relationships, and activities I saw people there engaged in. The *diaphoron* person also bears the implications of my own participation in such events, relationships and activities as a relatively young and unmarried male researcher, who conducted the majority of his research while residing in a small Islamic boarding school in the town's periphery. The concept of becoming that I explore here is hence intrinsically related to my own experiences during fieldwork. These I have narrated elsewhere (Retsikas 2008) as involving a process of becoming a moral Muslim subject despite having not converted to Islam. In a sense then, my own trajectory is echoed here in the very descriptions and concepts I am advancing and employing to render my interlocutors' personhood communicable to an audience unfamiliar with Java. At the same time, the figure of the *diaphoron* person is also embedded within a set of views provided by the library, having grown out of subsequent engagement with anthropological and non-anthropological literatures. As such, the *diaphoron* person is also a product of scholarly imagination, the parameters and overall problems of which are not to be conflated with those of my informants. Within my shifting back and forth between personal experiences, scholarly commitments, and what properly belongs to my fieldwork friends, neighbours and acquaintances is the very necessary and inescapable analytical movement of any ethnographic monograph as an assemblage of heterogeneous elements. This book is therefore not only about the *diaphoron* person but is *diaphoron* itself.

Becoming

It is perhaps impossible to write about Java, or Indonesia for that matter, without having to come to terms with Geertz's monumental work on the subject. This is due to Geertz's unparalleled influence on the ethnography of the area but also because it is often the case that people in Java seem only too ready to explicate themselves to foreign tourists and anthropologists alike through the very same categories and conceptual connections that Geertz established as paradigmatic. While his tripartite division of the Javanese religious landscape is well known and widely accepted by many educated Javanese, every student of anthropology at one point or another has had to cut his/her teeth by engaging with Geertz's classic essay 'From the Native's Point View' (1993). While the text is often taught as a critical response to the Malinowskian privileging of empathy as the very basis of anthropological knowledge, it is more directly concerned with elucidating alternative conceptions of the person to the Western one.

In his unique writing style and highly relativistic manner, Geertz's starting point is:

> The Western conception of the person as a bounded, unique, more or less integrated motivational and cognitive universe, a dynamic centre of awareness, emotion, judgment, and action organised into a distinctive whole and set contrastively both against other such wholes and against the social and natural background, is, however, incorrigible it may seem to us, a rather peculiar idea within the context of the world's cultures. (1993, 59)

To this odd conception that foregrounds uniqueness in an era of mass production Geertz counter-opposes a triadic set consisting of Javanese, Balinese and Moroccan conceptions of the person that differ markedly and dramatically both from one another and from the Western one. While the Moroccan way of conceiving persons grounds them in relational contexts and proceeds by way of arranging them in a series of nested categories, one more inclusive than the other, and the Balinese seem to view the person as an de-individuated performer in a theatre of status distinctions in which very exact positions are statically filled by subsequent generations, the Javanese view of the person revolves around two sets of contrasts that finding no resolution or integration into a higher order result in 'a bifurcate conception of the self' (1993, 61).

While Moroccans and Balinese in their different ways go about insisting that the person is social in the sense of being always already enmeshed in social relations, Geertz suggests the Javanese divide the person up by means of a two-fold partition. No longer an undifferentiated whole, the person is conceived as split in four. These partitions Geertz relates interpretatively both to the conceptual division between the 'inside' (*batin*, Ind.) and the 'outside' (*lahir*, Ind.), the emotional life of the human person versus his/her outward behaviour, and to the distinction between the 'refined' (*halus*) and 'vulgar' (*kasar*). The relationships between the two divisions are quite complex and can be summarized as follows. *Batin* and *lahir* correspond not only to highly autonomous, separate and independent realms of the person but are also thought of as in need 'to be put in proper order independently' (1993, 61). In this connection, the second pair comes into play with the goal being to avoid acting with vulgarity and coarseness, striving instead towards achieving refinement, subtlety and smoothness both inwardly and outwardly. The primary means for accomplishing this coveted goal involve firstly, the undertaking of religious regimes of asceticism that smooth one's *batin* and secondly, the regularization of *lahir* through conforming to social rules of etiquette. However effective the ordering of *batin* and *lahir* is, the person remains nevertheless the locus of dissonance as the difference between 'inside' and 'outside' can be neither surmounted nor displaced. Thus Geertz concludes that for the Javanese

> An inner world of stilled emotion and an outer world of shaped behaviour confront one another as sharply distinguished realms unto themselves, any particular person being but the momentary locus, so to speak, of that confrontation, a passing expression of their permanent existence, their permanent separation, and their permanent need to be kept in their own order. (Geertz 1993, 61)

Geertz's analysis of Javanese ontology – this is the term he himself uses – as premised on split subjects and foundational divisions is carried forwards in this book by the concept of the *diaphoron* person. The *diaphoron* person, I have already argued, is to be understood not as the site and source of a pre-given identity but as an unstable and shifting subject permeated by and constituted by means of difference, a self-differing person that assumes a multiplicity of forms which correspond to the pauses and rests of unlimited becoming. If this carrying forward exercise is to take effect, however, both Geertz's interpretative style of analysis that coheres around the cross-cultural translation of concepts as the differential representations of an objectively given and shared world and his emphasis on anchoring such representations to a sole theme – theatre in Bali, *nisba* in Morocco, dissonance in Java – need to be approached with caution. For what we are dealing with here is certainly not representations or worldviews but presuppositions and assumptions that belong to worlds that are differentially constituted and lived.[3] In order for us to better grasp these disparate worlds, it is not enough to simply emphasize different concepts. We have to rethink and reconceptualize difference itself, inclusive of culture difference. To this end, it is also necessary to avoid reducing the complexities of what we encounter in the field to a few principles, themes or foundations that act as metonyms for what is veritably a much more open and undetermined field.

---

3 As Viveiros de Castro puts it, 'the problem is not that Amazonians and Euro-Americans give different names to (or have different representations of) the same things; the problem is that we and they are not talking about the same things' (2009, 241). On the limits of cross-cultural translation, see also Retsikas (2010a).

While the present book makes no claims regarding the first task, i.e. the reconceptualization of culture difference, it nevertheless aims to show that the *diaphoron* person is not simply the result of the operation of two sets of 'contrasts' but a figure one runs into in a manifold of social plateaus. As such, it is neither simply anchored in nor merely reducible to a determinable and knowable set of factors, themes, or causes. Instead the *diaphoron* person will be shown in this book to proliferate acentrically in all kinds of directions and to thrive in a plurality of local ideas and practices that in turn have to do with what we conventionally call ethnicity, kinship, religion, sorcery and place. In addition to having two sides, one of which is eclipsed and the other revealed as a result of particular encounters and relations, the *diaphoron* person is also a multiplicity, containing within itself an assorted set of differences, with its form changing every time it crosses over and moves from one plateau into another.

In the plateau of ethnicity, the *diaphoron* person of East Java is stabilized as an assemblage of Madurese and Javanese parts. These parts are themselves related to the *halus–kasar* hierarchical distinction Geertz mentions above. The distribution of such parts among the current inhabitants of Probolinggo is intrinsically related to the demographic history of this part of Java – discussed in Chapter 1 – that during the nineteenth century saw large numbers of Javanese and Madurese migrating into, taking up residence in and making a living out of its resources that related principally to land and its products. Subsequent intensive processes of inter-ethnic marriage and of spatial intermingling in ethnically mixed neighbourhoods along with extensive and widespread patterns of exchange of food, prayers, and ancestors among the migrants and their descendants have contributed towards the self-identification of today's inhabitants as 'mixed people' (*orang campuran*, Ind.), i.e. as a people who are disjunctively connected both to 'Java' and to 'Madura'. Among the key contentions of this book, set out in Chapter 2, is the argument that this mixing has neither cancelled out nor displaced the distinction between Javanese and Madurese but has worked so as to foreground difference as constitutive of the experience of locals' sense of self. To be mixed, in other words, does not amount to the superseding of the hierarchy that marks the relation between the categories of 'Java' and 'Madura' and the people these categories are associated with. Quite the contrary is true. As I have shown before (2007b) and argue again here, ethnic difference is re-inscribed from a new and innovative point of view, that of mixed people that strive to portray themselves as the occupants of the apex of hierarchical pyramid in their capacity to act both in Madurese and Javanese ways and manners.

In the plateau of sorcery, the elements that make up the *diaphoron* person change and involve the unstable assembly of masculine and feminine capacities and affects therein. As every ethnographer of Java knows only too well, sorcery is a pervasive and constant concern among the peoples of this most densely populated island. In general, sorcery is intrinsically connected with acute anxieties and fears regarding the true intentions and feelings of significant others and intimates that includes ones' kin, neighbours, friends and work colleagues. The book's excursion into sorcery ideas and practices undertaken in Chapter 6 is carried out with the explicit aim of showing that the person is locally understood as an internally differentiated being also with respect to gender. In all respects and purposes, it is conceived as an androgynous entity that becomes singularly male or female in view of the specific relations it enters, voluntarily or not. In the case of sorcery, as in the case of ethnicity – remember the example of Guntur – what we often take to be formally opposed characteristics (male and female) are locally conceived as reciprocally implicated and presupposed terms, with masculinity held to subsist under and inhere in femininity. The internal gender difference that makes up the person along with its transformability from male to female, and vice versa, is the very ground on which sorcerers conduct their business. Their techniques are thus uniquely designed to use both such gendered difference and such becoming for their own and their client's advantage through the delivery of misfortune, pain and death to their intended victim whose gender, in the course of sorcery rites, is made to change from male to female; that is, from relatively closed and invulnerable to relatively open, porous, and susceptible to attack.

Quite paradoxically, sorcery's efficacy, I argue, stems partly from the evocation of weddings and marriage transactions as the fee the sorcerer's client submits to the sorcerer is construed as *mahar* (Ind.; *mahr* in Arabic; also referred to as *mas kawin*), an essential part of the validity of any marriage contract according to Islam that both Madurese and Javanese profess in their vast majority. The practice of *mahar* corresponds to the zone of indiscernibility as far as the differences that organize the plateaus of sorcery and kinship are concerned. *Mahar* is the threshold, the door that leads from sorcery to kinship and back; it is their intersection, the borderline on which the differences that make them up meet, communicate and cross over; it is the thread that ties such differences and plateaus together.

In distinct Southeast Asian fashion, persons in Probolinggo are conceived in sibling terms. Indeed, one of the three most important questions any newcomer in the area is asked to provide information about is how many siblings one has – the other two being where does one come from and whether he/she is married. The right way to answer this question is to include oneself in the counting, that is to render oneself as part of a set (of two, three, four, etc.) siblings and often to designate one's precise position in the set in terms of birth order, i.e. first, second, third, etc. The conception of person as part of a set,

I argue in Chapter 3, presents a number of interesting features. Firstly, the emphasis placed on the set is strongly associated with the identitarian union of siblings who are thought of as being and acting as one, in accord with reference to similarly constituted sets. Sibling unity is best exemplified and actively cultivated by the siblings' sharing a common set of progenitors, a common dwelling and a hearth, having access to a commonly held property that is yet to be allocated, etc. (see Carsten 1997; Errington 1987; Freeman 1970). Indeed, locals of Probolinggo place great emphasis on both the values of solidarity and co-operation that are said to permeate sibling relations and on the feelings of love and care that animate and motivate such values. At the same time, however, such a set is unequivocally conceptualized as dividable, with the operation of the incest taboo ensuring the parting of the members of the set. This divisibility, which is fully actualized with marriage and the distribution of the parents' property between the parties involved according a variety of rules and preferences, corresponds to a latent presence that always and already 'haunts' the unity of the set. Indeed, in Probolinggo as well as in numerous other societies in the Indonesian archipelago birth order more than gender arranges the set of siblings according to precise relations permeated by hierarchy, and thus, by difference. The singularity that sibling sets form, in other words, is both contingent and unstable for it is subject to processes of dissolution and separation the first effected by marriage and the second by means of the internal relations of hierarchical difference that regulate behaviours between birth order juniors and seniors. It goes without saying that such behaviours are equally elaborated in Java as involving the demonstration of respect and deference younger siblings owe older ones, and the duty of care and personal sacrifice even that elder siblings owe their younger brothers and sisters.

In Chapters 3 and 4, I reflect on the very important literature on kinship in island Southeast Asia. Taking inspiration from Lévi-Strauss's notion of the House (1988), I argue that sibling sets instantiate the *diaphoron* person in the plateau of kinship. The person the set so designates is pure becoming for two reasons. The first relates to what has been said above, i.e. the entanglement of the processes of singularity formation and hierarchical separation and dissolution that constantly evoke each other forth, corresponding to two sides of the same phenomenon. Such processes are never ending as each particular sibling set is but a momentary pause and rest of all those sets preceding it and flowing from it, a point that Errington eloquently conveys in observing that 'relationship terminology [in Southeast Asian islands] arranges people into [past, present, and future] layers of siblings' (1987, 409).

The second reason for siblingship realizing the *diaphoron* person is that it amounts to a very particular, very special topos as it connects affinity with

descent, and vice versa. The way this is achieved involves both mythology and
ritual praxis. In common with several other Southeast Asian island societies,
Javanese mythological accounts of the world's founding tell of the story of
the very strong attraction between a heavenly pair of brother and sister, of
their forced separation, and of the gift of rice agriculture that the sister made
to humanity. The myth, I argue, forms the background for the conduct of
wedding rituals which are dedicated to fashioning the bride and the groom
into younger sister and elder brother respectively, something that is both
reflected and enforced by the deployment of the relevant kinship terminology
that remains in place at least until the first offspring arrives. Condensed in
the relationship of siblingship, therefore, is an alternative conceptualization
of the social that previous anthropologists working in the region have done
well to emphasize though not fully explore. This alternative conceptualization
my argument is gives primacy neither to the doctrine of descent as vertical
encompassment nor to the principle of alliance as reciprocal recognition.
What the conceptualization of the social in terms of siblingship does is to
highlight the links that connect descent to affinity and the processes of their
mutual convertibility. More than anything else, siblingship brings attention
to the becomings which persons must undergo as a precondition for the
achievement of reproduction, fertility, abundance, profusion, excess and life
itself. To the extent that siblingship is synonymous with the attainment of
abundance, abundance is contingent on the person being seen from the outset
and forever as a member of a divisible set and/or part of a dissoluble pair. The
referential capacity of this pair is not limited to relations pertaining among the
offspring of a couple but in a distinct fashion encompasses the relations that
organize and make up the couple itself.

   The becomings that the incest taboo and siblingship set in motion do not
exhaust local conceptualizations of the person however 'constraining' and
specific they might be for every anthropologist working on island Southeast
Asia. The unstable assemblages of discrete and hierarchical parts that sibling
pairs form are supplemented – in the double sense of the term as addition
and displacement (see Strathern 1999, 238) – by other, equally contingent
assemblages one readily encounters in the plateau of religious devotion. Much
has been written about the place and relevance of asceticism in Java. The
works of Anderson (1990) and Keeler (1987) have done much to illuminate
both the links that the Javanese establish between religious asceticism and
power, on the one hand, and between abstinence and selfhood, on the other.
In particular, Keeler's argument about the Javanese ideal of selfhood is
highly pertinent for my purposes. Keeler shows how the Javanese sense of
self revolves around the vagaries, risks and dangers everyday encounters
entail, on the one hand, and, on the other, the promises of unsurpassable

self-assuredness, safety and ascendancy that asceticism is credited with bringing about. Asceticism, he writes, 'is a kind of reaction to the vulnerability people sense in encounter' (1987, 49, n.10) with the decision to disengage from the world being the result of an attempt to temporarily escape the incessant negotiation of status distinctions affected by, and manifested in, among other things, speech level use. Stepping out of the uncertainties of everyday encounters and getting engaged in silent meditation, Javanese men as well as some women willingly undergo ascetic practices inclusive of fasting and abstaining from sex, with the explicit aim that the more one suppresses one's desires and the more one is without selfish interest, the more one will be capable of defining, or imposing upon, other people one's own speech, wishes and claims.

Perhaps Keeler has overstated the extent to which 'encounter and asceticism [are] two opposite and complementary modes of action' (1987, 49). As I endeavour to show in Chapters 5 and 6, ascetic regimes do involve encounters with non-human beings that can be equally risky and dangerous as well as very promising in terms of accruing beneficial outcomes. Chapter 6 ventures into a consideration of the hazardous nature of social relationships established with non-human beings while Chapter 5 takes a close look into narratives associated with the acquisition of the capacity to heal by people who subscribe to traditionalist, Sufi-inspired modes of Islamic piety. East Java, within which Probolinggo is situated, is widely and validly considered as one of key strongholds of Nahdlatul Ulama, Indonesia's largest Muslim organization that is centred upon the figure of Islamic scholars (*kyai*) and networks of Islamic boarding schools (*pondok pesantren*, Ind.) similar to the one I found myself living in for more than a year. My close acquaintance with such figures and such traditions is conveyed in the narratives of two people who are locally renowned for their abilities in dealing successfully with the troubles and misfortunes that afflict humans. Such healers are endowed with what I argue can productively be thought of as heterogeneous assemblages of human and non-human parts and elements that are intensively connected through circuits of relations that ascetic regimes of religious devotion foster and maintain. The difference, on the basis of which such persons are constituted, is traceable to processes of becoming-sacred. Such processes are transformational as they involve the voluntary and temporary annihilation of the human and are accompanied by gifts of divine grace as semi-permanent attachments and additions to the make-up of the healers' bodies. Such non-human attachments are furthermore subject to detachment and circulation that proceed by means of both commodity logic and exchange relations in terms of their transmission to other human recipients who then become able to perform healing with a variety of degrees of efficacy.

The themes that the current book deals with are offered as an incitement for us to reflect on the implications this multiplicity of differences has for the *diaphoron* person as it, and the accompanying ethnography, crosses over from one plateau to the other. In a way, the current book is an old-fashioned sort of ethnographic monograph. I make no apologies for evoking here a certain ideal, that of a total ethnography which guided many anthropologists working during the discipline's classical era. Evans-Prichard's *The Nuer* (1969) and Leach's *Political Systems of Highland Burma* (1970) provide perhaps the most iconic examples of such a programme of study, containing descriptions and analyses of a bewildering variety of materials that encompass almost everything from ecological conditions and modes of livelihood to material culture, kinship and political systems, religious practices and ethnic relations. Beyond the crude and unreflexive functionalist 'cutting' of the social into distinct institutions and the simplistic task of organically relating back what had previously been rendered separate, beyond even a certain encyclopaedic ambition to match the ambitions of colonial governments, there was, it has to be finally admitted, among anthropologists of that generation an admirable lack of certainty about what was important to the people one studied with, and a marvellous dearth of *a priori* convictions about what constituted politics, or kinship, or economy in such faraway places. This was a moment of aporia that I want to recapture and redeploy.

During my fieldwork I had the privilege of finding myself with plenty of time to spare and this plenitude was matched with the generosity of the people I worked with who were more than willing to put up and assist with my rather awkward queries. For this I will be eternally indebted. Due to circumstance and good intentions then I was able to follow diverse lines of inquiry and diverge into all sorts of concerns, most of which have found their way in this book. However, the total ethnography I advocate here for is quite different from totalizing ethnography. Whereas the former is an exploration that moves laterally and stays on a level, flat surface, comparing and contrasting phenomena so as to evince their characteristic ways of diverging, the latter moves vertically and seeks to reach deep into unfathomable depths so as to unearth and extract the factor(s) that make things the way they are. In other words, whereas total ethnography is concerned with mapping the movements and the transformations incurred on such flat plane of a 'thing' that differs constantly from itself, totalizing ethnography is characterized by its recourse to an extrinsic element or a supplementary dimension that gives the observed phenomena their organic unity and organizational coherence (see Viveiros de Castro 2010). The systems the two approaches are therefore designed to set up are largely incompatible and irreconcilable. Total ethnography's complexity is related to describing both the processes of assembly and disassembly that permeate the empirical phenomena under consideration as encountered in each specific plateau, and the trajectory their crossings over various plateaus trace. In contrast, totalizing ethnography's complexity is connected to determining the system's transcendent unification by the operation of a limited number of principles. While the former conserves our aporia and leads to an opening that is directly associated with difference's acentric proliferation which is going all the way down, so to speak, the latter ends up projecting closure and certitude through the identification of the found and its naming. For all their brilliance therefore Evans-Prichard's 'discovery' of a Nuer politics conducted by means of lineage corporate groupings, and Leach's alternative of Kachin affairs organized around the oscillation of hierarchy and equality as the horizon and end point of anthropological inquiry simply won't do us any more.

For beginning from and staying with aporia, starting from and conserving wonder it is necessary to tear the person up *and* to keep it open. The first move involves paying attention to its becomings; such becomings are associated with the two reciprocally presupposed sides that the person consists of and their alternate manifestation in the process of forming relations with other persons in the space defined by particular plateaus. As an assemblage of heterogeneous elements, the becomings which *diaphoron* persons undergo therein are related to the person shooting up and down 'like a telescope', revealing this side and eclipsing the other, becoming male now and female later, Madurese yesterday and Javanese tomorrow, acting externally in sibling unison or in accordance to internal hierarchical distinctions. The relation between reciprocally presupposed differentials that the concept of becoming encodes is, however, only half of the story. In order to keep the *diaphoron* person open, and our curiosity amplified rather than satisfied, a second move is equally required. As Deleuze and Guattari have put it in the fabulous Chapter 10 of their *A Thousand Plateaus* (2004), it is also necessary to focus on the transversal relations pertaining among plateaus, the diagonal connections among the different sets of heterogeneities that make the *diaphoron* person up. This analytical move amounts to a further instance of foregrounding becoming, a becoming articulated in the intersections of assemblages, the zones of indiscernibility the meeting of two or more multiplicities sets up.

For Deleuze and Guattari, there is very little difference between the concepts of becoming and multiplicity. Indeed, they write that

> becoming and multiplicity are the same thing. A multiplicity is defined not by its elements, nor by a centre of unification or comprehension. It is defined by the number of dimensions it has; ... it cannot lose or gain a dimension *without changing its nature*. Since its variations and dimensions are immanent to it, *it amounts to the*

same thing to say that each multiplicity is already composed of heterogeneous terms in symbiosis,
and that a multiplicity is continually transforming itself into a string of other multiplicities,
according to its thresholds and doors. (2004, 275; italics in the original)

Becoming therefore summons the relations between the immanent assemblages as the latter continually transform themselves into each other, cross over into each other. The assemblages in question correspond to the various dimensions of the *diaphoron* person explored in this book in relation to specific themes organized in terms of separate chapters. Becoming, however, exceeds and surpasses such separations and purifications by means of the curve a discontinuous, broken line draws. This excess, which Deleuze and Guattari (2004) variously name as 'line of flight', 'the Body without Organs' and 'rhizome', has certain unmistakable effects; it both sets out to destabilize and deterritorialize the temporary and concrete forms the *diaphoron* person assumes in each specific plateau and to push or carry its becomings forwards and onwards onto new plateaus where fresh processes of form giving or territorialization are bound to begin their work. This second instance of becoming bound as it is with crossings-over is all about unhinged growth, immense proliferation, and lateral profusion. They argue that the rhizome 'assumes diverse forms, branches in all directions, and forms bulbs and tubers. [It] is multiple, giving rise to its own structure but also breaking that structure according to the "line of flight" it contains' (quoted in M. Strathern 1995, 21). It is in this sense that becoming achieves to generate and permeate everything there is and to present the best image of being we can hope for getting at.

Becoming as 'line of flight' not only keeps difference intact but its registered transversal movements have the capacity to increase difference exponentially. Becoming does not correspond to a singular entity nor does it present a type. It is neither an indivisible unity nor a static aggregate of assemblages but always an evolving difference-in-itself. As its trajectories push the assemblages it consists of towards change and transformation, so too the connections and relations becoming creates among them make it to differ constantly from itself. The more crossing over takes place the more passages through assemblages are accomplished; the more connections are generated the more differences are produced. The unlimited character of becoming brings about the unbounding and multiplication of difference as an internal and immanent dimension of the *diaphoron* person, and opens the door to aporia and astonishment once more as this profusion's adjunct, this acceleration's accompaniment.

In this regard, Deleuze and Guattari are as precise and succinct as possible.

A line of becoming is not defined by points that it connects, or by points that compose it; on the contrary, it passes *between* points, it comes up through the middle. … A point is always a point of origin. But a line of becoming has neither beginning nor end, departure nor arrival, origin nor destination; to speak of the absence of an origin, to make the absence of an origin the origin, is a bad play of words. A line of becoming has only a middle … it is the absolute speed of movement … the in-between, the border. (2004, 323; italics in the original)

In the face of this aporia of origins and destinations, the task the radical philosophy of Deleuze and Guattari sets out is at once much simpler and more challenging. The task consists of constructing a plane of immanence (sometimes also called a plane of consistency) that gathers all the dimensions, all the assemblages on a smooth, unstratified, deterritorialized, flat surface in such a way that all the becomings involved, all the crossovers and intersections, all the differences assembled are given due prominence and free rein to announce themselves, unencumbered as they are from unduly deterministic and reductionist temperaments. 'Can a given multiplicity flatten and conserve all its dimensions in this way, like a pressed flower that remains just as alive dry?' they ask (2004, 277). For ethnographers that strive to keep their experiences alive when transporting them to the dry page, this is the most apposite challenge and the task which I now turn to.

Map 1. Indonesia

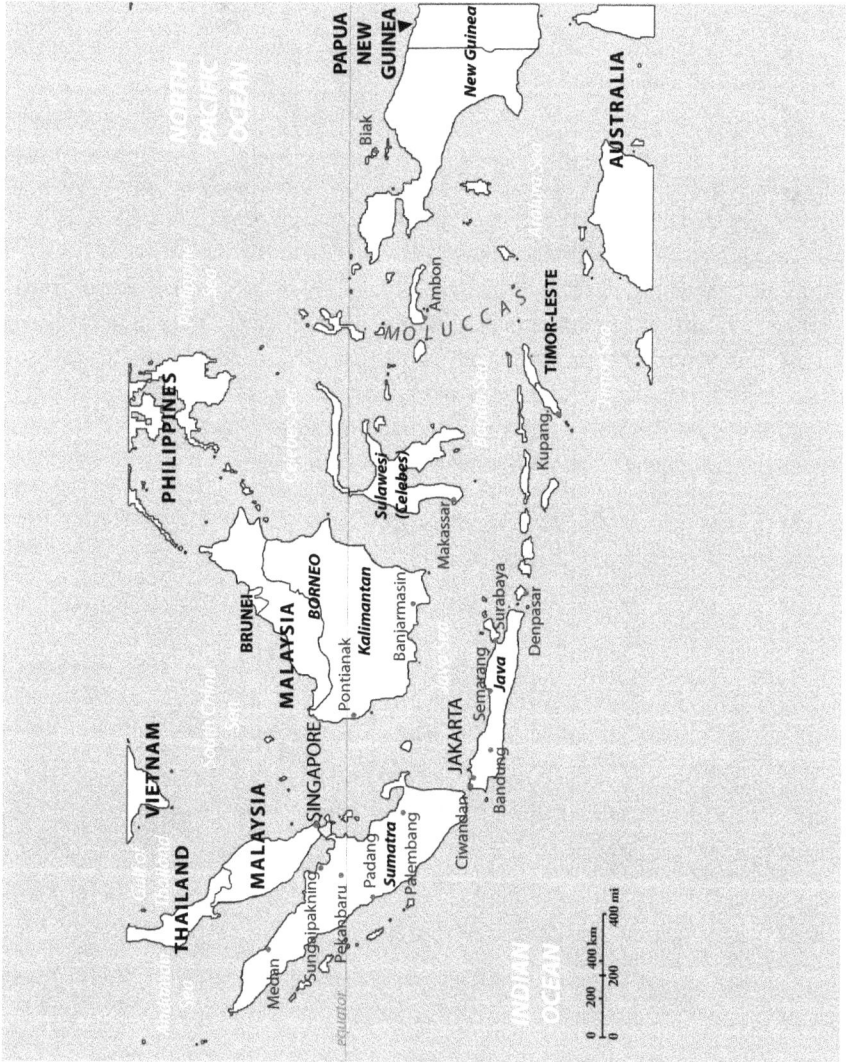

Map 2. East Java

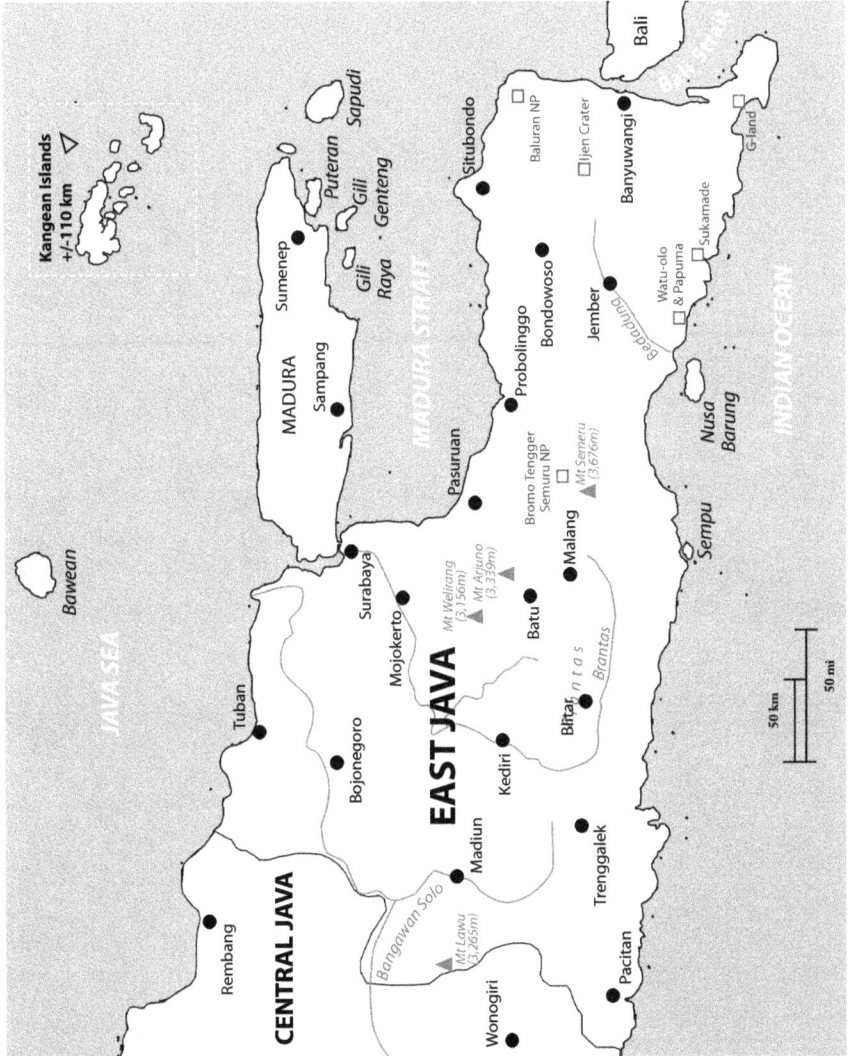

Chapter 1

THE BECOMING OF PLACE: MOVING, CLEARING, INHABITING

The unity of the beginning

> Rather than being one definite sort of thing, ... a given place takes on
> the qualities of its occupants, reflecting these qualities in its own consti-
> tution and description and expressing them in its occurrence as an event:
> places not only *are*, they *happen*.
>
> (Casey 1996, 27; italics in the original)

First time I visited Alas Niser was well into the fasting month of Ramadan
of 1998. Accompanied by my research assistant, I hopped on one of the
many yellow minibuses packed with an assortment of people, produce,
and commodities that connect downtown Probolinggo with its southern
periphery. It was a hot mid-afternoon right after the call for prayer, and our
co-passengers, tired from work and the fast, were returning home for a quick
rest. The minibus was travelling fast, overtaking schoolchildren in their bicycles
and uniformed civil servants in their Honda motorcycles, over a bumpy road
that had only been laid with asphalt in the early 1980s. The ticket collector,
a young man over-hanging from the side door, was shouting the name of
our destination while gesticulating wildly as we passed through the densely
populated neighbourhoods of the city centre. The latter soon gave way to
a kilometre-long stretch of irrigated rice fields planted with bright green
seedlings, interspersed here and there with a few white-washed brick houses
and a newly built mosque featuring a shiny, light blue dome.

Some ten minutes or so later, going past a Chinese cemetery and a vineyard,
we came across a village and the van pulled up in the central market, where
it offloaded its human cargo and readied itself for the return trip. We had
reached our destination. Much to my surprise, the market was lethargic.
Most of the stalls and indoor shops were now closed, while the few remaining
open were devoid of any customers, while their owners dozed off behind
the counters. There was no sign at all of the vibrant intensity and vitality

that one usually encounters in Southeast Asian marketplaces. The only trace of human presence came from an unidentified mix of male voices chanting away in Arabic coming from the adjacent mosque and other directions some distance away. For this most holy month at least, the excitements and hazards of trade had been largely substituted with the vigour of reciting sacred words, infusing the area's soundscape with tokens of devotion for the benefit of both reciters and listeners.

Following the sounds, we made our way southeast towards a rather small compound that featured a small prayer house and the residence of a *kyai* (Ind.), a much venerated figure of Islamic scholarship in this part of Java. The purpose of our visit was to inquire about the possibility of taking up residence in the vicinity after the approval of the headman and at least several of local *kyai* had been secured. Alas, a young man and a disciple of his informed us, the *kyai* had been away on business in Surabaya, the provincial capital, and he was not expected to return until after dark. Resigned to the necessity of having to come back the following day, we were engaged in conversation by Mas Bukhari – that was the young man's name – who asked us warily but politely about our reasons for being there. With the help of my research assistant, I managed to convey something about my interest in migration and local culture, saying that I was a student from Greece. When Mas Bukhari heard this, he hurried to introduce us to an elderly neighbour of his who was considered an authority of sorts on these issues. This would be the first time I heard the story of the coming into being of the area by a set of siblings.

Pak Mattasan, the elderly man in question, was said to be over one hundred years old; as Mas Bukhari put it, he had 'his skin changed like a snake seven times over'. Despite his old age and frail health, he went on to offer a narration of the area's founding that I came across several times in subsequent conversations with other locals. These stories commonly start with the arrival of a set of siblings who, some time in the past, crossed the Madura Strait, separating the island of Madura from East Java by means of a boat, made it to the port of Probolinggo and then headed further inland in an attempt to find or actually 'make' land. In Pak Mattasan's own words the story begins in the remote past.

> In the *jhaman krajaen* [Mad., the period of the kingdoms; i.e. before the arrival of the Dutch] my ancestor came over here from Madura. His name was great-grandfather Renten. He came here not alone but together with his five other *satretan* [full siblings, Mad.] from Omben [a village in the hinterland of Sampang district in central Madura]. If all of them were to gather here today, together with their descendants, my compound's space would not be enough. Their names were great-grandfather Renten, great-grandfather Siang, great-

grandfather Banjir, great-grandfather Sayanten, great-grandfather Sermatija and great-grandmother Sumi, who was the only woman. These were the first to settle in the area, for before their arrival it was not populated. ... It was covered by thick forest and only animals and evil spirits lived here. ... The whole area was covered by forest. ... That was in the past. These siblings were the first people to make [aghabay, Mad.] the village, the houses, the land. Although they came here as a set of siblings [setretanan], they later spread out and each chose a spot of the forest to clear. They made the village by clearing the forest [bhabhad alas, Mad.]. By doing so, they created rain-dependent fields, built the first huts and small prayer houses. Except for great-grandmother Sumi, there was no other women accompanying them. After they made land and huts, their wives followed them here from Madura ... and they all gave birth to a lot of children ... all of them were born here. Children and clearing the forest. ... It took four generations to reach my generation. ... Here, it is big Omben. Starting from the area further away from the bridge, to the west and to the south, we are all descendants of these first people [oreng situng, Mad.].

In other versions of this topostory,[1] the set of siblings numbered five instead of six; in others the set consisted of four. There were also some inconsistencies of the names of the ancestors involved. In some narratives the first settlers were said to have arrived together with their wives from the outset; in others they already had children. However, all the versions converged on a common theme, insisting that the siblingship ties connected the village founders, their place of origin was Omben and that they had cleared the forest, referred to as bhabhad alas (Mad.). The narratives were arranged similarly too, along generational lines proceeding lineally towards the present. Unlike in other parts of Southeast Asia where genealogical memories are commonly rather shallow, reaching back only three or four generations,[2] the cultural memory of that initial encounter with the forest and its subsequent appropriation by these 'first people' extended six or seven generations.

According to all versions of the sibling topostory, genealogy and ancestral acts of clearing the forest are intimately linked. The term bhabhad is particularly significant. As Giambelli notes (1999), the Old Javanese term babad, cognates of which are found in both the Balinese and Madurese languages, carries two different meanings. Within the context of the indigenous literary tradition, it refers to a genre of historico-genealogical chronicles narrating the founding

---

1 Topostory refers to 'the story of a place'; see Fox (1997) for more.
2 Examples of what is usually termed as 'genealogical amnesia' are to be found in Borneo (Freeman 1961, 208), Malaysia (Carsten 1995), Java (Jay 1969, 171) and Bali (Geertz and Geertz 1964).

of new royal dynasties and/or significant events. Within the context of agriculture, it designates the creation of cultivable fields through the chopping down of trees, the levelling of the ground, and the preparing of the soil for planting. What is common to both is the activity of cutting, as in the cutting down of trees and the cuts that pre-modern scribes were required to insert on palmyra palm-leaf *kropak* 'books' before the introduction of paper as a means of writing, a practice common throughout Southeast Asia. Pushing the issue a bit further, I would suggest that what this common stress may seek to establish is, firstly, the idea of a beginning, a point in history from where the current situation originates, and, secondly, the idea of becoming: 'the emergence of a new situation from a given existing situation' (Giambelli 1999, 498). In the case of Alas Niser, *bhabhad* stories emphasize the transformation of the landscape by the force of ancestral agency, and highlight the anteriority of siblingship and its centrality for precipitating such a transformation.

The narrative evocation of siblingship is a potent one. Siblingship establishes sociality as primordial, existing from the very beginning, both beyond history and at the root of it. In a sense, the sociality of siblingship is without a cause and origin, being simply and profoundly foundational. The same can be said about other narrative instances of place making in the Austronesian world that Fox (1997) calls topogenies (literally, the genesis of *topoi*, places). In broad terms, topogenies recount the journey of an ancestor, or the migration of a group from its point of departure, through its movement across spaces and encounters with other men and groups to the instantiation of habitable places and the erection of houses (8–9). Quite commonly, topogenic stories merge the idea of the 'path' with the idea of 'origin' and emphasize 'the botanic image of the growing and spreading "tree" that extends from its base' (1997, 9).[3] Images of extension and growth are images of dispersal and multiplication. This applies in our case too. The sibling topostory portrays the present population of Alas Niser as partaking in such an extension in the sense of having sprung up from a set of closely related people who, by virtue of being siblings, shared the same substance. In this regard, the present inhabitants are constructed as consanguineous in various, however distant, degrees. The precise nature of such ties remains unelaborated in everyday practice and genealogical knowledge is not utilized to accomplish greater clarity. Nevertheless, the multiplicity of the intimate links implied posits the possibility of tracing a common point of origin for

---

3 Ingold's (2009) work that sees places produced out of criss-crossing trajectories of human movement, forming knots and tied together by threads of migration forms a further illustration of the same idea on a more abstract, less regional specific level.

all inhabitants as a real one. The point of common origin is the point of the path of migration of the 'first people'.

The accomplishment of unity through the tracing of a common origin is only partial as it gives rise to certain problems. These have to do with the narration of the area as empty of humans, and an extension of Madura. Seen from a certain perspective, the claim that Alas Niser is a Madurese 'colony' sits rather uneasily with the general emphasis on mixing through affinal exchanges that is pronounced in other contexts (see below). Moreover, the emphasis on the emptiness of the area is equally problematic and, as such, of particular importance. This is best exemplified when certain aspects of pre-modern Probolinggo are taken into account.

From an analytical perspective, it is essential that the sibling topostory is interrogated for the aspects of the regional history it selectively seeks to highlight and those it seeks if not to deny then to push to the margins of relevance. According to the historical record, coastal Probolinggo was a thriving maritime and rice-growing area that was well-integrated within the administrative structures of Majapahit, Java's last Hindu-Buddhist kingdom which ruled in the fourteenth and fifteenth centuries, the capital of which was actually situated a short distance away (Pigeaud 1960, 63). The southern highlands of Probolinggo were, during the same period, the centre of a most important Sivaite cult whose clergy were members of religious networks stretching the whole of East Java and Bali. Today the descendants of this Hindu-Buddhist population still live in the Tengger Highlands (see Hefner 1985, 271–6; Smith-Hefner 1989, 260). It is clear, therefore, that the wider area was not depopulated in pre-modern times, and that, as Hefner (1990) has argued for the neighbouring Pasuruan, the arrival of Muslim Madurese and Central Javanese migrants in the nineteenth century pushed this Hindu-Buddhist population further upland, away from the more fertile plains, and changed the religious outlook of the area.

As several historians have argued, the depopulation of Java's eastern salient was primarily the outcome of two and half centuries of political violence, starting with Majapahit's fall to Muslim forces in the 1520s, Mataram's campaigns in East Java and Madura in the early to mid-seventeenth century, Trunajaya's and Surapati's rebellions of the late seventeenth and the early to mid-eighteenth century, respectively, and the Dutch campaigns against Balambangan in the late eighteenth century (Boomgaard 1989; Ricklefs 1981; Van Niel 2005). Kumar (1976, 1979, 1997) attributes the economic devastation and virtual depopulation of the area in particular to the atrocities and scorched-earth policies of the Dutch and their Mataram's allies against the rebels and the court of Balambangan that wiped out the local population and the Madurese, Balinese, Chinese, Buginese and English migrants who were also making a living there. Conversely, the subsequent repopulation of the eastern salient through the immigration of vast numbers of Madurese and Central Javanese was the outcome of the 'pacification' of the area and the establishment of effective administrative rule by the Dutch, as well as in the case of Probolinggo and the adjacent areas of Besuki and Panarukan to the east, a significant but brief period of Chinese overlordship. Both Chinese and Dutch sought to realize the economic potential of the territories under their control through a dual process of expansion of the land under cultivation and of the necessary manpower through encouraging immigration.

According to the genealogies and other scanty information that I have collected from descendants of the 'first people', I can hypothesize that their demographic movement out of Central Madura and into East Java took place sometime between 1830 and 1850.[4] Historians and anthropologists of Madura have repeatedly pointed out that around that time the island experienced an unprecedented rural exodus, precipitated by the combined effects of rapid population growth and the excessive tax demands of the local aristocracy, which imposed a huge burden on the population (de Jonge 1989; Husson 1995; Kuntowijoyo 1981; Tjiptoatmodjo 1983). Madurese peasants responded principally to these pressures by migrating *en masse* to sparsely populated areas of East Java.[5]

As Adas's (1981) work has shown for both pre-colonial and colonial Southeast Asia, issues of taxation were directly related to demographic movement as peasants would flee heavily taxed areas in protest of excessive demands from above to sparsely populated ones which were relatively removed from effective administration. The Madurese case adds further support to his hypothesis. In the course of the eighteenth century, the principalities that were to be found on the island of Madura transformed themselves from vassals of kingdom of Mataram of Central Java to vassals of the Verenidge Oostindische Campagnie (VOC), the Dutch East India Company (de Jonge 1982). From this

---

4 This is an estimate calculated on the basis of genealogical layers, allowing for 25 years to mark genealogical succession. In total, six detailed genealogies have been taken into account and cross-examined.

5 Madurese migration to East Java, of course, goes back several centuries. Husson cites Pigeaud who records the forced movement of Madurese serfs to East Java 'for opening up new lands for cultivation' in the fourteenth century (1997, 80). Similarly, in the seventeenth century the massive relocation of 40,000 Madurese peasants to the sparsely populated areas of Gresik and Jortan was a result of the military expeditions of Sultan Agung (de Jonge 1989, 48). Not all movement across the straits was forced however. Madurese migrants established pioneer settlements in parts of Java, such as that of Besuki, and traders, soldiers and labourers chose to make Java their home for a variety of reasons.

period up to the late nineteenth century, the Madurese princes were granted the right to govern their polities without the supervision or direct control of the Dutch. Starting from the early to mid-nineteenth century, according to colonial officials cited by Husson, 'the status of being an independent self-ruled province had bitter consequences for the local population which was crushed under exactions, abuses, taxes and corvées' (1997, 84). Taxation increases were partly the result of the payments in money, kind and troops the princes had to make to the VOC in return for its military 'protection', and partly due to the adoption of a lavish life-style by the aristocracy in a vain attempt to compensate for its colonial domestication through displays of conspicuous consumption. A third contributing factor was the widespread practice of tax-farming (i.e. the practice of renting out the right to levy taxes to third parties for a lump sum of money usually paid in advance) through which the aristocracy was trying to raise cash. It is highly probable that tax-farming had an inflationary effect as several layers of tax-farmers sought to increase their profit margins (see de Jonge 1986; Kuntowijoyo 1981, 1986).

Taxation increases imposed a further burden on the population and on the scarce resources of the island economy. Geographically, Madura is an offshoot of the north and east Javanese limestone hills. It is characterized by aridity, scarcity of good soil, and extended period of droughts (Husson 1995, 61–75; de Jonge 1989, 5–10). With the exception of the alluvial soils where irrigation is possible and which are concentrated around the major urban centres of Pamekasan, Bangkalan, Sampang and Sumenep, the rest of the island consists of rocky low hills. The barrenness of the soil is further exacerbated by the absence of volcanic elements, the low level of rainfall, and the absence of big river systems. The dominant mode of agriculture practised both today and the preceding centuries was that of *talon* (Mad.), rain dependent fields which produce only one yield per year and are extremely sensitive to droughts. Colonial commentators viewed Madura as an economically poor society that could barely grow enough crops to feed its mushrooming population (see Van Dijk et al. 1995, 2). In the period between 1815 and 1867, Madura experienced an almost tripling of its population which went up from 218,659 in 1815 to 254,123 in 1845 to 595,841 in 1867 (de Jonge 1989, 21). This increase was very much a consequence of political stability, and the lower incidence of disease. This increase led both to a rapid deforestation of the island's hinterland as peasants tried to expand their holdings, and to an exodus which saw thousands of Madurese leaving the island for the frontier areas of coastal East Java.

The Madurese peasants' flight took a specific form as they migrated to areas of East Java which are more or less opposite their area of origin (de Jonge 1989, 24; Husson 1995, 92–9). Thus, Madurese from Bangkalan migrated mainly to Tuban, Surabaya, Jombang, Pasuruan and Malang;

those from Sampang to Surabaya, Pasuruan, Probolinggo and Lumajang; those from Pamekasan to Probolinggo, Jember and Bondowoso; while those from Sumenep went to Bondowoso, Situbondo, Jember and Banyuwangi. The volume of this demographic movement is astonishing. According to Tjiptoatmodjo, the Madurese population of Surabaya increased from 12,376 in 1822 to 15,724 two years later (1983, 315). The same author cites colonial records that estimate that the population of the Besuki regency (*afdeeling*, Dutch) increased from 41,555 in 1828 to 59,792 in 1845. In Besuki, the Madurese formed the vast majority with 58,256 in 1845 (1983, 274–5). To the north of Besuki, in the regency of Pasuruan the Madurese numbered 92,463 out of a total population of 264,519 in 1832, while the Javanese retained the majority estimated at 170,049 (1983, 268, 315; see also Husson 1997, 85). Between these two areas is Probolinggo. In 1845, the population of the Probolinggo regency comprised of 18,456 Javanese and 56,317 Madurese (Tjiptoatmodjo 1983, 317). Between 1854 and 1855, the population increased by 3.9 per cent from 270,734 to 281,294. That same year, a further 5.19 per cent population increase was recorded and attributed to a further influx of Madurese (Husson 1997, 86). Whatever the accuracy of colonial statistics might be and in spite of the simplistic picture the latter introduce to what are extremely complex processes of identification, a very forceful image emerges out of them: namely that of the flooding of East Java with poor migrants from Madura.

This influx slowly but steadily transformed the character that coastal East Java had assumed during the eighteenth century as a result of the expanding interests of the Dutch East India Company and its attempts to create a stable Java with its centre in Mataram (Elson 1984; Hefner 1990). As the Dutch and their local allies eliminated their enemies through a long and bloody series of campaigns, they converted Java's eastern salient or Easthook into a cauldron of warfare. War devastated and depopulated much of the countryside as peasants fled from recurring strife in search of safer ground. According to Hefner, few of the indigenous eastern Javanese populations remained and 'a frontier culture emerged that incorporated Madurese, Malay, and Javanese traditions', itself focusing on Islam (1990, 39).

The devastation brought to Java's eastern salient, particularly during the campaigns against the Surapati's descendants and Balambangan, was such that by the turn of the nineteenth century the most densely populated areas were those of the environs of the towns of Surabaya, Pasuruan, Bangil and Probolinggo and the land around them was said to be well cultivated. Outside the administrative and commercial centre of these towns, however, lay areas that were sparsely populated and mostly uncultivated. In the early nineteenth century, Easthook had an average of 33.66 inhabitants per square mile, well below the average for Java as a whole which was a little over 100, and far from the average for the densely populated areas of Central Java which was a little lower than 150 (Carrey 1986, 105, n.167). Sparse population meant land under-utilization. Citing colonial sources, Elson argues that by 1820 'only 6 per cent of the land area of Probolinggo regency was *sawah* [Ind., irrigated fields] and 87 per cent remained uncultivated' (1984, 6).

The 'pacification' of Probolinggo brought about the redevelopment of the area in terms of agricultural production and the encouragement of the settlement of Madurese and Central Javanese migrants. Actually, Jayanegara, the late eighteenth-century regent of Banger (as Probolinngo was then known), was considered by the Dutch to be a model ruler because of his successful efforts at land expansion, *sawah* conversion, irrigation system construction and the attraction of large numbers of migrants from both East and West Madura (Kwee 2006, 202). This trend continued well into the beginning of the nineteenth century, when Probolinggo was sold to the brother of the captain of the Chinese of Surabaya, Han Tik Ko (Bastin 1954). The sale, which was cancelled in 1813 as a result of a rebellion led by the disgruntled relatives of the dismissed regent, was instrumental both in the colonial state raising revenue and in enhancing the political role of the Chinese community of Java's eastern salient. The Chinese overlords of Probolinggo, as well as those of Panarukan and Besuki to the east, did much to encourage the movement of Madurese and to a lesser extend Central Javanese into their territories of ownership, in an effort to augment their tax base, recuperate the capital spent on the purchase and increase their profit margin (see below). Until the crushing of the rebellion, Chinese-leased and Chinese-sold lands were considered by the Dutch to be a model of both effective administration and economic management. After 1818, however, the colonial state adopted a policy of purging *peranakan*[6] Chinese regents from the eastern salient.

In Alas Niser, the process of opening up new land is attributed not to the opportunities afforded by the administration but to the mystical powers or potency (*kesaktean*, Mad.) of ancestors. 'Potent persons' are those who have inherited and maintained or acquired divine powers by means of sustaining ascetic regimes and elaborating modes of religiosity prescribed in the performance of Islam. Such persons are able to perform extraordinary deeds such as healing and entering dangerous and haunted places such as forests. The descendants of *bujuk* Banjir, one of the 'first people', remembered him as possessing a special *keris* (Ind., a dragon-shaped dagger) for clearing the forest. The *keris* he had made himself consisted of a mixture of soil, chopped

---

6 *Peranakan* refers to descendants of early modern Chinese migrants to the archipelago, born of marriages with local women, and speaking Indonesian or another regional language as their first language.

banana leaves and *kapok* tree bark (*Ceiba pentandra*, Lat.) and was infused with a secret incantation. His *keris* was said to be stronger than metal tools and able to cut high *jati* trees (*Tectona grandis*, Lat.) with a single stroke. This magical aspect of the area's founding aligns its founding with the powers that emanate from Allah and are bestowed to his most pious believers. The strength of the association between religion and locality is also manifested in portrayals of *bujuk* Banjir as an evangelist who persuaded neighbouring Hindu-Buddhist populations to convert to Islam through the demonstration of the powers of the *keris* to generate prosperity and wealth and his founding of several small prayer houses in the area.

The diversity of poverty

In contrast to the sense of place as vertically encompassed, as it is embedded in the topostory of the sibling set, a sense of horizontal encompassment emerges out of other contemporary accounts. This sense was primarily voiced by descendants of migrants from Madura and other locales of Java who arrived to Alas Niser at later times from the 1850s to the present. These narratives stress not only the diversity of ancestral origins, but also marriage at the expense of siblingship. In these accounts, affinity was central to the transformation of what was a foreign, potentially hostile space into a familiar and safe one. Such transformations were mediated by horizontal networks of sociality founded on intermarriage. Thus, while descendants of the first settlers emphasized the production of locality through a 'unity of descent' (*situng toronan*, Mad.), claiming it to be an extension, if not a colony of Omben, narratives of descendants of people who entered the area at a later date construed Alas Niser as founded on a great mixture of origins bridged through marriage. That was the case with the narratives of the descendants of people who arrived in Alas Niser from both Madura and Central and western East Java, the latter two being areas associated strongly with Javanese people, language and culture.

Despite this apparent difference in the mode of conceptualization of place, all narratives shared a common sense of newly founded locality emerging out of the demographic movement of destitute ancestors. Migrants who arrived in Alas Niser as late as the first decades of the twentieth century are remembered as continuing to 'make' land through forest-clearing.[7]

---

7 For Javanese conceptions of the forest as a dangerous and forbidding place full of natural and supernatural dangers and powers, see Wessing (1995) and Headley (2004, 251–74); for colonial views of the forest as a resource to be scientifically managed, see Peluso (1992, 44–78).

Forest-clearing is registered in collective memory as an act that generates rights of hereditary private tenure.[8] Although there is no space here to enter into a detailed consideration of the issue, both colonial administrators and historians of Java have long debated the precise nature and types of land rights (see Boomgaard 1989a; Carey 1986). From this debate, two things seem highly probable. Firstly, as Boomgaard (1989a, 1989b) notes, the perceptions and policies of colonial authorities during the nineteenth century did much to effect the strengthening of communal tenure according to which peasants had rights of usufruct rather than rights of ownership over the land that they cultivated. Such rights were tied to corresponding obligations of labour and to deliver produce to local and supra-local authorities. In addition, the majority of peasants were rather tenuously attached to specific plots of land due to a variety of mechanisms that, from time to time, redistributed land among a village's population in response to demands from above. Secondly, certain areas of Java's northeast coast, in particular the eastern salient seem to have been exempted from these trends (Boomgaard 1989a, 27–30). In Probolinggo, as well as Besuki and Panarukan, hereditary private tenure seems to have been predominant throughout the nineteenth century. This, in turn, was the result of a series of factors, including low population density, light taxation, the abolition of appanage holdings by the Dutch due to the local aristocracy's participation in the Surapati rebellion (Kumar 1976) and the predominance of Madurese settlers who were unfamiliar with communal land tenure since in Madura such arrangements were virtually unknown (de Jonge 1989, 64–75). In addition, it is also clear that this phenomenon occurred mainly in those areas that had been leased and then sold to wealthy Chinese families. Indeed, if we are to believe in the reports of a British administrator named Hopkins, the individualized landholding arrangement was introduced by the Chinese leaseholders as a way to attract sufficient labour force (see Van Niel 2005, 269). According to this arrangement, settlers were assigned pieces of forest to clear or land to plant and they were subject to give half of their produce to the Chinese overlord, with all *corvée* labour abolished and waged labour preferred. This, in turn, contributed both to a stronger grip over the land by the peasants and the recognition of full inheritance rights (Elson 1984). Such rights were maintained by subsequent authorities and must have had a direct effect on

---

8 In Central Java, forest-clearing was equally associated with individual rights of possession. However, these rights were a lot weaker. Boomgaard notes that in mid-nineteenth-century Pacitan, 'the first reclaimer could regard his soil as private property for three years, where after the leaseholder (*bekel*, Jav.) could rent it out to the highest bidder' (1989a, 34–5). The operation of more effective systems of administration and their greater proximity to rural communities meant that in Central Java newly opened land was quite often subject to the arbitrary appropriation of power holders.

imbuing a sense of emplacement and rootedness among migrants and their descendants.

While the account of Madurese migration I presented in the previous section highlights avoidance protest caused by a crisis in agrarian relations, the descendants of the 'first people' as well as those who arrived in Alas Niser later in the nineteenth century emphasize poverty avoidance as the root of their ancestors' movement. The difficulties of making a living in Madura as a peasant were primarily related to the ecological conditions of the island rather than to its politics of surplus labour extraction. Echoing this view, Pak Sukoco, a 65-year-old man whose ancestors moved to Alas Niser from the district of Pamekasan in Madura in the late nineteenth century, commented with the accuracy any sociologist strives to attain that

> My ancestors came over here in search of a living [*nyareh nafkah*]. Life in Madura was not easy … the land was infertile and arid … so they migrated [*ongghe*, Mad.; literally moved upwards, ascended] to Java; they came here as poor migrants. Over there it was difficult to find a job besides being a farmer. … There was some fishing and trading done but actually the situation was desperate … even drilling wells for finding water was hopeless. So, one had to wait for the rains to come. If there was no rain, one could not plant. It was far better being a farmer here … land was plentiful and we get three yields a year while over there they only got one.

The relative availability of land for clearing, the dream of having enough to get by and the fertility of soil in East Java were defined in opposition to the barrenness of fields and the scarcity of alternative economic opportunities in Madura. These characterizations were a constant feature of the way people remembered the orally transmitted experiences of their ancestors. This mediated remembering portrays Java in general and Alas Niser in particular as a newly discovered heaven and a land of plenty waiting for people to work it with dedication, commitment and energy so as to make it habitable and productive. The ancestors' involvement with Alas Niser sits at the heart of narratives of the locality's becoming.

In narrative terms, the ecological poverty of Madura was coupled with the economic plight of its inhabitants. The infrequent consumption of rice meals and the predominance of maize and cassava as staple were evoked extensively by locals when talking about the life of ancestors in Madura, marking in stark fashion the difference between here and there, the present and the past. This sense of poverty was embedded within descriptions of ancestor's rarely having enough rice to eat and of being forced to make do with maize and cassava for extended periods of time, sometimes even

Figure 1. Ploughing the field for rice planting

for the whole agricultural year. In addition, the ancestors' diet was limited to one meal a day instead of the three their descendants can afford to eat these days. For locals, both maize and cassava are considered as of lower nutritional value in relation to rice and are said to lack in taste too. Today maize and cassava are consumed only by the poorest of households. While these conditions were said to be routine rather than exceptional in Madura, certain historical events have contributed to their exacerbation among which one could count the famines of 1877, 1903, 1918 and 1933 as well as the world economic depression of the 1930s. Exceptional was also the impact of the Japanese occupation (1942–45), a period locals remember vividly for the devastation impacted by Japanese policies of confiscation of produce and livestock and the use of villagers as forced labourers across Indonesia as well as Malaysia, Burma, and Vietnam.

Such recollections focusing on a past of shared poverty, both direct and indirect, make better sense when set against the background of the diversity of origins of which Alas Niser's inhabitants are very conscious. Leaving aside for the moment the issue of ethnic diversity, an issue I deal with in the following section, the crux of the matter is not, as one might expect, ethnic similitude and solidarity, but 'regional' differences within broad ethnic categories that are emphasized locally. While the majority of Alas Niser's inhabitants portray themselves as descendants of Madurese migrants, it is not their shared Madurese-ness that is stressed but diversity within.

Having recorded the story of the foundation of the area by a set of siblings, I set about eliciting reactions to it by repeating what I had heard to people who did not claim descent from the 'first people'. Their responses countered the unity of descent by insisting on the different paths that brought their ancestors to Alas Niser and the lack of kinship and other ties among them. Pak Sukoco's imagining of Madura (and Java) as a fragmented assortment of localities is particularly relevant here.

> We may have come from Madura … yeah, but you have to know that there is Madura Sampang, Madura Pamekasan, Madura Sumenep, Madura Bangkalan; there is Madura east and west; Madura north and south. … We came here from all directions and our ancestors were strangers to each other [*oreng laen*, Mad.; literally 'other people'], they were not kin previously; they just met here … the same goes for Javanese … there are Javanese from Yogya and Blitar, from Jombang and Kediri … they did not know each other before [coming here] but they are all living here today.

On another occasion, I was accompanying Pak Muharom, a trader of sheep in his mid-40s, to a *slametan* (Ind., ritual rice meal) in a nearby neighbourhood.

Strolling along the narrow street, the father of four teenage children, and fluent speaker of both Madurese and Javanese, voluntarily introduced his neighbourhood to me along similar lines to Pak Sucoko's, emphasizing the heterogeneity of origins of his daily associates.

> Here is the house of Pak Indang who originates from Malang [western East Java]; [pointing to the opposite side] that's where Pak Hosein lives, his family descends from Madurese from Sampang but they have been living here for a long time; beside his is Pak Sugeng's house whose grandfather was from Sumenep [east Madura].

In these two as well as other numerous instances, the sense of place privileged is that of a locality comprised of a diversity of people who converged in the same area while following distinct paths of movement.[9] Their gathering was accomplished over a long period of time, stretching from mid-nineteenth century to the present. The sharing of the same place in the present and the sociality that this sharing allows for is accompanied by a conspicuous lack of belonging to an imagined community conceived in terms of the ethnic categories of Madurese and Javanese. Moreover, as far as the locals' ancestors are concerned, these are not remembered as primarily Madurese or Javanese but as Madurese or Javanese from a specific, named part of Madura or Java.

There are several reasons that account for stressing the internal diversity of ethnic categories with which ancestors are associated. As far as the category of Madurese is concerned, it has to be noted that the application of the name 'Madura' to the whole island is a historically recent phenomenon. Up to early nineteenth century, 'Madura' referred to a single regency located on the western part of the island, ruled by the famous Cakraningrat family (Kwee 2006, 248, n.88). Research into the chronology and precise conditions that marked and facilitated the extension of the name to the rest of the island and the associated emergence of a unified, homogenous Madurese subject remains to be undertaken. Nonetheless, it is important to observe that a lot of people's ancestors left the island during a period when such identification was in all probability still in its infancy. Furthermore, the fact that Madura never formed a single, unified political entity but remained fragmented in various regencies is compounded with the poor lines of internal communication that prevailed until at least the beginning of the twentieth century. According to

---

9 Colonial statistics confirm to a certain extent this diversity. The last colonial census of 1930 lists a total of 238 Madurese migrants born in Sumenep, 1,252 born in Pamekasan, 2,577 born in Sampang, and 237 born in Bangkalan as living in the regency of Probolinggo that year (see Husson 1995, 374).

Niehof (1982), such factors make Madura's sociological and conceptual unity rather deceptive. Moreover, ethnographers of Madurese society argue that today the principal components of identity refer to either kinship-based *tanean* (Mad., yard/farmstead) groups, or the neighbourhood (de Jonge 1989, 17, 48; Jordaan and Niehof 1980). Taken together all these factors explain the lack of a Madurese consciousness prevailing in contemporary memorializations of ancestors' identities. On the other hand, the long history of immigration to Alas Niser that allowed for the gradual incorporation of newcomers into the local community, as well as the rare occurrence of chain migration involving close kin,[10] has discouraged the formation of groups or associations based on similarities in areas of origin and the privileging of kin at the expense of non-kin. Similarly, exclusively Madurese or Javanese associations have not been part of the fabric of local social life.[11] The availability of plenty of unclaimed land and the relative abundance of work opportunities and other economic activities created in East Java by the Cultivation and Plantation systems during the nineteenth century has meant that there were few material grounds for the emergence of competition that could lead to the formation of ethnic-cum-interest groups among migrants; groups which would otherwise be equipped with rigid boundaries, engaged in fighting for control over scarce resources. In addition, the emergence of Indonesian nationalism early in the twentieth century that construed the Dutch colonialists as the ultimate Other also mitigated against the stressing of ethnic exclusivity, not to mention the fact that both Madurese and Javanese migrants professed to follow Islam.

Madurese migration patterns show great fluidity. Some migrants arrived in Alas Niser as single men and women; some others though already married came alone in the first place and brought their families over at a later date. Some came together with their spouses and children from the outset. Others arrived together with a sibling of the same or the opposite sex. In some cases one of the siblings settled permanently in Alas Niser, and the other moved to another area in Java, usually after he/she got married, or returned to Madura. I recorded four cases of chain migration in which either a migrant moved to Alas Niser after a relative had already settled in Java, or it was s/he who motivated others to follow her/him to Java. Several people had

---

10 Out of a total of 67 detailed cases of migration I have collected and numerous others which are not as complete, I have encountered only four cases of chain migration. These involved people who were either full siblings or first cousins.

11 Even Budi Utomo, the first native political society of colonial Indonesia that is usually portrayed as a Javanese association in the literature used Malay as its preferred language and its membership, encompassed all the people of 'Javanese culture' inclusive of the Sundanese of West Java, the Madurese and from 1918 the Balinese (see Elson 2005).

Figure 2. Harvesting onions

made many seasonal trips back and forth before deciding to stay permanently. Their seasonal movements involved leaving Madura at the start of the dry season and returning for the sowing and the harvest, as well as for *Lebaran*, the end of the fast festivities. Some others left with their minds already set on the move being permanent. In general, people of both sexes and of variable ages participated in this demographic movement, although it was mainly young people in their early and mid-twenties who formed the bulk of migrants. Although the majority of migrants came without having secured employment, there were also people who arrived from Madura with a job earmarked for them in the sugar mill that operated during colonial times in the area.

While land clearing for cultivation is emphasized in oral history accounts as the principal pre-occupation of ancestors, Madurese migrants also found work as labourers in the port cities of Pasuruan and Probolinggo, working for Dutch, Chinese, and Arab owned trading companies and storehouses, as well as in Chinese-owned shops such as restaurants and general stores. According to informants, Dutch, Chinese and Arabs preferred Madurese workers who were assumed to display physical power, endurance, and reliability, despite their fierce reputations. Migrants from Madura were also (and still are) engaged in informal sector activities providing services that required the acquisition of small capital they either raised themselves or accessed through loans. Plenty of women were employed as peddlers, fruit and vegetable sellers, and food-stall owners. Men, on the other hand, made a living as rickshaw drivers, scrap metal dealers, as well as cart owners and labourers. Some others yet who stayed in coastal areas instead of moving inland found employment in the fishing industry. In Probolinggo, as well as in the neighbouring Pasuruan and Situbondo, fishing came to be almost exclusively in the hands of Madurese migrants who acted as unskilled or semi-skilled boat crew, fish traders both small and large, and fish processors (see Kusnadi 2001). However, during the nineteenth century and early twentieth century, opportunities in the agriculture sector provided most jobs. The Cultivation System and, after the Agrarian Law of 1870, the establishment of private plantations meant that the great majority of migrants proceeded inland to work as labourers in the sugarcane fields and sugar mills that dominated lowland East Java or in the coffee plantations that were to be found in the highlands. According to Husson, plantation owners relied on travelling recruiters who offered migrants a free ticket to enable them to make the trip to East Java, organized them in work groups and arranged for free lodging and business deals because they considered them reliable (1997, 87). Through forest clearing, hard work and savings, some of these plantation workers acquired their own land and transformed themselves to peasants. Still others remained landless, making a living either through entering into sharecropping arrangements with their landed patrons, working for wages, or engaging in small trade.

The fluidity that characterizes demographic movement and the multiplicity of origins of migrant ancestors are mediated by an emphasis on sociality founded on intermarriage. As in other parts of Southeast Asia characterized by migrant populations (Carsten 1995), cultural memories of past heterogeneity are coupled with discourses of mixing and the establishment of relations through marriage. In Alas Niser, the alternative to the 'first people' founding myth is related to the multiplicity of affinal relations that crisscross the wider area, tying together previously unrelated people and establishing commonality through reference to the co-production of future generations. As Errington (1987) has argued, in the exogamic societies of the 'Centrist Archipelago' that both Java and Madura are a part of, future generations – which she aptly calls 'apical children' – are of central importance in the conceptualization and enactment of sociality, for they correspond to nodal points allowing people to be linked together over ascending generational layers.

The importance attached to affinity and marriage in the local imagination was best exemplified in Pak Putro's comments. Pak Putro is the non–Alas Niser born son of a couple originating from the village of Propo in the district of Pamekasan, Madura. His parents moved to Java in the 1920s to make a living as labourers in the sugar mill, and stayed on after buying to a small plot of land to erect their house. Pak Putro was raised in Alas Niser as a child and had gone to marry three times over his lifetime, something which was quite usual for people of his generation. Asked about how did his family got on with the villagers, he replied that

> People in the past, that is female ones, rarely had a fiancé. So a lot of newcomers from Madura like me married local women. Then, it is mainly women who inherit land … so it is easy. … The man, the newcomer gets a woman, gets land and a house. … It's nice to get married, isn't it? You should do the same.

To marry a local woman, to acquire land and a house and have children is to acquire new roots, to ground oneself in a new place. Time and again people would point to marriage between a local woman and a foreign man or vice versa as the primary means though which sociality was established between successive waves of immigrants and those already living in the area. The relative severance of relations between people and the land of their origins created by migration, as far as the connections of a permanent out-migrant and his locale of origin are concerned, found relief in the creation of new social relations in the locale of destination. Getting married is about the acquisition of new relatives and the occupation of a specific place in the kinship terminology people commonly use to identify each other.

The data I collected readily attests to the regular seeking of spouses among migrants from either Alas Niser itself or from surrounding villages; that is, places located in East Java and not in Madura. Although my data lacks statistical precision, this tendency is quite clear. Out of 27 interviews I conducted with first-generation migrants who arrived as single men or women, all but two had married people who had been born in Java. Their spouses were either descendants of migrants or were migrants themselves. The remaining two cases involved Madurese migrants who had sought a wife in their origin place in Madura and had brought her subsequently to Java. First-generation migrants who arrived as couples also had their children and grandchildren married to people living in the area. Out of eighteen cases, all but one couples encouraged their children to look for spouses from Alas Niser rather than their own places of origin. The place of affinity is also acknowledged in statements such as 'we are all kin [here]' (*sengko' kabbi tretan*, Mad.). Despite its stereotypical tone, it points to a mode of self-representation that assumes the primacy of affinity as producing familiar place out of alien space. Affinity is conceived as being endowed with the agency of transforming space into place and ensuring the accomplishment of sociality through the channelling of human reproductive capacities that marriage and the sharing of offspring entail. In other words, becoming-kin is both facilitated by and based on the becoming of place: place is immanent in sociality.

Marriage and affinity occupy prime of place in the identification of people from Alas Niser and Probolinggo as 'mixed people'. The mixing in question has two interrelated components. The first one relates to the corporeal make-up of persons as established in and through marital transactions. The second one relates to place and its attributes.

Locals identify themselves as *orang pedalungan* or *orang campuran* (Ind.). While *pedalungan* (Ind.) is used by non-*pedalungan* people in other areas of Java to connote Madurese of the diasporas, in Alas Niser the word *pedalungan* refers to all those who have been born as a product of a Javanese person and their Madurese spouse and to those who have been born and socialized in Alas Niser. In general, children are believed to be created out of a combination of the role played by both sexes in the production of human beings. The body of the foetus is regarded as a mixture in which the 'man's liquid' (*aeng lake*, Mad.; i.e. sperm) can no longer be differentiated from the 'female liquid' (*aeng binne*, Mad.; i.e. uterine blood). Thus, the father and the mother contribute not only equally in the formation of new bodies, but also in an indistinguishable fashion. Children of a marriage between a Javanese woman and a Madurese man, or vice versa, are therefore considered to be composite sites of affinal exchanges and thus 'of mixed blood' (*campur darah*, Ind.).

The registration of affinity on the space defined by the human body is replicated in social space and the way it has come to be historically arranged While during the colonial period, and probably during the first decade of independence, one could argue that specific residential quarters in Alas Niser, which were composed of Javanese or Madurese migrants, were the unmistakable result of the colonial policies that mapped ethnic difference in the distribution of space; this is no longer true.[12] The advent of the Indonesian state and the instigation of more flexible patterns of social mobility have meant that, across urban centres in the country, residential quarters are today more easily identified in terms of class than ethnicity (see Evers 1980). Moreover, the class structure in postcolonial Indonesia and in most of Southeast Asia is ethnically plural. This historical trend towards the de-ethnicization of social space is accentuated further by factors such as local pressures to convert agricultural fields into new residential areas, the increased commoditization of land and the higher rates of geographical mobility, itself due to improvements in transportation and demands for a flexible labour force. Taken together, these factors have contributed in the emergence of a situation in which villages that were once rigidly distinguishable

12 The situation is unlike that depicted by Clifford Geertz (1965) in his study of a small East Javanese town in the 1950s, itself based on the concept of 'hollow town', a term employed to describe the lack of interaction among the various ethnic groups that remain spatially and socially discrete.

are now increasingly intermingled. Alas Niser has benefited from this process. As a result, the purely spatial component of the term *campuran* (Ind., mixed) means that the community is not polarized along ethnic or regional lines by the existence of culturally distinct neighbourhoods. In common with other places in East Java characterized by equivalent processes of flexibility and fluidity (Beatty 1999), the neighbourhoods of Alas Niser are today composed of people of diverse origins leading interconnected and mutually dependent lives.

The civility of emplacement

In the late nineteenth century, the newly opened land of Alas Niser attracted the attention of a Dutch entrepreneur who proceeded to capitalize on the opportunities arising from the abolition of the forced cultivation of cash crops and from the opening up of the sugar industry to the private sector. The 1882 establishment of a sugar mill in Alas Niser forms the point of emphasis of official, state-sponsored narratives of Alas Niser's origins. The official narrative focuses on the equally historic and mythic persona of this Dutch entrepreneur, elevating him to the status of *oreng sakte* (Mad., potent person), a status he shares with the uniquely skilful forest-clearing ancestors. The establishment of the sugar mill marks not only the transformation of forest into a fully man-made and named place but also the incorporation of the locality into the colonial and, later, the independent nation state. This is a case of reciprocal domestication; as the locality became more tightly integrated into the larger political community, it too sought to domesticate this community and its forces into its own universe. At the same time, the locality's administrative inclusion in the colonial state, a process initiated by the establishment of the sugar mill and government representation at the subdistrict level, brought about an influx of Javanese migrants. Although Javanese migrants were present in the locality from earlier times, it was during the twentieth century that the diversity of origins of Alas Niser's inhabitants was greatly enriched by the arrival of skilled, professional workers and civil servants the majority of whom originated from areas conceived as the homeland (*daerah asal*, Ind.) of Javanese people, language and culture in Central and Eastern Java.

In 1998, a huge poster dominated one of the three Alas Niser village headmen's offices. The poster informed visitors that

> The origin of Murno [Ind., pseudonym] – the name of the village Murno, the subdistrict Murno and the municipality of Probolinggo – is related to the foundation of the sugar factory Murno by Tuan Ardih [*tuan*, Ind., meaning mister; a term reserved for foreigners] who was of Dutch nationality.

The quote is taken from a report written for the local branch of what was then the Department of Education and Culture by Pak Warsito, a middle-aged civil servant and head of the local branch (see Warsito 1994). The investigation into the area's history was in partial fulfilment of a directive from Jakarta as to the importance of collecting information about 'history and traditional values'. Such information, Pak Warsito explained, was valuable for the Indonesians to be able to resist the process of westernization, by being made aware of their ancestors and their distinctive *adat* (Ind., customs). Acting as a true historian and dutiful civil servant, Pak Warsito put together an account of Alas Niser's origins using the oral narrations of elderly locals who had worked in the sugar mill. Although, it made no mention of either the sibling or the affinity story, this account was a corroborative rendition of 'Tuan Ardih' topostories I heard over the period of my fieldwork. The elevation of one kind of topostory into an authoritative account is primarily related to providing the historical *raison d'être* of the village as an administrative entity.

The Tuan Ardih topostory construes him as an *oreng sakte*, a potent person. His potency is manifested in several ways: the building of the factory and the resevoir to store water which was '3 metres deep and 150 metres in diameter' or 'as wide as the sea itself'; the erection of a mountain, the '*ringgit* [Ind., gold coin] mountain', from the proceeds of the pool excavation process; the sacrifice of a water buffalo and the use of its skin to make a tape-measure; the operation of the factory that required 'hundreds of workers', forming a kind of personal entourage; the naming of the factory and the place as Murno. From the villagers' perspective, the establishment of the sugar mill did not so much integrate the locality within the colonial and global economy, transforming it into what the Dutch called a 'circle' (i.e. a land area encircling a sugar factory and comprising of the immediate villages and the agricultural land under sugar cane cultivation) (see Elson 1984, 72), as it endowed the landscape with monuments one can still encounter today and provided it with a name, thus making it distinct. From this perspective, Tuan Ardih's actions are equivalent to ancestral deeds. Although unrelated by either descend or affinity, Tuan Ardih stands as an ancestor to today's inhabitants in the sense that his actions were a triumph of hyperhuman activity over unnamed, poorly marked, asocial space.

However, neither Tuan Ardih and his family nor the rest of the Dutch workers in the factory during colonial times are thought of today as part of the moral community of mixed persons. Quite the contrary is true. The iconoclastic memories of locals speak of a fence of tall trees encircling Dutch houses, making them inaccessible to the lower strata of the community which comprised of what the Dutch pejoratively called 'the natives'. Despite being migrants in the same place, the differences of power, race and religion between the Dutch and the 'natives' did not succumb to blurring. The same goes for a small number of Chinese-Indonesians (*oreng Cina*, Mad.) that made a living in Alas Niser as shop owners and wholesale merchants. Out of the four Chinese-owned shops that were to be found in the area during colonial times, only one remained by the late 1990s. Significantly, the family running it was totally absent from local events and happenings, favouring instead the city centre to visit other Chinese and participate in Christian activities.

Simultaneous to the establishment of the sugar mill, the area witnessed the foundation of the headman's office and the subdistrict (*onderdistrik*, Dutch) office. The three key buildings housing these institutions defined the administrative centre of Alas Niser and co-operated closely on the production of sugar cane, the allocation of the agricultural land to cane cultivation, the authorization of contracts and the overseeing of payments and disputes. The administrative centre also included the residences of the Dutch managers, which according to oral sources totalled five families, the temporary residencies of 'native' high-skilled workers such as engineers and administrators, and the residencies of the 'native' subdistrict head (*wedono*, Jav.) and his assistant. Those belonging to the latter two categories are remembered as newcomers (*pedeteng*, Mad.) from various localities of Central and East Java and, because of that, they are categorized as Javanese. Thus, narratives focusing on Tuan Ardih serve another purpose too; namely, they account for an increase in the Javanese migration into the area, which formed the background of the mixing that was to follow. Far from providing actual rates of migration but rather an indication of such rates, my own research into local genealogies attests to the close relationship between the influx of Javanese migrants and the expansion of state bureaucracy and services in the locality. However, Javanese migrations to the frontiers of the eastern salient did not begin in the late nineteenth century; they go back to at least the early nineteenth century. In addition, not all Javanese migrants to the Easthook were employed in the state sector; some came as war refuges and poor agricultural labourers.

According to Hefner, the migration of both Madurese and Javanese to the eastern salient goes back to the final years of the eighteenth century when the Dutch consolidated 'peace' (1990, 10). Javanese migrants were equally attracted both to Pasuruan and Probolinggo by the tax breaks and the free farmland provided by the authorities. However, in Probolinggo, Javanese newcomers were by far outnumbered by Madurese.[13] Further impetus for movement out of Central Javanese principalities was the onerous fiscal and

---

13 Elson writes that 'In 1820, the population of Besuki Residency (of which Probolinggo then formed a part) was composed seven-eights of Madurese and only one-eight of Javanese' (1984, 4).

corvée demands of the post-Mataram rulers and appanage holders in the early nineteenth century, and the rapid population growth of the same period. These factors led to a fast evolving agrarian crisis and the Java War of 1825–1830 (see Carey 1986).

The impact of the Java War can not be underestimated. Governor General Van den Bosch estimated that one-third of the population of Central Java were exposed to the ravages of war. Over 200,000 Javanese lost their lives and one-fourth of the cultivated area sustained damage (Peper 1970, 82). Despite these circumstances, the Easthook was largely unaffected by the hostilities and must have attracted substantial numbers of Javanese peasants fleeing the conflict. Post–Java War, the attractions of migration included a different set of factors. The appropriation by the colonial power of the *mancanegara* (Jav., outlying regions) of Madiun and Kediri, a key outcome of the Java War as far as the curtailing of the powers of the Central Javanese courts is concerned, undermined individual land rights. Instead there was a push towards communal rights and the spread of taxation obligations to a wider part of the population (Boomgaard 1989a, 36). At the same time, the eastern salient was undergoing heavy investment in infrastructure, was seeing the establishment of agricultural estates and provided plenty of opportunities for opening up new land. According to Gooszen, migrants from Madiun and Kediri moved to Pasuruan, Jember and Besuki in the late nineteenth century to work in rail construction, port and irrigation expansion as well as to cultivate land and tend sugar cane, thus working and living along side Madurese migrants (1999, 57–65). In the early decades of the twentieth century, the province of East Java saw lots of people moving between adjacent residencies, while in Central Java thousands of Javanese left their home villages for the plantations of Sumatra's east coast (Gooszen 1999, 69).

Not all of Javanese migrants were destitute peasants. In Alas Niser, some of the earliest Javanese migrants were highly educated for their times; their literacy and numeracy were much sought after skills. Pak Sugeng's and Pak Sunarman's family histories exemplify this trend. Pak Sugeng was a frail man in his seventies and a retired civil servant who talked to me at length about his forebearers on several occasions.

> My father and my mother were from Yogyakarta. While, they were born and raised there, they never returned to Yogyakarta after they moved here to work in the sugar mill [in the 1920s]. My father was a graduate of a Dutch primary school. He was actually brought here by Tuan Ardih together with his brother to work in the factory as mechanics. He was a smart man, a graduate, and it did not take him long to learn the job. He liked living here. So he bought land, built a house and raised all five of his children here.

Figure 3. The central market in downtown Probolinggo

Pak Sunarman's grandfather was from Surakarta, another Central Javanese principality. Described as of aristocratic descent, Pak Sunarman's grandfather had attended an exclusive school for upper-class children in Solo. He was forced to flee the city because of his involvement in the independence movement of the 1930s. 'He sought refuge here and took up a new identity,' Pak Sunarman said to me and continued:

> Because of his education, he found a job at the subdistrict's head office; he could read and write in three languages, Dutch, Javanese and Indonesian. Later on, he took a loan and built the animal market, married my grandmother, a Madurese newcomer from Sumenep, and erected the house we live in now.

At the root of this kind of migration lies education differentials, as the Probolinggo regency at that time was one of the less developed areas of Java as far as literacy is concerned. Elson, citing colonial sources, observes that 'at the time of 1920 census, for example, only 4.4 per cent native males [of the Pasuruan Residency, of which Probolinggo then formed a part] over 15 years of age could read or write, and only the residencies of Madura and Besuki had lower levels of literacy' (1984, 212). As such, the inauguration of Ethical Policy by the colonial state in the beginning of the twentieth century, which was based on the premise of a growing availability of formal schooling for 'natives', did not have much success in Probolinggo. But in other areas of Java, and especially in Central Java, the availability of formal schooling was marked by growing enthusiasm as the graduates of government schools found employment in the lower and middle ranks of the colonial bureaucracy or in enterprises (Benda 1958, 25; Sutherland 1979). Both capitalism and colonialism necessitated the creation of an educated middle class of skilled professionals. In the case of Alas Niser, these were mostly imported from afar.

This pattern of Javanese immigration to Alas Niser and Probolinggo has occurred in a more or less continuous stream throughout the twentieth century and has picked up in the decades of the New Order state as the latter sought to combat underdevelopment and create a political power base through a crusade against illiteracy and an overgrown bureaucratic sector respectively. The number of civil servants employed for the *kabupaten* (Ind., district) administration of Probolinggo increased from 684 in 1978 to 1,764 in 1980 while the number of those working for the *kotamadya* (Ind., municipal) administration of Probolinggo increased from 1,293 in 1984 to 3,410 in 1994.[14] Accordingly, the number of residents of the subdistrict of Murno who were officially registered as civil servants/military personnel went up from a total of 1,535 in 1990 to 1,918 in 1997. Although official statistics are lacking information about the employees' areas of origin, I suggest a great number of them were newcomers since the local population was still lacking in terms of education. Official statistics show that in 1987 only 1,608 individuals out of a population of 31,158 had progressed further than primary school in the subdistrict of Murno. In contrast, newcomers were graduates of teacher schools, other technical/vocational institutions of secondary and further education, and a good number of them had received university degrees.

In 1998–2000, I collected detailed information about this type of immigration to Alas Niser and the figures I obtained, though far from the strict requirements of statistical analysis, do convey a clear picture of its main characteristics. The majority of Javanese immigrants originated from the traditional *nagara agung* (Jav., core) areas of Javanese culture in Central Java (Yogyakarta, Pacitan, Kedu and Surakarta) and the *mancanegara* (Jav., outlying)

---

14 All statistical information in this paragraph is taken from the annual reports of the Kantor Statistik Kotamadya Probolinggo and the Kantor Statistik Kabupaten Probolinggo. Information regarding the 1980s and 1990s is generally reliable given the agency's much improved methods of data collection. In the early 1980s, the subdistrict of Murno was transferred from Kabupaten Probolinggo to Kotamadya Probolinggo, becoming thus part of the municipality. The transfer was accompanied by the electrification of all households, improvements in the road network and the establishment of a clinic.

areas of the western parts of the province of East Java (Madiun, Kediri, Blitar, Tulung Agung). There were also Javanese from Banyuwangi, Surabaya, Malang and Jombang, all in East Java. There were few cases of migrants from further afield (Bali, Sumatra and South Sulawesi). There were also some new arrivals from Madura and from Probolinggo city centre, working as civil servants. Although the overwhelming majority of recent Javanese migrants were employed in the state sector, there were few cases of self-employed migrants involved in petty and wholesale trade and the construction industry. For some civil servants, residence in Alas Niser was only temporary, amounting to a couple of years' stay over a long line of official appointments. They hoped that their movement across the territory would eventually see them return to their place of origin. However, others had already decided that Alas Niser was the end of the journey. The cases of two of my neighbours illustrate the situation.

Pak Danang was a 40-year-old primary school teacher, originating from Kediri. He had moved to Alas Niser 16 years ago, after having taken part in a provincial examination for the appointment of teachers. He had avoided sitting for inter-provincial exams; the idea of having to live in a far outlying area somewhere in Eastern Indonesia was too distressing, as it would make visiting his relatives difficult. His first posting was to Alas Niser where he took residence in a boarding house for bachelors. He met his wife, who was born in Alas Niser, at a wedding celebration. After getting married, he moved to a newly erected house his wife's father had built. Pak Danang was a regular participant in all kinds of neighbourhood rituals and activities and recently had been voted treasurer of a rotating credit association. When asked whether he ever thought of returning to Kediri, he replied negatively saying that he was 'compatible' (*cocok*, Ind.) with the people in Alas Niser and it was enough for him to visit his ageing parents once or twice a year, mostly during *Lebaran*. After all, he added, Alas Niser is where all his 'siblings' now lived; significantly, Pak Danang used *tretan*, a Madurese word, to describe his relationship to his affines and fellow villagers.

Pak Mu'allim was another neighbour. He originated from Tulung Agung, another town in western East Java. Pak Mu'allim used to work in the local branch of the department of agriculture while his wife was a nurse in the government clinic. Pak Mu'allim had first come to Alas Niser as a bachelor, some thirty-eight years ago. Having managed to evade several marriage proposals by locals, he finally settled for Ibu Suharni whom his parents had insisted he married. Ibu Sunami was also from Tulung Agung. After getting married, they lived for four years in rented accommodation. Then they bought the land on which their current house stands; impressive by village standards, it is a two-storey house with an additional outbuilding housing three pairs of oxen which they rented out for ploughing. The oxen represent their security since they retired. Asked whether they had thought of returning to Tulung Agung, they both replied that such a move would be too difficult since it would necessitate a process of re-adjustment. They had lived for so long in Alas Niser that their fluency in Javanese was now somewhat compromised and their accent was already influenced by Madurese in which they were fluent. Moreover, most of the people they knew in Tulung Agung had either died, a reference to their parents, or had migrated elsewhere, a reference to their siblings. In addition, neither had any property left there. Most importantly, their three children, all married, were living either in Alas Niser or in the Probolinggo city centre.

I collected several other life stories that stressed a similar process of acquiring new roots in the place of destination. This process of emplacement involved marriage and the production of children, the acquisition of property in the form of land and/or a house, and the establishment of meaningful relations of co-residence founded on neighbourhood participation. Emplacement is facilitated by learning another language (i.e. Madurese for the Javanese newcomers, Javanese for the Madurophone locals), as people seek to interact cordially and respectfully with each other on an every day basis. Such processes are accompanied by a parallel process of gradually distancing from and eventually rupturing ties with the place of origin as visits tended to become less frequent, especially as parents and other senior relatives die, siblings move on, kin disperse and property gets divided. This sort of distancing is more pronounced among second-generation migrants, both Madurese and Javanese, who admitted to having visited their parents' place of origins mostly as children, but who have maintained few active connections with their kin there as adults, although from time to time such connections do get re-activated depending on circumstances. In most cases, the process of distancing turns into rupture by the time the third generation comes of age. They enjoy little if any contact with distant relatives. Rupture and emplacement are twin processes, taking place at the same time, pulling in two different directions. The diversity of origins, therefore, is counterbalanced by practices of emplacement that emphasize the here and now of the convergence of diverse paths of movement: the production of a shared generation of descendants born and bred in Alas Niser, the generation of wealth and the performance of rituals involving neighbourly exchanges. These practices are at the heart of the process through which 'mixed personhood' has emerged historically and is maintained on an every day basis. In other words, mixed personhood is the product of a history of lived experiences of sharing the same place with equally dislocated, equally uprooted people. Due to relations of affinity and relations of neighbourliness that stem from spatial interspersion, the self-identification of people in Alas

Niser as mixed means that, to their eyes, its fruitless to try to distinguish them as Madurese or Javanese.

We have already seen that as far as Madurese migration is concerned, memories of poverty work to establish commonality within the heterogeneity of origins. Oral accounts of Javanese migration also stressed the unfavourable economic circumstances that faced migrants in their places of origin. Getting educated and pursuing a career in the civil service was an investment and the primary means available to them and their families to set themselves relatively free from the 'vicious circle of poverty, inequality, underproductivity, and population growth' (White 1976, 286) that had engulfed rural Javanese society for the last two centuries. Although few of the Javanese migrants in Alas Niser came from landless families, there were few from rich trader and big landowner households. The vast majority belonged to middle-income families of *sawah* (Ind.) smallholders, lower-level civil servants, or other professionals such as small shopkeepers, petty traders, tailors, etc. For these people, formal schooling was a way of reproducing or slightly furthering rather than dramatically advancing their social position and, most importantly, avoiding falling into poverty.

A number of studies that have focused on rural to urban population movements in Java since the 1960s have highlighted certain factors that force people in rural Java to look for employment opportunities outside their locales of origin both in Java, in the outer islands, or abroad (Kano 1981; Harris and Speare 1986; Hugo 1982; Jellinek 1978). These factors include high population growth,[15] limited or no access to land, few other employment opportunities and low wages. These factors have stimulated an emphasis on obtaining education certificates as a way of securing prestigious salaried jobs either in the government or in the private sector among those who can afford it. For those unable to do so, migration to urban centres as unskilled factory workers and self-employed petty traders is an alternative taken up by large numbers. Migration to urban centres is complemented with state-sponsored transmigration to the outer islands, and construction work and domestic service abroad. However, few of these poorer Javanese migrants have been attracted to the city of Probolinggo, despite the presence of big factories and a burgeoning informal economy. For the most part, as in Surabaya, and Jember, the lower echelons of Probolinggo's economy continue to be filled by recent, mostly circular or temporary Madurese migrants. The latter are to be found

---

15 According to some estimates, the population of Java (including Madura) grew from a mere 5 million in early nineteenth century to 80 million in 1976 to 125 million in 2005. For a discussion of debates relating to the reasons behind Java's extraordinary demography, see Gooszen (1999, 3–13).

in the transport business, petty trade, street selling, scrap metal salvaging, butchering, etc.

The education differentials that set more recent Javanese migrants apart from Alas Niser locals do not translate easily into sharp and rigid class differences as all the big landowners of the area are locals who convert their economic capital into political and symbolic one through pursuing patronage relations with the landless and advancing their own and their children's religious education. In the latter case, they form parts of networks of religious learning that span across localities, and find institutional expression in the founding and running of independent religious schools (Ind., *madrasah* and *pondok pesantren*). The heads of these schools, the famous *kyai*, command both deference and respect among locals and newcomers alike. The top strata of the local society also include rich traders of agriculture produce and other commodities, such as timber, agricultural tools, pesticides and animals. Such wealthy traders are commonly people who come from the locality. It is among people of this class that secular and religious education is pursued as a strategy for social mobility; often they can afford for their children to study both in the provincial and national capitals, as well as abroad. However, not all educated civil servants and military personnel are Javanese. There are Balinese, Bugis and Batak too. In 1998, the subdistrict head was a newcomer from Madura.

Among the middle class, those originating from Java do have an overwhelming presence. But in terms of income, at least, they are joined by local shopkeepers, mid-level traders, factory supervisors and those running their own home industry who may employ as many as five or six people. There are locals also among the teachers and the lower civil servants. However, among the landless agricultural workers, petty traders of a bewildering variety of goods, unskilled factory workers and shop assistants it is locals that predominate.

Becoming-place

Reflecting on Heidegger's concept of dwelling, Keith Basso states that 'dwelling is said to consist in the multiple "lived relationships" that people maintain with places, for it is solely by virtue of these relationships that space acquires meaning' (1996, 54). Here, I have traced the meaning of narratives of dislocation, movement and subsequent emplacement to stories that begin somewhere else, are associated with historical events of power struggles and the scarcity of means of living, and end up with the active creation of a new spatial belonging in a new location. These narratives are accounts of lived or told experiences of diasporas and dispersal, mobility and movement, but contrary to expectations they do not lament a paradise lost. Rather they celebrate a paradise gained.

Issues of agency are integral to the emergence and constitution of place. Through human agency, place becomes, via a process of transformation, the turning of environment into equipment for survival and of undomesticated space into familiar, inhabited and meaningful dimensions of sociality (Ingold 2000). As such, place is not fixed; it has no stable, pre-given essence. Rather, it is shifting and capable of change. In the case of Alas Niser, the making of place as a cultural process is intimately related to the transformative agency of ancestors who, by means of their mystical powers and labour, converted a forested and previously uninhabited area into cultivated fields and houses that, in turn, have provided for and sheltered an expanding community of humans. The stress on the shaping of the topographical features of the landscape is intimately related to the historical transformation of the kindness of these humans and of their descendants. In local ontological terms, both *wong Jawa* (Jav., Javanese people) and *oreng Madura* (Mad., Madurese people) are said to be different kinds of people. However, the Javanese and Madurese who have arrived in Alas Niser as migrants and settled there permanently are described as being entangled in a long process of becoming-mixed. Getting married with a local man/woman, acquiring property, having children and being active in neighbourhood and other public affairs (i.e. getting involved in the very commonplaceness of established situations and dimensions of local social life) has fundamental consequences for forms of identification and the production of personhood. Over a period of successive generations and waves of immigration, such a process of place creation has resulted in the common designation of the people of Alas Niser as *orang pedalungan* or *oreng camporan*; that is, 'mixed people'. As I argue in the next chapter, 'mixed people' are conceived as fundamentally different in corporeal terms from both Javanese and Madurese. In this regard, the becoming of place is coupled with the becoming of persons, i.e. the emergence of a new kind of persons who are conceived as being distinct from their remote ancestors, despite the acknowledgement of having derived from them.

It must be emphasized that Alas Niser is not to be taken as typical of Java. Its history has been shaped by distinct patterns of demographic mobility, landownership and Islamization. Moreover, the emergence of 'mixed persons' concerns those of Madurese and Javanese ancestry only. This inclusiveness stops short of being extended to Hindu Tengger people and Indonesians of Chinese origin who, although present in the wider area, are considered as too different in terms of origins, class and religion. Because they remain outside this circle of engagements, they are also construed as 'out of place'. The idiom of mixing is founded on a selective historical memory that is constructed so as to omit the presence of Hindus in pre-modern times and deny the roles of Chinese in the making of modern Probolinggo. However, the case of Alas

Niser exemplifies in a highly specific manner the ways in which an attachment to place is generated. Such an attachment is radically different from our understandings of it as primordial and given. As I have shown, neither persons nor places are conceived as static. Furthermore, the fundamental correspondence between persons and place as of a particular kind is not rooted in deep histories of sedentary habitation. Rather, it is predicated on short histories of mobility and a facility of incorporating *particular* instances of difference. The ways that difference is incorporated are the subject matter of the chapters that follow.

Chapter 2

THE PERCEPTION OF DIFFERENCE: EMBODYING, REVERSING, ENCOMPASSING

Kinds of bodies

> My body is the fabric into which all objects are woven, and it is, at least
> in relation to the perceived world, the instrument of my comprehension.
>
> (Merleau-Ponty 1962, 235)

Downtown Probolinggo, March 1999. Gatot and I were having lunch in Sumber Hidup, an upmarket restaurant owned by Chinese-Indonesians in downtown Probolinggo. Gatot had been helping with the transcription of some interviews I had conducted over the past week. He was a young unmarried man in his mid-twenties, working in the soya sauce factory on the outskirts of the city. Born of a local woman and a Madurese migrant, he was fluent in Javanese and Madurese, as well as Indonesian, as do several of the inhabitants of Probolinggo with varying degrees of competence. Across our table, there was another young man sitting all by himself, eating silently; a rare sight in this part of the world where food and sociality go together. It was probably for this reason that Gatot invited him to our table and, despite the young man's repeated and polite refusals, Gatot's insistence eventually won him over. The slender but well-built man approached our table with great hesitancy, asked for our *permisi* (Ind.), took to the seat slowly and placed his plate on the table with such a care and attention as if the slightest noise would be tantamount to a gross offence. Speaking in Indonesian mainly but interjected with polite, mid-level Javanese pronouns, we introduced ourselves. Yusuf, our guest, showed none of the usual signs of sheer bewilderment and animated curiosity that initial interaction with a white foreigner usually arouses. He refrained from asking many of the usual questions, and remained calm and collected for the duration of our conversation. He was in Probolinggo on business, he said, looking for an associate whom he had paid in advance for the delivery of forest timber. However, he had been unable to find him – the man's wife had informed him that her husband was away on business – and was starting to suspect that he had been deceived. Yusuf, a native of Sumenep, East Madura, was set to catch the early morning bus to Surabaya and return home empty handed, although he was to try the man's home once more before leaving. Showing neither anger nor any overt exasperation over the whole incident, he blamed his bad luck on the ease with which he trusted others. Not long after having finished his lunch, he excused himself and with the same grace he had come to our table paid his bill and left the restaurant. After he had gone, Gatot admitted to being totally bemused; this was not at all what he expected: a Madurese who does not get quickly angry (*orang Madura yang tidak cepat marah*, Mad.)!

In Probolinggo, ethnic difference is generally described in terms of the concept of *sifat* (Ind.; *watak*, Jav.; *sepat*, Mad.). *Sifat* means one's character, attribute, quality, disposition, nature and temperament. *Sifat* qualifies personhood as in *sepat niser* (Mad.), meaning of charitable or merciful temperament, or *watak gemi* (Jav.), denoting thrifty disposition. Although humankind is believed to come from the same source, namely Allah's creation of Adam, humanity is held to comprise a variety of disparate attributes culturally encoded as *sifat*.

The dispositions of Madurese *sifat* are invariably (and relatively incontestably) depicted as coarse, crude, hard and lacking in refinement; in short as *kasar*. In contrast, the Javanese are construed as the epitome of gentleness and smoothness, endowed with subtlety and exquisite refinement; that is, *halus*. Being of *kasar* or *halus* disposition and temperament includes a number of other qualities. For instance, the Madurese temperament is perceived as brave (*berani*, Ind.), daring, adventurous, hard (*keras*, Ind.), hard working (*kerja keras*, Ind.), tough (*teguh*, Ind.), loud, arrogant and stubborn (*keras kepala*, Ind.), touchy, vengeful, hot-tempered and prone to violence (*cepat marah* or *cepat panas*, Ind.), but also loyal, generous and fair. Javanese temperament is perceived as soft, tender and delicate (*lembut*, Ind.), timid and cool-tempered, avoiding open conflict, agreeable and reserved, lacking in desire for adventure and the capacity for hard manual labour.

The hierarchical contrast between *kasar* and *halus* as qualities of personhood is pervasive. Pak Idris, a man born in Probolinggo of a Madurese mother and a Javanese father, gave me an early lesson in how people in Probolinggo perceive their universe, saying that

> The *sifat* [Ind.] of human beings is diverse. There are some who are honest and there are those who are not. Because humans are not all the same, we have to be alert. The *sifat* of Madurese is different from the *sifat* of Javanese. Madurese *sifat* is *kasar, keras* [Ind. unpolished, hard]; more emotional [*lebih emosi*, Ind.], more hot

lebih panas, Ind.]; it is easier for a Madurese to become angry [*marah*, Ind.] than a Javanese. If a Madurese feels offended for whatever reason, his or her blood will soon start rising [*naik darah*, Ind.], making it difficult for him or her to control the emotions and then, there will be a fight [*carok*, Ind.].

Pak Idris cited a Madurese proverb that encapsulated this: '*angor pote tolang tembeng pote mata*', which can be translated as 'death is preferable to shame'. Pak Santoso, a man in his late fifties who was born in Madura but had been living in Probolinggo for some 30 years, joined in. He said that *sifat Jawa* is, by contrast, *halus* and *lembut* (refined and gentle), calm (*tenang*, Ind.) and assured/quiet (*ayem tentrem*, Jav.) to such an extent that insults are not avenged through open, public violence but through either avoiding further contact with the other party, or employing mystical means, i.e. sorcery. Mixed persons, like Pak Idris, largely perceive themselves as combining these characteristics; they are assemblages of two unequal dimensions or halves, characterized by tension and instability. Stressing this combination and its volatility, another informant in a rather different context commented, 'Probolinggo people are 50–50. We are both *halus* and *kasar*. Depending on circumstances, in cases of conflict mixed people can respond either with anger or just give in.'

During the 18 months I stayed in Probolinggo, I was astounded by the alacrity and insistence with which people kept reminding me of their differences from Madurese or Javanese. Locals of Probolinggo assert that they, and more generally the people who lived along the east coast of Java facing the arid south of the island of Madura, are *orang campuran* (Ind., mixed persons). They placed themselves at the juncture of two kinds of people that demographically dominate the area outside the *campuran* region, namely the Javanese and the Madurese. Such self-denotation as mixed people indicates a sense of self-perception founded both on intimacy and fractional similitude with their significant others and a substantial degree of separation from them. By describing themselves as a kind of people produced out of the combination of Javanese and Madurese, they assert their distinctiveness *vis-à-vis* the very people they are composed of.

As composites of Javanese and Madurese dispositions and attributes, mixed persons are made up of an internal difference. Located at the juncture of Madurese and Javanese, they cannot help but face in two opposite directions at once, noting and displaying their partial resemblance and incomplete departure from the people from which they derive. Mixed persons therefore correspond to a particular instance of what I term the *diaphoron* person. Rather than endowing themselves with a seamless and distinct identity, the *diaphoron* person is a site brought about by the articulation of difference; it is an 'entity' that has two sides and contains within it two opposing forces at once.

Within the plateau of ethnic differentiation, the *diaphoron* person becomes present through the refusal to choose between two equally exclusive identities. Instead, the *diaphoron* person asserts the power of an excessive combination that converts the other into a dimension of the self. In other words, the extent to which mixed persons understand themselves to be both Javanese and Madurese requires that they simultaneously perceive themselves to be both connected to and separate from peoples belonging to these categories.

The difference the *diaphoron* person articulates is not simply that of an assemblage, i.e. the combination of heterogeneous parts. Equally important is the fact that the 'others' in question are both 'non-selves' and 'part-selves' to mixed persons. Contexts wherein distinctiveness, *vis-à-vis* the Madurese and the Javanese, is judged as paramount, mixed persons assert their separation from them, effectively rendering the Javanese and Madurese as different. However, in other contexts where connections and resemblances are of direct concern and importance, Madurese and Javanese are recognized as intimate part-selves to mixed persons. The paradoxical character of the self–other relation means that no taxonomic line of demarcation is drawn between them once and for all. In East Java, the other is taken to subsist and inhere in the self as much as it is taken to be distinct from it. This paradox is partly rooted in the fact that connections between self and other always already implicate and presuppose their separation, and vice versa. Indeed for relations to be established certain forms of distinction must come into play; the opposite is equally true that is, distinctions always point to and anticipate certain forms of connection even if only some of these will be realized. Furthermore, the paradox of self–other articulation is grounded in the ways that the hierarchy underlining the *halus–kasar* distinction is played out. Specifically, in terms of encompassment with the other being subsumed into the self as a lower part of a higher and larger whole, an issue I elaborate below.

Along with the composite, detotalized character of mixed personhood, I also discuss the relation between the body and the person as conceived locally. In the conversations I have had with the people of Probolinggo, the body, its growth, attributes and capacities were of particular importance. In the local imagination, modes of bodily constitution and comportment encode an array of differences that set Madurese and Javanese people apart. The linking of different kinds of people with particular sets of sensibilities and capacities for action means that alongside the corporeal, material body another kind of body makes its appearance. I call this body 'phenomenal' and elaborate on its dual character as both sentient and sensible. My discussion of the phenomenal body aims to underscore the lived rather than representational dimensions of ethnicity and show the body's social character as well as its grounding in perceptual engagements of intersubjective character. However, before we are ready to explore the centrality of the body in the economy of the *diaphoron* person, we have first to grapple with certain theoretical issues in order to create a clearing for our discussion.

The flesh of the social

In the previous chapter, I outlined the historical emergence of locality in terms of demographic mobility and the performance of certain activities such as forest clearing, land ownership, house building, spatial interspersal, neighbourliness, marriage and the production of children. The performance of these activities is central in the becomings of place and the becomings of people as mixed. This is recognized as much by the people this study is about as by myself. However, certain analytical difficulties arise by the unreflective employment of this terminology. The concepts of process and performance currently used in the social sciences and the humanities are built around an assumed opposition between the fluidity of the subject that is recognized by an emphasis on process, historical contingency, and practice and the immutability of being posited by an emphasis on the body. Questioning this distinction is a necessary step before we proceed further.

It has become a commonplace in anthropology and other social sciences to state that identities are socially constructed, i.e. rather than given by nature. This argument permeates the literatures of ethnicity and nationalism, gender and kinship and has become the orthodox position in anthropology's study of humanity. As Ingold observes, persons are imagined as constituted within culture for they are made by processes of socialization or enculturation 'through the imposition of a specific cultural form upon a pre-existing and undifferentiated material substrate' (1991, 358). This material substrate is commonly taken to correspond to what is given to persons by nature and its formation is thought of as guided by genetic inheritance.

The distinction between the given and the acquired rests on a further distinction, that of things interior and things exterior to the person. While nature is thought of as internal to bodies, society is portrayed as an external to them. The social is generally conceived to exist between persons rather than within their bodies. It thus corresponds to the 'networks of relationships' and the 'shared webs of significance' that link pre-existing, monadic entities together. Persons are conceived of as physically discrete and bounded; as organisms they have absolute boundaries between them; they do not extend beyond their skin. Nevertheless, they are conceived of as living interdependent lives within the domain of the social. This interdependence is described as both extrinsic to and antithetical to the body. As individuals, persons become social, and thus fully human, through entering into life trajectories designated by the society in which they are socialized, enacting specific roles and acquiring identities through the performance of specific activities and the occupancy of particular positions. Identity is thus the result of the act of the social on an undifferentiated body; it is produced out of acts of inscription on the material nature provides.

Curiously the metaphysics espoused by social constructivism find some definite echoes in certain ethnographic descriptions. Several studies focusing on the Southeast Asia (Astuti 1995; Tooker 1992; Kammerer 1990; Carsten 1995) and beyond (on South America, for example, see Slaney 1997; Canessa 1998; Gow 1991) argue that identities are understood as processual and performative from an *emic* perspective as well. Rather than seen as 'rooted within', personhood is described by ethnographers as emically conceived, acquired 'from without' and predicated 'not on what one is but what ones does' (Canessa 1998, 241). The Vezo of Madagascar, for example, are said to construe different kinds of people in terms of the everyday economic activities they undertake; for instance, fishing as opposed to agriculture (Astuti 1995). Similarly in Malaysia, Langkawi personhood is described as being moulded and shaped 'gradually through life as [people] acquire different attributes derived from the activities in which they engage and the people with whom they live' (Carsten 1995, 329). In Mexico, Tarahumara ethnicity is contingent on the undertaking of both fire and water baptism (Slaney 1997). Indigenous conceptions of personhood are depicted as informed by metaphysics bearing a certain similitude to those of social constructivism in the sense that they share the same stress on the exteriority of the social and the processual acquisition of identity set against the immutability of the body and its natural givenness.

These presuppositions are particularly present in studies that consider cases of religious conversion, which have actually led the way for the conceptualization of Southeast Asian identities as contingent on performance (see Bowen 1995, 1060). Both Kammerer (1990) and Tooker (1992) argue that the unproblematic status of the conversion to Christianity among the Akha people of northern Thailand is grounded in an indigenous understanding of identity as a bundle of practices. Given that practices are assumed by the ethnographers and locals alike to be dissociated from bodies and thus easily discarded and substituted with new ones, becoming a Christian for the Akha is simply a matter of doing, such as being baptized, following the Sunday mass or receiving communion, and discontinuing ritual practices embedded in the 'traditional' religion.

The distinction between an exterior society and an interior nature that gives us the antithesis between the person as becoming and the body as fixed is, however, totally absent from the presuppositions the people in Probolinggo hold. In locating the difference between human beings in their bodies, the people of Probolinggo do not employ an understanding of the body as a natural substratum. They presuppose neither a distinct domain that of the social, as an external force shaping persons from without, nor do they presuppose that it is this very same domain that provides the connections amongst 'individuals'. Taking local ideas seriously amounts to a cultural critique of presuppositions we hold dear. The orthodox position of constructivism I must add is not so much a false position as far as my informants are concerned but an oddity and a peculiarity.

Throughout this study I maintain that, for the people of Probolinggo, bodies do not come into being before the entry of persons into social relationships. Rather bodies are conceived as co-extensive and co-incident with the social relations that have produced them and which such bodies proceed to perpetuate, enact, change and transform. As such, bodies are both effects and quasi-causes of previous and future becomings respectively. Because there is no presumption in East Java of an absolute line separating the social from the natural (Retsikas 2010a; see also Chapter 3), bodies are not understood as biological outcomes which are then inserted into the social. Bodies are perceived as nodal points, concrete manifestations of the social relations which precede them and which are enacted and produced by them. As such, bodies are wholly social (i.e. made up of relations) and wholly co-extensive with the persons they index, forming body-persons. Such body-persons evince in their corporeal make-up and in the modes of acting the history of the social relationships that have given them flesh and which they carry about inseparably with them. To paraphrase Merleau-Ponty, their flesh is made of the same flesh as that of the social. In this respect, they are more like places which, as we have seen in the previous chapter, arise out of and are brought forth simultaneously with the social relations that have created them. Body-persons embody the trajectories social relationships have travelled, encoding their continuities as well as ruptures, and manifesting their future contours as well as the unexpected directions they might follow.

Origins, originals and ruptures

People in Probolinggo recognize various categories of persons. The category of the person corresponds to the noun *orang* (Ind.; *oreng*, Mad.; *wong*, Jav.) Rarely, though, does *orang* appear unqualified in conversation. It is usually followed by an epithet designating a particular and relevant attribute of the person addressed or referred to. Thus, *orang kecil* designates a commoner in opposition to *orang besar*, a dignitary; *orang kaya* defines a rich or well-to-do person as distinct from *orang miskin*, a poor or less well-off person; *orang dagang* is a tradesman, while an *orang petani* is a farmer; *orang sedapur* is a person 'of the same hearth' (a kin person), an *orang jauh*, 'of the afar' (a stranger). *Orang* is also the most common term used to describe kinds of people in an ethnic sense. Thus, the categories of *orang Jawa* (person of Java), *orang Madura, orang Bugis, orang Banjar, orang Dayak*, to name a few, are used more extensively than the terms *suku* (Ind., tribe) or *etnis* (Ind., ethnic group) that are privileged by official discourses emanating from state institutions.

As much as they assert the existence of different kinds of people, the inhabitants of Alas Niser and Probolinggo identify themselves as mixed people, i.e. as *oreng camporan* (Mad.; *orang pedalungan*, Ind.; *wong pedalungan* Jav.). The idea of mixing refers to the collapse of 'pure' and 'original' categories of people in the locality and asserts that their personhood is composite and plural rather than elemental and singular. Such a conception draws on the history of demographic movements and transposes images of newly found place, interspersal and intermarriage to the level of the person. To be a mixed person means to be of different kinds of people simultaneously, emphasizing the innovative and novel character of the persons involved. Quite early in my fieldwork, I was given the following definition of mixed people:

> Alas Niser and Probolinggo as a whole do not have their own original people [*oreng asle*, Mad.]. Unlike other places in Java such as Banyuwangi which has its own original people that is, the *oreng Osing*, or West Java with its own original people of *oreng Sunda*, Probolinggo consists only of mixed people [*oreng camporan*, Mad.]. The meaning of *oreng camporan* is that a person is both of Javanese and Madurese descent [*toronan*, Mad.], that one is not exclusively of Javanese descent or Madurese one, that one is both a person of Java and a person of Madura [*awaq-duaq oreng Jebbeh-Madura*, Mad.].

To be mixed both involves and displaces the purity of *ke-asli-an* (Ind.). *Asli*-ness is a quality of the other. The self of mixed persons is both part of and yet different from the other to the extent that it consists of several others; it is marked by multiplicity, its presence is excessive. In contrast, *asli*-ness is characterized by singularity; its presence is elemental, static and internally undifferentiated.

Asli is difficult to translate. In certain contexts, it refers to that which is original, true and genuine and thus distinct from those that are fake and fabricated. In yet other contexts, *asli* carries connotations of autochthony in the sense of a lack of rupture, parting and estrangement. While both mixing and purity rest on particular notions of origins and growth, the way that such origins and growth are played out and realized marks their difference. Notions of origins are encapsulated in the concept of *asal*. *Asal* means beginning point, source, basis, cause and reason, and refers as much to genealogy as to place. *Asal* corresponds to the social relations that precede the person and which it is made of. The purity of *asli* is predicated on the close, uninterrupted correspondence of genealogical relations and spatial ones and the likeness of the genealogies that have produced a person. In contrast, the multiplicity of mixed persons emerges out of the disjunction of genealogy from place, as well as from the junctures formed by the meeting of two distinct lines of genealogy.

Madurese and Javanese persons are understood as having different kinds of blood. *Asli* refers to the genealogical engendering of persons and is contingent on the corporeal links between generations, the vertical flow of blood (*dereh*, Mad.) from the past to the present that connects the bodies of ancestors and descendants. Thus, a person who identifies himself/herself as *orang Madura asli* maintains that his/her blood is pure Madurese in the sense that both his/her mother and father were of pure Madurese blood, that they too were *orang Madura asli*. Similarly, the hetero-categorization *orang Jawa asli* is taken to mean that a person is of pure Javanese ancestry. The genealogical connotations of *asli* refer to the fact that persons are conceived as the embodiment of relationships of affinity and made from the undifferentiated mixture of blood their fathers and their mothers contribute to their formation (see Chapter 3).

The category of *orang campuran* rests on the same premise. To the extent that it has to do with procreation, *orang campuran* means that the flesh of mixed persons is the outcome of acts of intermarriage of people of pure blood. The narrowest definition of *orang campuran* I encountered during fieldwork centred on children produced by unions either of a Javanese man with a Madurese woman or of a Madurese man and a Javanese woman. This definition privileges neither 'sex' in the significance of either contribution in blood to the offspring's identity. In this respect, it is different from the definition that Husson provides in her monograph. She notes that 'sometimes, this term also describes the children of a Madurese father and a non-Madurese mother, born as a result of migration' (1995, 20; my translation). Husson's definition ascribes to semen a priority and efficacy that women's contribution to the formation of the person lacks. As will become apparent in the next chapter, the people I worked with did not subscribe to a theory of conception that privileges semen at the expense of maternal blood.

In Probolinggo, the category mixed people refers only to people born of marriages between Javanese and Madurese, and transforms the history of demographic movements and intermarriage into an embodied process resulting in the creation of new kinds of persons. In other words, it transforms history into bodies by means of procreation. Other kinds of ethnic intermarriages are recognized, too. However, the children of such unions are referred to using different terms. Children born of unions between an *orang Cina* (Ind., Chinese-Indonesian) and a Javanese or a Madurese are described as *orang blasteran* (from *blaster*, Ind. which means to cross-breed). Similarly, children born of marriages between an *orang Indonesia* (Indonesian) and *orang asing* (a non-Indonesian, a foreigner, usually a Westerner) are called as *orang Indo*.

Questions of origins and growth are not limited to procreation, but involve another set of relationships. This is so for *asli*-ness has a spatial component of equal significance to the vertical flows of blood. In its spatial capacity, the self-identification of *orang Madura asli* means that a person was born and bred in the island of Madura. Similarly, the hetero-categorization *orang Jawa asli* carries the connotation of being born and raised in the island of Java. Central to this is the idea of a 'homeland', an ethno-locality. This is partly conveyed by the term *dhere'k* (Mad.) which designates an expanse of space, its inhabitants, its natural environment and the activities people undertake there. From this perspective, *asli* is used interchangeably with *lahiran* (Ind.). *Lahiran* refers to place of birth and socialization. The self-designation *lahiran Madura* or *lahiran Jawa* construes a person born in Madura or Java and belonging to a place in the sense that its origins and growth are predicated on its embeddedness within spatial sets of relationships. Persons are conceived of in the widest sense possible, as literally grown out of the land. Those whose ties to ethnic homelands have been severed due to demographic movement and who have taken up new spatial positions are described as *pedatang* (Ind., newcomers). A *pedatang* is a person born of another locale who has recently moved to a new settlement and is living and working there. The term captures the rupture with *asal* that demographic movement entails and new sets of ties fostered with and in the locale of destination. Mixed persons are created by similar ruptures to those characterizing the condition of *pedatang*, but their relation with the place they inhabit involve deeper histories of settlement.

Campuran's spatial component is more apparent when the term's synonym, *pedalungan* (Jav.), is considered. The term *pedalungan* is itself a composite term firstly because it consists of two lexical items, and secondly because these items belong to two different Javanese language levels which are kept separate in most circumstances. The first lexical item *pedalungan* consists of is that of *medal*. *Medal*, meaning to emerge, to take a route, to leave, belongs to the higher language level (*krama*) of Javanese (the lower level, *ngoko*, equivalent for *medal* is *metu*; see Horne 1974, 369, 378). The second lexical item is *lunga* and belongs to the lower level. It means to depart, to go, to be out (the *krama* for *lunga* is *kesah*; see Horne 1974, 352). As a category, *pedalungan* designates those people of Madurese genealogical origin who live outside the island of Madura, most commonly in East Java. This is the meaning given by Javanese speakers living outside Probolinggo, in Jakarta, Solo and Surabaya. It describes the disjunction of genealogy from space, i.e. the introduction of a discontinuity between the genealogical and emplaced ways of engendering and growth. Although the inhabitants of Alas Niser and Probolinggo have adopted the term, they have given it a quite different meaning, wholly synonymous with *campuran*. To them, it stands for both the children of mixed (Madurese–Javanese) marriages and the kinds of persons who are born, live, work, produce, reproduce and die in the wider locality, irrespective of their precise genealogy. In this sense, *pedalungan* retains a refashioned spatial referent, designating a place as somewhere where mixing takes place and a mixed place.

The corporeal and the phenomenal

Asal's importance in indigenous ways of perceiving ethnic difference has to do with it providing the means by which the body becomes, designating the sources and springs of its formation and growth. The vertical flows of blood across generations require the formation of junctures for bodies to spring forth. These junctures correspond to the marriages contracted in the past. As such, *asal* is about past social relationships that have come together in order to produce bodies. But this engendering is also contingent on the relations bodies entertain with the land and the people that occupy it. *Asal* therefore encodes a different set of relationships to genealogical ones as well, pointing to spatial relations that have occurred in the past and which are still taking place in the present as the additional sources of growth for the body.

The body, considerations regarding *asal* relate to, has a corporeal, material dimension. Its sources of growth are basically semen, blood and food (on the relations between the two, see Chapters 3 and 5) that make up its bones, organs and skin. The sociality of the corporeal body is attested by the affinal junctures and spatial engagements that form and sustain it. *Asal* is therefore about the first articulation of the body as a social process; it is about its becoming material. The body's second articulation relates to its phenomenal dimension, i.e. the fact that it is both perceiving and sentient, sensible and perceived. This phenomenal dimension takes the presence of others as axiomatically given. These others are the quasi-objects the body perceives and in relation to which it acts. The phenomenal dimension of the body also rests on the reversibility of such relationships with one's body corresponding to a quasi-object for others and a point of orientation for the undertaking of actions. The people of Probolinggo place great importance on the phenomenal dimension of the body and to the ways that the materiality of the body becomes actualized in every day activities. Indeed, the ways in which ethnic difference is perceived are closely related to the attention paid to how Madurese and Javanese bodies behave, realizing persons in intersubjective practice.

I opened the chapter with reference to the pervasive influence that the hierarchy of *halus* and *kasar* qualities has on the perception of difference between Madurese and Javanese. The perception of these qualities takes place within the parameters of intersubjective engagement and presupposes the occupancy of a position or a perspective, a fixed point of view from which perception, evaluation and judgement proceeds. The following ethnographic description records the perspective of the mixed people of Probolinggo as they engage with and evaluate the manifestations of their significant others' bodies.

From the perspective of mixed persons, to be a *halus* person (as a distinct quality of being Javanese) involves the deployment of a particular set of sensibilities and a mode of being-in-the-world that is manifested in concrete activity and behaviours. Such behaviours include gentleness, smoothness, subtlety of expression, ethereal mannerisms and exquisite refinement. In opposition, being *kasar* involves the Madurese body in its entirety. In this case, *kasar* is inferred from everyday activity. Such activity is aesthetically and perceptually evaluated as lacking in refinement and characterized by a certain hardness, harshness or roughness. To be mixed involves a certain indeterminacy manifested by and reflected in the capacity of acting both *halus* and *kasar*. As I discuss later, the combination of *halus* and *kasar* qualities in mixed bodies upsets and redraws the hierarchy that this distinction is based on in some significant ways.

The corporeal and the phenomenal dimensions of the body are not related by any simple form of determinism. Euro-American forms of essentialism privilege the determination of the phenomenal by the corporeal, of action in the world by the substance of which the body is made. In contrast, social constructivism privileges the action of the phenomenal on the corporeal, of exterior social events on the passive receptacle that the body assumedly is. However as Deleuze and Guattari remark, we must move beyond this simplistic dichotomy and seek 'reverse causalities' or 'advanced determinisms' (2001, 371). The most common cases of reverse causalities are feedback loops which involve effects reacting to their causes and presuppose the relative autonomy of one another. The interchangeability of causes and effects combined with their relative independence means that the relation of the corporeal and the phenomenal entails two possibilities. The first is that they are closely articulated with each other. This sort of circular, mutually reinforcing causality ensures that the corporeal and the phenomenal are finely attuned and aligned with each other (see Errington 1989; Tsintjilonis 1997). In our case, this translates in the understanding that bodies that are Javanese in origin behave in characteristically *halus* ways and that *kasar* practices are supported by Madurese sources of growth. In this regard, the phenomenal dimensions of the body actualize in practice the materials (past social relations) of which the body is made, with the body's current sources of growth (present social relations) continuing to provide further supports for these actualizations. The second possibility is one of disarticulation. The phenomenal and the corporeal become less perfectly aligned, less closely attuned. The case of Yusuf, the young Madurese trader from the start of the chapter, who acted in markedly *halus* and characteristically un-Madurese ways, is a case of dissonant articulation. Here we could say that the phenomenal acted independently of the corporeal in the sense of not actualizing it.

Sensible distinctions

From the perspective of Probolinggo locals, the perception of difference is intimately related to the phenomenal dimensions of the body, the kinds of sounds it is capable of producing and receiving when speaking and hearing, the colours it is enveloped in, its degrees of heat and coolness, its dryness and hardness, its softness and dampness. These qualities are neither asocial nor simply given. They are the outcome of acts of perceptual engagement and evaluation and so are embedded in social interaction. Thus, the perception of the body is contingent on the presence of another person who occupies a specific position and perspective in relation to it. Phenomenal bodies are instantiated and realized within a relational field of mutual engagements. They are communicated and perceived in terms of their speech, gestures, tastes and distastes. Such bodies are sensible and sentient; they are perceived through the senses and manifested as sensibilities.

As elsewhere in Java, in Probolinggo the violent and the non-violent approaches to disputes and conflicts arising from every day life are traced to dispositions, *kasar* and *halus* respectively, themselves imagined as a difference in the propensity of one's blood to remain cool or to become boiling hot. *Kasar* and *halus* refer to specific courses of action and behaviour related in turn to one's body temperature. The direct association people in Probolinggo draw between *sifat Madura* and violence was a constant feature of our discussions. When a Madurese was ashamed, I was told, he would pull out the sickle he carries concealed beneath the clothes and engage the other party in a duel (*carok*, Mad.; see Husson 1990). In contrast, *sifat Jawa* is construed as one who is able to successfully restrain feelings of embarrassment from becoming overt and public, by keeping them hidden in the *hati* (Ind., heart/liver) while maintaining both an interior and exterior quality of calmness and tranquillity. In this case, *halus* draws its superior ontology from a disposition of exercising control over unsettling and socially disturbing emotional states, in particular those attributed to *nafsu amarah* (Ind.), the drive of anger and rage.

Kasar's and *halus*'s thermal attributes interact with other sensory material such as certain chromatic qualities. Typical Madurese dress is perceived by mixed persons as involving a taste for colours which are gleaming and dazzlingly bright (*cemerlang*). These colours are worn in combinations which seek to achieve a high contrasting effect. 'Madurese women like bright coloured clothes,' commented one person. 'They usually rely on red and other reddish colours, such as yellow and orange. Light blue and green are also their favourite,' he added. Female attire usually consists of a *krudung* (head cloth), a *kebaya* (clothing the upper body) and a *samper* (a batik cloth wrapped around the waist and covering the lower body), and draws several of these preferred colours together with the aim of enhancing beauty and attractiveness. Beauty products and the choice of jewellery are also carefully chosen to enhance conceptions of Madurese femininity. However, several of the people I spoke to were critical of these choices, claiming that Madurese women often opt for unsuitable lipstick colours that are too bright for their brown complexion, while their gold earrings, bracelets and necklaces were all thought to be 'too big' (*terlalu besar*). Madurese male dress was usually described in comparison to 'traditional' Indonesian dress. The tastes of Madurese males are equated again with a certain chromatic contrast. The contrast is conveyed by the combination of *klabih pesa* (Mad.), a black two-part cloth consisting of a short jacket and a pair of trousers, the latter wrapped around the waist rather than buttoned up, and a *kaos dalem* (Mad.), a red-and-white striped T-shirt.

Javanese dress is usually considered calmer (*tenang*, Ind.) and softer (*lembut*, Ind.) in terms of the effect its colours has on the eyes. This softness is thought to be a quality of dark (*gelap*, Ind.) colours such as white, black, ink blue and brown, as well as of the way these are combined in the decorative batik textile designs produced in the principalities of Yogyakarta and Surakarta, situated in the heartland of Javanese 'authenticity' (see Boow 1988; Schulte Nordholt 1997). During colonial times, such batik designs were highly regulated by edicts issued by the Javanese courts; in recent decades, they have undergone a certain resurgence.

Thermal and colour dispositions are interrelated; the hotness of blood is directly associated with the colour red, the colour par excellence of Madurese *sifat*. Reddish colours and bold combinations are commonly interpreted as manifesting the turbulent tensions imagined to inhabit the Madurese person, his/her uncontrollability of emotions and extrovert disposition. On the other hand, the coolness of Javanese blood is denoted by the neutrality of colours in the items of Javanese clothing. These colours are said to be highly harmonious or suitable (*cocok*, Ind.) to each other. In this regard, coolness is associated with introversion, timidity and refraining from public boasting.

Issues concerning the sense of taste are also highly significant. The island of Madura is arid, dry and infertile. Low levels of rainfall, combined with the limestone composition of the soil make the practice of irrigated agriculture far from common and necessitate the cultivation of un-irrigated fields (*tegal*). Due to these ecological factors, rice cultivation is complemented with the cultivation of maize and cassava, as well as other crops. Both maize and cassava are seen as characteristic of the hard (*keras*) Madurese diet. In particular, in Probolinggo, Madurese are seen as maize eaters in the sense that their staple diet consists mainly of maize, and only secondarily of rice, while cassava is consumed in periods of marked shortages of maize and rice, usually during the months preceding the new harvest. *Keras*-ness is perceived through the taste as well as touch, conveying a certain hardness and firmness felt by the teeth and the tongue. The *keras* quality is regarded as inherent to the texture of these foodstuffs, the direct result of the quality of the land on which it grows and of which it is an extension. By extension, Madurese corporeality is *keras* for Madurese bodies grow out of the consumption of *keras* food.

By contrast, the staple diet of Javanese consists of rice, which is designated as *halus*. The volcanic soil of the island of Java is rich and benefits from the generally high level of rainfall. These factors are construed as contributing to the high productivity of irrigated (*sawah*) agriculture and the softness of produce. Although none of the people I spoke to articulated explicitly a direct link between irrigated agriculture, humidity and food texture, such a connection was clearly established in their minds, nevertheless. The Javanese diet, consisting of rice which is soft (*lembut*) and juicy (*banyak airnya*), was seen reflected in Javanese displays of a similar softness. In Probolinggo, as in the rest of Southeast Asia, rice is thought to be far superior to any other foodstuff in terms of its contribution to human growth and health. Babies are fed rice as soon as they stop breastfeeding and generous portions of rice, consumed three times daily, are seen as absolutely essential to ensuring an adult's strength and well-being. Similarly, healthy bodies are said to be soft for they have flexible and elastic muscles. By contrast, hard bodies bear the signs of illness, usually related to bad blood circulation and the formation of blood clots. In cases such as this, a series of massages will be performed by specialists to reconstitute the body's texture to a healthy state.

The hierarchy that underlines the *halus–kasar* distinction has kinaesthetic effects too. Travel between the islands of Java and Madura is experienced as movement across uneven terrain. The kinaesthetic experience of space is manifested in the verbs used to mark movement. Several first-generation Madurese migrants in Probolinggo, who made regular short trips to their villages in Madura to visit family and friends, refer to their movement across the Madura Straits with the verb *toron*, which literally means to climb down, to descend, to move in a downward fashion. Their return journey to Java is denoted by the verb *ongghe* meaning to move upwards, to ascend.[1] Here, difference is perceived through travel and the movement of the whole body across space.

Thus, between the perceived uplands of Java and the lowlands of the island of Madura lies the land of mixed persons. To my interlocutors, this land covers most of the eastern coast of East Java, from the north of Pasuruan to the south of Situbondo and Asembagus and from the mountains of Jember and Lumajang to the southern regions of Malang. Such a land is construed as both *halus* and *kasar*, less *kasar* than the land of Madura and less *halus* than the land of Java. By being more fertile, less hot, less dry and more humid than the island of Madura, *camporan* land is thought of as giving life to persons of smoother appearance than those of Madura. In the same vein, *camporan* land is seen as being less fertile, more hot, more dry and less humid than Central Java. It is thus conceived of as engendering and sustaining persons with a more volatile temperament and more colourful appearance than those of Java.

Along with movement in space, gestures are accorded a particular significance in the qualification of ethnic bodies. In a series of discussions with members of the Sangar Bayu Kencana, Probolinggo's most famous dance troupe led by Pak Priyono, differences of gesture and movement acquired a particular importance. Pak Priyono, a multi-award-winning dancer and choreographer from Banyuwangi in East Java, had been living in Probolinggo for the past 21 years. He explained the differences between Madurese and Javanese dance as founded on different ways of being-in-the-world. 'Madurese dance is characterized by *leter* (Mad.) movement … movement that aims to attract somebody's attention. This is so, for *sifat Madura* is proud (*bangga*, Ind.) and likes showing off in public,' he asserted. Madurese dance movements are also perceived as spontaneous, corresponding to *sifat Madura* 'outspokenness', and marked by sharp, ungraceful and rapid movements, corresponding to *sifat Madura* 'bravery'. Such modalities of movement take place within a particular aural environment characterized by a percussion orchestra that produces a loud (*kasar*) frenzy of rhythm. The *kasar*-ness of sound is commonly attributed to the dominant roles of *gendang* (Mad.), a kind of drum made using animal skin, and *soronen* (Mad.), a short wooden flute.

Javanese dance movements are construed as soft (see Brakel-Papenhuysen 1995; Hughes-Freeland 1997). 'Javanese dance is full of movements that show indecision for *sifat Jawa* is reserved (*malu*, Ind.) and thinks a lot before acting,' Pak Priyono added. The choreography places particular emphasis on the smooth and effortless transition from one gesture to the next. In Geertz's

---

1 On the importance of 'up' and 'down' as spatial orientations in the Austronesian linguistic family that covers most of island Southeast Asia see Adelaar (1997) and Blust (1997).

words, 'every gesture [is] a calm defiance of anatomy and gravity' (1960, 284). These gestures are accompanied by a percussion orchestra that members of Bayu Kencana describe as inducing the dancers and the audience to feel calm (*tendrem*, Jav.) and satisfied (*puas*, Ind.). The smoothness of this music is attributed to the inclusion of the *gambang* (Jav.), an instrument similar to a xylophone which is quite important in Javanese music.

As well as gesture and movement, speaking and hearing play a significant part of the perception of ethnic difference. Writing about the ways in which speaking style is related to both gender and status differences in Java, Keeler notes that it is both the content of speech and its overall tone that are of particular importance to the Javanese. Noting that women are thought of as inferior to men in part because of their greater informality in deploying Javanese speech levels and their more casual tone, Keeler observes that conveying 'information carries some threat of discord. If contrary to its receivers' wishes, [speech] may startle them, causing disarray to their thoughts and feelings, and so endangering both their health and self-possession. It may, most dangerously, arouse disappointment or anger. ... [Thus, speech] should be diluted in a warm broth of agreeable sentiments, phrased in appropriate vocabulary' and using the appropriate language level (1990, 137).

> Particularly, when addressing someone of significantly higher status than oneself, but even with one's near equals, one should attend carefully to the tenor of any encounter as well as to the information that is being exchanged. (1990, 142)

Due the inherent risks and dangers of communication, hearing and speaking receive particular attention. Both the Madurese and Javanese languages, which are mutually imperceptible (i.e. despite the geographic proximity of the respective groups, Madurese speakers do not understand Javanese, and the reverse), consist of several speech levels. Differences between the two languages, as well as the difference between the distinct speech levels within each language, is construed in terms of the *halus–kasar* distinction. Here, the aural and oral qualities of speech are given as much attention as its content; the referential quality of words is of as much important as the sounds people produce and receive. Words are not simply 'carriers of referential meaning', meaning is also to be found also 'in the sounds of the words' (Stoller 1984, 568). That is, language is a communicative activity taking place in a world created, animated and experienced through sound.

In mixed Probolinggo, as in other parts of Java, the Madurese language is described as *kasar*: cacophonous and lacking the delicate, swirling melodies of the Javanese language. The relative inferiority of Madurese personhood therefore rests on the lesser degree of oral and auditory perfection a Madurese person is capable of displaying in linguistic interaction. *Kasar*-ness is largely a quality of the lower speech levels – *ngoko* in Javanese and *ta' abasah* in Madurese. The lower speech levels are employed in specific contexts, primarily among people of equal social standing who are engaged in long and intimate exchanges, or by a social superior speaking to a social inferior but not vice versa. Such contexts permit the expression of relaxed conviviality that involves jokes, teasing, gossip, as well as dissatisfaction and frustration, and sometimes even anger. The semiosis of these relations by *ngoko* is marked by *ngoko*'s blander, coarser sounds and a certain kind of speech performativity, such as speaking faster and less evenly. The contrast with the long, drawn-out tonalities of the highest speech level, *krama* (Jav.), is obvious. *Krama* is employed in formal occasions, when speaking to people one hardly knows or to whom one owes respect and deference. *Krama* is characterized by an extremely stylized, slow and flat mode of delivery. Indeed, Geertz observes that speaking in *krama* has 'a kind of stately pomp which can make the simplest conversation seem like a great ceremony' (1960, 254).

In Probolinggo, both Javanese and Madurese are spoken, along with Indonesian. However, it is almost invariably the lower, less formal and less differentiating language level (*ngoko*) of both Javanese and Madurese that is used, sprinkled with a few middle-level (*madya*) honorifics to mark certain occasions as more formal and hierarchical. Mixed persons have therefore partial command of both languages, manifesting their lack of *asli*-ness due to a lack of complete fluency. Such a lack becomes shamefully evident when the second-generation migrants visit their parent's origin places in Madura and Java, and find themselves unable to address their elder relatives properly, i.e. in *krama*. From the perspective of their relatives, this inability, as well as being rather offensive, is also a manifestation of the 'inauthenticity' of their junior kinsmen from Probolinggo who are invariably seen as more *kasar*.

While a substantial number of people in Probolinggo are able to converse adequately in both lower-level Javanese and Madurese, as well as Indonesian, Javanese and Madurese are unevenly distributed in the municipality. Javanese is primarily spoken in the neighbourhoods of the city centre, while the periphery's soundscape is dominated by Madurese. This distribution partly reflects the habitation of the city centre by civil servants and professionals who are primarily migrants from other areas of Java. In contrast, the agricultural periphery and the port area are populated by speakers of Madurese. However, such dichotomies are not clear cut. Madurese is also spoken in the city centre's market places and in many traders' homes, both small and big, while Indonesian is spoken in schools, government offices and banks. Similarly, Javanese is spoken in some homes in the agricultural periphery. In addition to those people who learn both languages at home, due to being born of inter-ethnic marriages, others learn a second language as a result of being brought up in mixed areas. Dual fluency depends also on profession, age and gender. Older Madurophone women in Alas Niser who earn a living as agricultural labourers and do not have extensive networks outside the immediate neighbourhood generally speak Madurese only. This is in contrast to men who work as traders, who have extensive networks and can speak both languages. Those fluent in both Madurese and Javanese deploy either language contextually, according to assumptions about the interlocutor's range of competence and origins; while there is also a lot of language switching going on and a tendency towards a hybrid language that combines Madurese, Javanese and Indonesian. The success of Indonesian as a secondary, national language cannot be underestimated either, especially since knowledge of it is not exclusive to those who have attended school. Several people of older generations have mastered it through casual conversations.

The distinctive capacities of mixed persons are further manifested in the absence of 'traditional' *campuran* attire, a mark of the novelty of the body involved. The modern status of mixed bodies is underlined by the adoption of forms of everyday clothing that register it as belonging to national and supra-national communities. In today's Probolinggo, men typically wear long trousers and shirts for formal occasions or T-shirts for more informal events. These items were introduced to Indonesia by means of the colonial 'civilizing' mission. As in other places in Indonesia, male government employees don the safari suit or the long sleeved *batik* shirt worn loose over long trousers. This style of clothing was propagated in the New Order state (1967–1998) as the official dress. Middle-class professionals usually adopt the full Western suit or a combination of trousers, shirt and tie, while youths generally opt for jeans and a T-shirt. Professional men rarely appear in public in a *sarong*, the chequered tubular cloth fastened around the waist, except for Friday prayers or other religious occasions. Men wearing *sarong* in public are usually encountered in the agricultural periphery of the city as they move between neighbouring houses visiting, hanging around in the market place sipping coffee and exchanging news, or performing prayers.

For formal occasions such as betrothals and weddings, women in Probolinggo, especially those of the older generation, comply with the elevation of *kain kebaya* as the national dress for women by the Indonesian state, which defines them as the repositories of a distinctive, non-Westernized, pan-Indonesian identity (Taylor 1997). Irrespective of class and status, the costume consisting of a *batik* cloth wound around the waist, and a long-sleeved blouse extending to the hips is worn by all women. Class and status are usually signified by whether the *batik* is handmade or printed and by the quality of the fabric with silk being highly prized. In addition, while upper-class women appear in *kain kebaya* only in specific occasions, working class women wear it as their daily and ceremonial attire. In Probolinggo, *kain kebaya* involves colours which are both vivid, bearing a striking resemblance to Madurese female costumes, and sombre, taking their cue from Javanese court traditions. However, vivid and sombre colours are rarely combined with greens, pinks and yellows, which are worn separately from and alternatively to browns, blues, and blacks. Younger women have a strong preference for jeans and T-shirts. A minority of women can be seen wearing the *jilbab*, the Islamic headscarf, even though local religious authorities were remarkably relaxed about the strict application of Islamic rules of dress.

If Probolinggo femininity is marked by the separation of *halus* and *kasar* qualities in terms of clothing, the dietary habits of less well-to-do Probolinggo households freely mixes *halus* and *kasar* together. Especially among the peasants of Probolinggo's periphery, diet is characterized by the daily consumption of rice and corn. Meals provide a balance of harder and softer substances, which is seen as essential to maintaining the body in good health and providing an excellent source of strength. This diet is interrupted only at ritual occasions in which rice features prominently, along with other foodstuffs, mainly chicken. The higher value accorded to rice is reinforced by better off people who consume rice as a staple and eat meat more often and in larger portions.

In order to provide for the dietary needs of the people of Probolinggo, the cultivation of irrigated fields on the periphery alternates during the agricultural year between rice and maize. Other products such as cassava, soya beans, green peas, peanuts, and onions are also cultivated, both for domestic consumption and the market. In general, maize is seen as a more commercial a crop than rice. Peasants plant maize twice a year, reserving the rainiest months of the wet season for the cultivation of rice. This rice is usually destined for meeting household consumption needs, though part of it might be sold to traders if there is plenty.

The oscillation of fields between *halus* and *kasar* products and the oscillation of femininity between vivid and sombre colour combinations is also encountered in certain efforts by the Bayu Kencana dance troupe to create dances with *ciri pedalungan* (mixed features, Ind). *Ciri pedalungan* alternates between soft gestures and gestures that are undeniably assertive. These dances are usually referred to as 'creations' (*kreasi*, Ind.), the product of individual choreographers and are often performed in provincial and nation-wide competitions and festivals. They invariably consist of *halus* and *kasar* elements combined in a tense, alternating fashion. For example, Pak Priyono composed a new dance called *mlijho* (Mad.) that narrates the hard work of street-sellers in Probolinggo. The song is delivered in low Madurese throughout. However, both the music and the dance movements alternate between sections marked by slow rhythms

Figure 4. The key members of the Bayu Kencana

and delicate sounds with the dancers moving with self-confident and gracious humility and reservation, and parts characterized by rapid rhythms and high-pitched notes with the dancers adopting angular and assertive poses to indicate flirtatiousness and pride.

Reversibility and the *diaphoron* person

From the mixed person's point of view, ethnicity is neither solely a metaculture in the sense of modern processes of inventing ethnic distinctiveness for purposes of legitimacy as Hobsbawm and Ranger suggest (1992), nor is it simply dependent on the instrumental use of culture diacritics for purposes of boundary demarcation in conditions of competition over resources as Barth advocates (1969). However, culture diacritics such as language, dress styles, dietary habits and dance do feature heavily in the indigenous logic of perceiving difference. They emerge as actualizations of the social relationships that have engendered persons, manifesting the sources of origin and growth (e.g. imagine someone who was born in Madura but moved to Java when he was very, very young) of the corporeal body in intersubjective encounters. As such, they amount to displays that at once unfold the body-person in the presence of others and inculcate and cultivate its sensibilities and specific modes of being-in-the-world through repeated performance. Dress habits, language capacities and dietary tastes therefore correspond to devices that communicate the social relations persons are composed of, making them visible, tactile and audible to others. At the same time, culture diacritics amount to techniques that transpose the social relationships, which compose the corporeal body, to the phenomenal body in the form of dispositions and capacities through the honing of particular sensibilities and tastes by means of repetitive practice.

The unfolding of *asal* in intersubjective praxis is an instance of becoming a person. *Asal* is not a given but the means by which the given is given. What is given though demands actualization. Genealogical connections demand confirmation, spatial relationships require verification. These demands are met by the unfolding of the person as a set of sensibilities, dispositions and capacities in an intersubjective field populated by other persons that are perceptually oriented towards it. The first articulation of the person as the effect of social relationships of genealogical and spatial kind is always incomplete. It can only be completed if it is succeeded by the second articulation. What is given is opened up to the world and the relationships of which it is made are revealed in the form of dispositions, qualities and attributes. The stage in which the second articulation takes place is a social one; others are always already there to elicit this opening and act as its witnesses. The second articulation completes the person, transforming it from an effect of *asal* into an agent capable of affecting others, i.e. from a given into an effecting subject.

This intertwining of the corporeal and the phenomenal, of the past of the body and of its present and future, sits at the centre of becoming. During my fieldwork, I sought to understand why it is that the Madurese act '*kasar*' and what makes the Javanese behave '*halus*'. I frequently asked people in Probolinggo these very questions. Pak Idris put it more eloquently than others, saying that difference 'inheres in the blood' (*ada di darahnya*, Ind.). When pressed for an example, he explained that the offspring of a *kyai* (Islamic scholar) are held to possess an inborn knowledge (*ilmu laduni*, Ind.) that gives them a special advantage over others in terms of religious learning and leadership. The supporters of Megawati Sukarnoputri, the daughter of Indonesia's first president, Sukarno, also believe her to possess at least some of her father's potency (*kesaktian*, Ind.) which was thought to be instrumental in Indonesia gaining its independence. So too is the case with the *kasar* and *halus*: they are *diturunkan* (Ind., passed down genealogically). However, this passing down does not involve the formation of a passive, pre-determined person. What is given is very much expected to be actively taken up and actualized in intersubjective praxis.

Not all the descendants of a *kyai* are necessarily going to become *kyai* themselves; some might, some generations might be bypassed altogether. *Ilmu laduni* demands demonstration and cultivation in the form of religious virtues such as piety, generosity, politeness, a lack of self-interest and an indifference towards wealth. It also requires evincing, such as the acquisition of religious knowledge through years of education, and the capacity to explain the scriptures with clarity and wisdom to an audience (Retsikas 2006). Succession to *kyai*-ship is not a right and stories abound locally of people who thought that it is with disastrous consequences. Rather, *kyai*-ship rests on the actualization of capacities in relation to others who judge and evaluate its performance. It is in this sense that the other completes the person. 'So too with Megawati,' Pak Idris continued. 'We will know whether she's got her father's *kesaktian* or not only if she is successful in becoming president and leading Indonesia out of the current [1998] crisis' (something that did take place in 2003 with mixed results). The unfolding of the corporeal body within the field of the social, i.e. the body's second articulation, evinces *asal* through the actualization of past relationships in the form of dispositions and capacities in the present. The second articulation therefore makes the phenomenal body into a personification of the very attributes it displays, manifesting the person in action.

When attributes passed down from previous generations are not actualized, people in Probolinggo conceive them as having gone missing (*hilang*, Ind.), as having disappeared, remaining unclaimed and unsought for. The reverse causalities I describe above as linking the corporeal and the phenomenal rest on their relative independence of one another. This results both in the phenomenal taking routes that distance it from the corporeal – e.g. the case of Yusuf, Megawati, unsuccessful claims to *kyai*-ship, etc. – and in the phenomenal acting as a cause on the corporeal, shaping and informing it in highly distinctive ways. The latter possibility is well attested in the explanations I was given as to why the Madurese act *kasar*. Drawing on the reputation of Madurese as brave seafarers and able fishermen, some people traced the coarseness of Madurese ways of speaking to the demands made by the fishing activities several Madurese living in coastal areas engage in. 'The people living on the coast have a more *keras* voice for when they are at sea fishing they have to speak loud so that they can communicate,' one person explained. The noise generated by the waves and the wind as well as the long distances that sometimes separate boats make specific demands on the people engaged in fishing and this is in turn is taken to shape both themselves and their descendants. On another occasion, Ibu Suhartini, a well-off civil servant, attributed *sifat keras* to the hard work Madurese peasants have to perform in order to ensure their livelihoods. 'In Madura, one has to work harder than here in Java. Because the land in Java is so much more fertile, the Javanese can be *ayem* [Jav., calm, assured] that they will have enough to get by without too much effort.' Hard manual labour she said makes one's blood more prone to heat which in turn makes restraining one's anger more difficult to achieve. The excessive heat of Madurese blood was attributed by others to the hot and dry climate of the island of Madura. In contrast, the cooler and wetter climate of Java, especially of Central Java with its big river systems and fertile valleys, is taken to shape and account for Javanese refinement. These and other comments made it clear that the relations persons maintain with one another and with the natural environment in certain climatic and labour conditions are acknowledged as affecting them directly, producing specific sensibilities and capacities for action that accord with the climate and the labour demands it makes. The attributes persons thus acquire are in turn also thought of as affecting their descendants, of passing down through genealogical relations, inhering and subsisting in the blood that makes their bodies and which flows vertically connecting the past with the future.

The indigenous logic of the mutual constitution of the person and the social world in which it is situated carries strong parallels with the phenomenology of Merleau-Ponty and his understanding of what one might term the 'body-subject'. His philosophy is dedicated to showing how, as Priest writes, 'the subject is the body: not the inanimate objective mechanical body that I may observe in the external world but the living moving experiencing whole human body that one is: the body, so to speak, I am co-extensive' (1998, 67). The body-person cannot be conceived through the series of Cartesian dichotomies of body and mind, subject and object, the person and the social. For Merleau-Ponty, such distinctions are the products of reflective, abstract thought and far from being absolutes. He redefines these distinctions in his unfinished work entitled *The Visible and the Invisible* as 'relational, intertwined and reversible aspects of a single fabric' (Crossley 1995, 47). This fabric he designates as flesh (1968). Flesh refers both to the reversibility of the sentient-sensible dimensions of the body-person due to its double-sidedness as at once an object for others and the lived immediacy for the subject, and to the intertwining of the body-person and the world as alternately seer and seen, touching and being touched, active and passive.

Merleau-Ponty's point of departure is echoed in my comments above regarding the peculiarity of the assumptions informing social constructivism. He puts his critique more succinctly and eloquently than I have, writing that

> it is false to place ourselves in society as an object among other objects, as it is to place society within ourselves as an object of thought, and in both cases the mistake lies in treating the social as an object. We must return to the social with which we are in contact by the mere fact of existing, and which we carry about inseparably with us before any objectification. (1962, 362)

I have tried to capture the quality of the inseparability of the person and the social through the deployment of concepts of the corporeal and the phenomenal body, the body as the given of past social relationships and its actualization in intersubjective encounters. I have also made a lot of the reversibility Merleau-Ponty speaks of. This reversibility I have attested to in a number of ways: firstly, with respect to the subject-object distinction as encountered in the second articulation of the body-person. In this instance, the body is actualized as a person through deploying its senses, perceiving, orientating and acting towards others; in short, through achieving sentiency. In doing so, the body becomes an object of attention by others; it is sensed, perceived, scrutinized and evaluated. The assumption of the subject's status calls forth the assumption of the status of the object with subjecthood inhering and subsisting in object-hood, and vice versa. This inherence is a crucial dimension of the *diaphoron* person within whom I see indigenous metaphysics as foregrounding and privileging. Secondly, I have brought attention to the reverse causality that characterizes the relation of the corporeal and the phenomenal and have highlighted the feedback loops that are held to develop between these two kinds of bodies. According to such feedback loops, the corporeal and the phenomenal body take turns in acting on and shaping each other. Or to put it slightly differently, the corporeal and the phenomenal body proceed to occupy the positions of cause and effect in an alternating and interchangeable fashion. Not only do the people of Probolinggo conceive of the phenomenal body as the undetermined unfolding of the corporeal body in intersubjective action; they also point to the ways that the social relationships people develop in the course of pursuing livelihood activities in specific climates affect and shape their own corporeality as well as the corporeality of their descendants. The reverse causality and relative independence of the corporeal and the phenomenal body means that the two are never fully coincidental and commensurate with the gaps, divergences, and differences inhering therein amounting to a further manifestation of the *diaphoron* person I speak of.

Despite obvious similarities, the accounts provided in interviews and Merleau-Ponty's writings display an acute divergence of emphasis. While Merleau-Ponty is concerned with elaborating a philosophy of existential beginnings, concentrating on the universal, pre-objective structures of experience that inform human embodiment, my informants' pre-occupation with the body comes in the shape of elaborating on the hierarchy that informs the experience and perception of having or being one. In East Java, the perception and experience of bodies is, in other words, embedded within sets of evaluative statements that construe certain body-persons as refined and others as coarse; mixed bodies, in addition, are understood as unstable combinations of *halus* and *kasar*. While it is indeed possible to distinguish between experience and its objectification in language from an analytical perspective, these two 'moments' are not radically separate but closely linked and interpenetrative (see also Strathern and Lambek 1998, 15). In what follows, I discuss the hierarchy of *halus* and *kasar* in terms of the history that informs the emergence of the categories of Javanese and Madurese and the politics that have shaped interactions among people belonging to these categories. My analysis, however, seeks to avoid subordinating experience to language and perception to political history. Keeping true to reverse causalities necessitates going all the way analytically. The inseparability of the person and the social, the political and the historical included, demands the terms of analysis be kept level, that analysis is flat, conducted at the surface. I thus intend to show the ways that bodies are living histories and highlight the experiential and embodied surface of politics.

Living hierarchy

Genealogically speaking, the emergence of the category of 'Java' as a recognisable cultural identity, endowed with a particular set of practices involving custom, arts, language and literature, is traced by historians and anthropologists in the dislocations and disruptions that Dutch colonialism heralded during the nineteenth century, particularly after the Java War (1825–1830). As Pemberton (1994) has amply made clear, the category of 'Java' came to be objectified and promoted in the Central Javanese courts as a possible resolution of a series of contradictions born out of the disjunction between the historical reality of the courts of Surakarta and Yogyakarta, as established and maintained in conditions of colonial intervention and support, and the courts' own rhetoric of divine kingship. Under conditions of colonial domination, and in the midst of the accelerated modernization of the economy and the administration contributing to the economic and political demise of courtly society, the courts sought to re-establish their legitimacy as rightful and powerful leaders of the native society by portraying themselves as upholders and promoters of all things quintessentially 'Javanese'. The crisis of legitimacy was met with the courts becoming entangled in a process of defining and elaborating in minute detail the contents of 'Javanese' tradition through compiling lengthy mytho-historic accounts of Java's glorious past, writing moral stories in verse and prose extolling obeisance, order and tranquillity, conducting extravagant weddings, sponsoring the arts and standardizing cultural practices (see also Ricklefs 1981).

The category of 'Java' that the courts and the *priyayi* class, so elaborately developed postulates a certain correspondence between morality, aesthetics and politics, on the one hand, and embodiment on the other.[2] This correspondence is directly related to the distinction between *halus* and *kasar*. *Priyayi* political distinction came to be based on the behavioural display of signs of refinement as signs of

---

2 The term *priyayi* (Javanese) corresponds to the semi-hereditary aristocrats turned civil servants (see Sutherland 1979).

potency (Anderson 1990; Keeler 1987). This potency consisted of the cultivation of a *halus* self through the undertaking of ascetic practices (meditation, fasting, etc.) and the mastery of elaborate codes of interaction, both linguistic and bodily (pointing, sitting and so on); together with aristocratic descent, these were taken to manifest high degrees of control over socially unacceptable drives for pleasure (*hawa nafsu*) and thus, to validate claims of political nobility and superiority. As both Geertz (1960) and Errington (1984, 1988) have observed, *priyayi* culture equates moral and spiritual excellence or *halus*-ness with political eminence and correlates degrees of restraint over inner desires with social status. According to this conception, the peasantry's inferior status and *kasar*-ness is largely the result of its inability to curb overpowering emotions of pleasure through discipline or to smooth in interaction. This conceptual nexus was also applied to understandings of space. The closest one was to the court and the sultan, the highest degree of *halus*-ness one was thought to have attained. The courtly centres of Central Java were fashioned as the very epicentre and source of *halus*. This quality and style of living and conducting oneself faded away the further one moved outwards towards its periphery. Thus, the peoples of the eastern salient in which Probolinggo is located and of Madura were construed as lacking in etiquette and inner control, of being ill mannered and unrefined (see also Hatley 1984; de Jonge 1995).

As far as the genealogy of the category of 'Madura' is concerned, we know remarkably very little. In the eighteenth and early nineteenth centuries, the term 'Madura' applied to a single regency located on the western part of the island, ruled by the famous Cakraningrat family (Kwee 2006, 248, n.88). The regency was one of three to be found on the island at that time, the other two being Pamekasan and Sumenep. It is important to note that with the possible exception of Sumenep which withdrew into a similar position of championing the cultivation of Madurese arts as a result of its colonial domestication (Bouvier 1995a, 1995b), the Madurese courts were in general not as successful in legitimating themselves as the repositories of Madurese authenticity. The political void in Madura was filled by the roles assumed by rural Islamic scholars (Kuntowijoyo 1981; Mansunoor 1990). The question, however, still remains: exactly when and under what conditions was the name 'Madura' applied to the other regencies and extended to the whole island's population? In addition, what was the process under which a single, unified 'Madurese' subject came to emerge historically?

In 1919, the Java Instituut was founded in Surakarta with the journal *Djawa* as its official organ. However, the 'Java' that both the Instituut and the journal envisioned was not coterminous with the island's geographical boundaries. The journal was devoted to researching 'the indigenous culture of Java, Madoera, and Bali' by 'promoting and disseminating knowledge of their culture' (Tsuchiya 1990, 91). The inclusion of 'Madoera' in 'Java' was not a twentieth-century innovation. Rather, it reflected a political imagination according to which 'Madura' was encompassed by 'Java' in the Dumontian (1998) sense of the term, i.e. enveloped, subsumed and appropriated by the 'whole' as a lower order part of it (see also Baumann 2004). This imagination furthermore belonged properly speaking to the *longe durée*.

From the eleventh century to the sixteenth century, the East Javanese kingdoms of Kediri (1050–1222), Singasari (1222–1292) and Majapahit (1292–1527), ruled over the various Madurese principalities (de Jonge 1989). Ties of subordination expressed in the submission of annual tribute were intersected by the politics of affinity. During the Majapahit period, the royal families of the various Madurese principalities enjoyed affinal bonds with the Majapahit royal family. As Lombard notes, 'the name Madura appears three times in the *Nagarakertagama* [chronicle composed during the Majapahit period], in particular in canto XV, where it is said that Madura is not to be counted among the foreign kingdoms because it has always just been part of the land of Java' (1972, 259). This pattern of relationships survived the demise of Majapahit with the rise to power of the Javanese coastal city-states. Pigeaud writes that 'in the sixteenth and seventeenth centuries, [with] the flourishing of the *pasisir* [coastal] culture, the Madurese districts [were] governed by sultans, probably of mixed Javanese and Madurese blood' (1967, 136). These Madurese districts were parts of larger 'wholes' with centres located in Java's northeastern coast.

A case of reverse encompassment comes into view, however, when the Madurese origin myth is examined. The story of Raden Sagara, of which many variants exist, portrays the Madurese as having partly Javanese, partly celestial origins, a potent admixture which permits the first prince of Madura, Raden Sagara, to encompass Java. According to D. Zawawi Imron's (1993) version, Raden Sagara was the son of Raden Ayu Tunjungsekar, the daughter of King Prabu Gilingwesi of the legendary Javanese kingdom of Medang Kamulan.[3] While a virgin, the story goes, Raden Ayu conceived her son in a dream (or dreamlike state); while under the spell of the full moon she allowed it (i.e. the moon) to slip into her body. As a result of the shame she brought to her family and kingdom, her father sentenced Raden Ayu to death but the prime minister secretly helped her escape by sea. Raden Ayu gave birth on a raft to a baby boy,

---

3　According to myths, Medang Kamulan is Java's first kingdom with Betara Guru, the supreme deity of Hindu Java, sometimes identified as Siva, as its founder. Raffles argues that it was located in the Prambanan valley of Central Java (1830, 57), while Imron and others point to the area of Bromo in East Java which is right next to Probolinggo. The latter version, of which few people in contemporary Probolinggo are aware, transforms the demographic movement of their ancestors into the area into a return to the origin place.

Sagara (sea, Mad.), and soon after they came across an uninhabited island to the north of Medang Kamulan. They named the island Madura after a bees' nest they came across on a tree in the middle of an open country (from *madu* for honey and *oro* for open country). In the years that followed, Raden Ayu and her son presided over the gradual population of the island by peoples coming from Java, Bali and Lombok, as well as other further afield. According to the version supplied by the Madurese poet Abdul Haji Wiji Muthari, Raden Sagara returned to Medang Kamulan as head of a powerful army and managed to save the kingdom from an invading army of Chinese. For his success he was coroneted as the prince of Medang Kamulan (see Husson 1995, 375–7).

The mythical theme of Madura encompassing Java came close to being repeated during the Trunajaya rebellion of the 1670s. In the aftermath of Mataram's campaign into the island of Madura, the decimation of the majority of its royal houses and the forced relocation of some 40,000 Madurese to East Java, the legendary prince of Sumenep Trunajaya fought against Mataram and the Dutch East India Company (VOC) and came very close to taking over Java and establishing a new royal dynasty in Mataram (Ricklefs 1981, 66–77). Trunajaya's eventual defeat had unexpected effects as it convinced the Dutch of ending the subordination of the Madurese principalities to Mataram. Thus, after Trunajaya's defeat, the eastern principalities of Sumenep and Pamekasan were ceded to the VOC and had their relations with the latter governed by a series of contracts that allowed the local aristocracy a considerable degree of autonomy (de Jonge 1982). The process was concluded in 1743 when Madura proper, i.e. the western Madurese principality, became a vassal of the VOC and was formally removed from the influence of the Javanese court. However, this disentanglement was severely resisted by the successors of Mataram, the two newly founded Javanese royal courts of Yogyakarta and Surakarta.[4] Surakarta sought to renew its affinal ties to Madurese nobility several times, and elevated such ties to a new level of literary recognition by the sponsoring of the writing of *Babad Prayut* (*The History of Ties*) in the eighteenth century and *Babad Madura* (*The History of Madura*) in the nineteenth century. Both of these texts detailed and celebrated such affinal ties (see Pemberton 1994, 39–40, 73–5). As far as Surakarta was concerned then, 'Madura' was safely encompassed once more through the arts of literature and affinity.

During the nineteenth century, Java's northeastern coast was subjected to the infamous Cultivation System, which transformed the existing relations

---

4 The splitting of Mataram actually resulted in the founding of two major and two minor courts. The major ones were the Sultanate of Ngayogyakarta Hadiningrat in Yogyakarta, and the Sultanate of Surakarta Hadiningrat in Surakarta, both founded in 1755. The two minor ones were the Mangukegaran, located also in Surakarta, and the Paku-Alaman, located in Yogyakarta, and established in 1757 and 1812, respectively.

of production, intensified the monetization of the economy and opened Java anew to international trade networks, heralding investments in infrastructure, education and services. The Madurese regencies, however, never became part of the Cultivation System nor did they attract the attention of private entrepreneurs. The Madurese economy remained stagnant. As we have seen in the previous chapter, in these circumstances, increasing numbers of Madurese migrated in large numbers to coastal East Java. In all respects, Madurese society remained in the shadow of developments centred on the most fertile, economically vibrant and politically dominant island, i.e. Java, and grew dependent on it. This trend continued into the twentieth century as Java became the epicentre of political developments in Indonesia both before, during and after the establishment of an independent nation-state, a process characterized by what Drake has called 'the growing Javanization in government' (1989, 257–8, 269). During this period, Madurese society provided much of the labour needed for industries and urban growth in Java, as well as other places like the transmigration sites of West Kalimantan, contributing huge numbers of low-skilled workers both in the formal and informal sector.

The experience and perception of Javanese persons as *halus* and of Madurese as *kasar* in contemporary Probolinggo captures the contours of the regional political history with 'Java' looming large over 'Madura', and transforms the relations of encompassment as developed over the *longe durée* into distinct and hierarchically arranged dispositions, attributes and capacities. This history which I have traced here through the use of secondary literature was never a topic of discussion or an explicit concern for the people I worked with, and in our conversations an awareness of its details never arose. Although the people I interviewed were familiar with some of the kingdoms and historical figures, such as Trunajaya mentioned above, their hierarchical entanglements were never specified. For the most part, such kingdoms and figures remained hazy and vague, spectres of bygone eras. However, this should not blind us to the undeniable presence of history in the ways persons and bodies are perceived and evaluated today. History, in the sense of past social relations, is alive in the perception and embodiment of ethnicity. In other words, it is by means of the body that the past hierarchies continue to be lived and experienced. History is manifested, remembered and reproduced both in the myriad activities that bodies perform and in the ways that such bodies are perceived and evaluated by others. The body is not simply in history; it is living history in the present.

Mixed personhood is itself embedded within the logic of encompassment. Instead of trying to transcend hierarchy, mixed personhood works in tandem with it and makes a serious claim to pre-eminence. By portraying themselves as combinations of *halus* and *kasar* qualities, mixed persons place their bodies as 'wholes' in relation to those of their intimate others, which supply the lower parts of a higher, more encompassing way. In literally incorporating both 'Java' and 'Madura', they subvert the contours of the hierarchy of the past, transforming what was once a marginal region into today's centre. However, their contestation of the superiority of Javanese personhood and claims to distinction are performed within a broad affirmation of the *priyayi* unity of ethics, aesthetics and embodiment as outlined above.

Mixed bodies are endowed with a certain unreflexive givenness. For all their elaborate commentary on the embodied differences between Madurese and Javanese, locals have steered clear of forming a self-reflexive discourse beyond the point of stressing that their mode of conduct and style of action 'combines' (*campur*) *halus* and *kasar*.[5] My insistent questioning into the qualities and dispositions of mixed personhood was met with short answers of the kind that 'we are all mixed persons here' or that 'mixed persons are those coming from a marriage between a Javanese and a Madurese'. Such answers lacked the density, precision and eloquence of the descriptions locals provided of Javanese and Madurese persons. The lack of a self-objectifying discourse is crucial politically. Their eagerness to objectify the intimate others they consist of and to avoid objectifying themselves to others, including myself, expresses the assumption of the position of the subject and the power associated with it to remain a 'who', never to be reduced to a 'what'.

The argument for mixed personhood achieving pre-eminence due to its encompassing character is related to a deeply felt ambiguity towards *halus*-ness. On the one hand, locals of Probolinggo admit that the attainment of Javanese *halus*-ness is a much-desired goal. The refinement of Javanese character with its superiority based on control over emotions and the ability to conduct oneself with humility and deference in the process of acknowledging status differences and of avoiding putting things in a blunt way is a prized quality, for it ensures a certain predictability and smoothness in social interaction. On the other hand, *halus*-ness is readily associated with dissimulation and pretence, even with hypocrisy (*kemunafikan*), as well as a lack of self-assertiveness. Successful control

---

5 This situation might be about to change with plans for the establishment of *pedalungan* museum in 2011 already in place. The museum will be displaying the 'unique' qualities and attributes of mixed persons through its collections of every day objects, dances, and costumes. The municipality of Probolinggo, which is the driving force behind this plan, hopes to attract both foreign and domestic tourists and to generate further income for the town. Starting in 2006, a culture festival (*pawai budaya*) has also been taking place annually with the participation of local troupes and troupes from neighboring cities. Municipal officials are in the process of cataloguing, comparing and contrasting various regional art forms and styles for the purpose of identifying those which are uniquely *pedalungan*.

over emotions is said to conceal intentions and to allow for the possibility to mislead, even to deceive others. Furthermore, the self-conscious avoidance of open conflict and the adoption of extreme forms of humility run counter to the very qualities that locals admire in Madurese temperament. Among these are self-assertiveness and honesty. By being incapable of controlling their emotions fully, the Madurese have the advantage of spontaneity and relative transparency of intentions, albeit in a blunt and excessive form. *Kasar*-ness is also prized, as *kasar* bodies are capable of working hard to earn a living doing whatever jobs come their way to sustain the family. In contrast, *halus* bodies are a good match for white-collar jobs only, and too timid to protect successfully the family honour when it is under pressure as in cases of accusations of arrogance, adultery, etc.

The combination of *halus* and *kasar* qualities and styles of conduct that mixed persons reserve for themselves carries a strong parallelism with one of the hallmarks of potency, namely the concentration within the potent person of antagonistic principles of being. Anderson (1990), in his seminal exposition of conceptions of power in Java, notes that the attribute par excellence of a charismatic leader is his capacity to combine opposing forces. The classic iconographic image is to be found in the *ardhanari* (Jav.) statues. 'In ancient Javanese art', he writes, 'this combination does not take the form of the hermaphrodite of the Hellenistic world, an ambiguous transitional being between the sexes, but rather the form of a being in whom masculine and feminine characteristics are sharply juxtaposed … [with] the left side of the statues [being] physiologically female, the right side male' (Anderson 1990, 28–9).[6] This emphasis on the concentration of opposites as a sign of power was, as Anderson himself notes, very much at the centre of Sukarno's politics of *Nasakom* in the late 1950s, a politics that attempted to reconcile nationalism, religion (Islam) and communism as the foundation of the state. It is also present in the postcolonial nation-state's official policy. The national motto *Bhinneka Tunggal Ika*, usually translated as 'Unity in diversity', is the founding principle of the modern Indonesian nation. As Liddle writes, it reflects 'the idea of coexistence or of a permanent balance between the many and the one, each legitimate in its own ways' (1988, 4), i.e. the multitude of the different ethnic groups found in Indonesia and the one-ness of the nation-state with the ensuing tensions between the many and the one acting as a source of strength and vitality rather than of weakness and instability, even

---

6 Another manifestation of the same principle is Semar (see Christie 1978), one of *wayang kulit*'s most famous characters who is both a god and a clown, both one of the most spiritually refined and senior characters and one of the most *kasar* looking with a bulging belly, a taste for obscenities and uncontrollable farting. Semar's is also androgynous with his/her gender oscillating between male and female. For the relevance of androgyny to my overall argument, see Chapter 6.

though, as events in the archipelago during the past decade attest to, such an emphasis is not always successful.

The fabric

Contrary to Euro-American assumptions that imagine society as exterior to individuals and a mathematical aggregate (a collection of alike monads), the people in Probolinggo conceive of the social and the person as inseparable in the sense of the former inhering and subsisting in the latter, and vice versa. This inseparability and reciprocal immanence means that the social is conceived as always already present in the person and that the person is always already co-extensive with the social. The inseparability I have traced through the notion of reversibility, borrowed from Merleau-Ponty, designates the space that the single fabric the social and the person form. This fabric is a thin, flat surface with no outsides and no insides; only two sides that as Deleuze might put it 'converge asymptomatically ... since they meet one another only at the frontier they continually stretch' (2001, 32).[7]

The asymptomatic convergence of the fabric's two sides is realized through the work that the double articulation accomplishes. The first articulation produces the corporeal body as the effect of past social relations, while the second articulation completes momentarily the person in the course of specific intersubjective encounters. In these encounters, the person is made present to the other as phenomenal, as having both a sentient and a sensible body. The phenomenal body unfolds and reveals the social relations that the person is made of in the form of qualities and attributes which are manifested in action. It is only on the condition of this unfolding taking place that the person can claim the status of an agent and become capable of acting on the world with efficacy and force. We might also safely say that to the extent that the person is completed by the other, the person owes its agency to this very other. This is so for the other's perceptual activity is a necessary requirement for the elicitation of the attributes and capacities of a person's phenomenal body. In other words, the other is not only the external point towards which the action of the subject is directed but the very condition of the actualization of the person's agency.

The notion of reversibility allows us to grasp the play of self and other as the interchangeable dimensions of the single fabric their continuous

---

7 Deleuze (1994, 2001) was, of course, not a phenomenologist and his work on cinema was highly critical of Merleau-Ponty's thesis of grounding perception on the human body. However, as the work of Bell (1998) makes clear, Merleau-Ponty and Deleuze do share some common ground and the importance attributed to reversible connections shapes much of it.

entanglements weave and expand. The infinite stretching of the fabric amounts to the unlimited becomings of the person. The work of double articulation never stops. Effects that go on to act as causes combine with other causes to create new effects that in turn assume the status of causes that produce ever new effects and so on and so forth. The unlimited becomings of persons do, however, know of rests and pauses. In this chapter, I have concentrated on one such pause and on the stable forms persons temporarily assume.

The processes of the becoming of place examined the previous chapter have produced the mixed persons of Probolinggo as assemblages of Madurese and Javanese qualities and capacities. The *diaphoron* person that this sort of assemblage encodes is a site of difference that holds together two opposing and contrasting ways of acting and situating oneself in the world. In combining *halus* and *kasar* attributes in a tense and often oscillatory manner, the metaphysics on which mixed personhood is based foregrounds difference as constitutive of the person. In other words, the persons with whom people in Probolinggo are endowed are split apart and divided down the middle. They have two sides: one is refined, the other is coarse; one seeks bright colours; the other dark; one speaks with a soft and slow voice, the other loud and fast; one grows with rice, the other with corn. The oscillatory manner in which these sides manifest themselves, as, for example, in the *pedalungan* dances of Bayu Kencana or the ways that women in Probolinggo dress, means that when the *kasar* side comes into view, the *halus* side is eclipsed, and vice versa. The dynamism this oscillation unleashes renders dictates in favour of equilibrium, and the achievement of stable identity very much at the centre of Western assumptions of the subject, as peculiar and strange. Mixed personhood is disinterested in observing its identity for it is always in motion, always becoming, indefinitely moving to and fro the directions of *halus* and *kasar*.

As well as engaging in oscillation, these two halves are unequal. The relationship that connects them is a hierarchical one; the lower part is encompassed or subsumed by the higher one. However, the exact content of the hierarchy remains undetermined. In certain contexts, the *kasar* half with its qualities for bravery, honesty and assertiveness ranks higher than the *halus* part; in other cases, *halus* qualities, such as control over socially undesirable emotions and ability to show respect and deference, attain pre-eminence. In contrast to Dumont (1998) who described the encompassment of the impure by the pure in India as fixed once and for all, the trajectories encompassment traces in East Java are bi-directional, with *halus* and *kasar* occupying interchangeable and reversible positions as to the encompassing and the encompassed.

In the chapter that follows, I discuss yet another instantiation of the *diaphoron* person through a consideration of ideas and practices of kinship that portray the person as always already social, this time looking at the case of the person as part of a set of siblings. I also seek to advance the concept of the *diaphoron* person, by paying attention to the ways that affinity and descent, which we have seen as central in the conceptualization and experience of place in Chapter 1, converge asymptomatically in siblingship as it connects them through an affirmation of their difference.

Chapter 3

THE BLOOD OF AFFINITY: MARRYING, PROCREATING, HOUSING

Disjunctive synthesis

> The whole function of noble houses, be they European or exotic,
> implies a fusion of categories which elsewhere are held to
> be in correlation with and opposition to each other, but
> here are henceforth treated as interchangeable: descent can
> substitute for affinity, and affinity for descent.
>
> (Lévi-Strauss 1988, 187)

In the previous chapters, I have noted that the makings of mixed persons are explicitly attributed by the people of Probolinggo to the marriages of people of Javanese and Madurese ancestry, enacted over successive generations in the area locals designate as *pedalungan*. In addition, I have shown how the perception and experience of place centres round the unfolding of two key relations, i.e. relations of descent and relations of affinity. The present chapter affords the opportunity of delving deeper into the intersections of ethnicity, place and kinship through pursuing the ways that people in Probolinggo connect descent to affinity. This connection comes to the fore and is realized in the institution of the House.

In the present chapter and the following one, analytical concerns over body will be back-staged and the House will be foregrounded as the primary form the *diaphoron* person takes in the plateau of kinship. The House affirms the *diaphoron* person as pure difference for it amounts to the disjunctive synthesis of relations established through genealogy and relations traced through marriage. Such a synthesis is tense, unstable and far from equilibrium. The House is a becoming in the sense that it actively deterritorializes or deaggregates, as Deleuze and Guattari (2001) might put it, the verticality of relations of genealogy and the horizontality of relations of affinity, and reterritorializes and rearranges them via a 'partial connection'. This partial connection is the relation of siblingship.

In Probolinggo, as in the rest of island Southeast Asia, a multiplicity of relations are encoded as siblingship. These include the relations the foetus forms in the womb and the relations between persons who share the same parents, as well as the relation of newlyweds until their first born arrives. They also include the relation of people who have breastfed from the same woman and, as we will see in the next chapter, the relation of neighbours who in the course of ritual commensality are actively fashioned as siblings. As well as registering multiplicity, siblingship is also a differentiating relation as it points at once to similitude and hierarchy. As similitude it connects persons through highlighting the things they have in common. These might be blood, property, food or dwelling. At the same time, it connects persons through establishing distinctions as siblings are always hierarchically related to each other by means of birth order. Neither simply about similitude/ sharing nor merely about hierarchy/distinction, siblingship bypasses the logic of naming its identity and insisting on being double-headed, pointing towards both directions at once.

The institution of the House and the relation of siblingship challenge our thinking for they invite us to think neither in terms of a vertical totalization provided by models of kinship that privilege descent, nor in terms of a horizontal wholeness emphasized by models of kinship that privilege alliance. Instead they call on us to employ the alternative concept of immanent becoming (Deleuze and Guattari 2001, Chapter 10) that is irreducible to serial segmentation and structural correspondence. Becoming designates an affirmation of difference, privileging a particular mode of connecting heterogeneous terms without having to reduce them to some pre-existing identity found at a deeper level. It moreover assigns an affirmation of process in the sense that the connections are never stable and permanent but are forever made and unmade with the terms moving transversally across different series. More important for my present purposes, becoming's immanence makes it wholly distinct from metamorphosis, the change of A into B that takes A and B as separate from each other and from becoming. The immanence of becoming means that B is already part of A in the sense of a virtual presence that anticipates its possible actualization, and that A and B are inseparable from the process of which that they are parts. Returning to the issue at hand, the implication is that the concept of becoming allows us to grasp the House as a site of difference where descent and affinity are reciprocally presupposed with affinity inhering in descent, and vice versa. It also allows us to define siblingship in a similar manner, disjunctively and intensively, acknowledging that similitude and hierarchy are reciprocally implicated with hierarchy subsisting in similitude, and vice versa.

The House

Lévi-Strauss defined the House as a

> corporate body holding an estate made up of both material and immaterial
> wealth, which perpetuates itself through the transmission of its name, its goods
> and its titles down a real or imaginary line considered legitimate as long as this
> continuity can express itself in the language of kinship or of affinity and, most
> often, of both. (1988, 174)

This standard definition has been subjected to intense scrutiny by researchers
working in island Southeast Asia. With respect to Java, there is some argument
about whether the notion of House societies can be applied productively (see
also Newberry 2006). Headley notes that the Central Javanese society sits
at the weak end of the spectrum of House societies (2004, 92); the 'idiom'
of siblingship is restricted in its application, never extending to the 'whole',
never reaching the totalizing image found in other parts of the archipelago
where society and the House are made synonymous. As a result, in Java the
permanence of Houses is rather short lived, with Houses failing to act in an
encompassing manner. This kind of problem is also echoed in Schrauwers's
(2004) study of the Central Highlands of Sulawesi who notes the continuum
of structural transformations House societies form and highlights the problems
some societies encounter in creating durable Houses because of constraints in
the intergenerational passing of the estates they command. While both authors
draw attention to siblingship and its role in constituting the House, they fail
to explain why permanence or durability should be treated as the singlemost
important criterion for deciding whether a society falls within, without or at
the limits of the spectrum.

This attention paid to siblingship is widespread in the respective literature
on the region, especially so in texts concerning the cognatic societies of the
archipelago, as anthropologists have sought a way out of their definition as
'loosely structured'.[1] In particular, Carsten and Hugh-Jones argue that the
original Lévi-Straussian definition needs to accommodate itself to the relation
of siblingship which is a 'far more important principle' in organizing social life

---

1 The term was proposed by Embree (1950) in a most impressionistic essay on Thai
  kinship. For a critique of the concept, see the essays in Evers (1980b). H. Geertz
  (1961), Koentjaraningrat (1960) and Niehof (1985, 1992) who follow Embree, analyse
  Javanese and Madurese kinship as founded on the nuclear family and stress its lack
  of internal systematicity and minimum contribution to the articulation of an overall
  'social structure'.

in the region (1995, 27; a call repeated by Gibson, writing in the same volume with respect to South Sulawesi).[2] Carsten's own work on a Malay fishing community emphasizes the performative aspects of the House as a dwelling which is constituted by the every day activities of women and the sharing of food and children. These aspects together with the relation of marriage are described as more crucial than the transmission of property. The impermanent nature of the House highlights for Carsten the constant requirement for the performance of relatedness on an every day level; unless this is done, the House runs the danger of decomposition. The emphasis on performance is reinforced by the seminal work of Errington (1989, 406), who portrays Houses as coalescing around sacred objects (*pusaka*, Ind.) and forming worship communities that trace their mythical origins to ancestral sets of siblings – either to cross-sex twins or cross-sex siblings – with her work complementing that of Carsten's in the sense that she brings cosmology and ritual back into the fold.

In the course of this chapter, I argue that the multivalent nature of the criteria used for the delineation of the House is replicated in the multiplicity of relations that qualify as relations of siblingship. In Probolinggo as well as other parts of the archipelago, siblingship is a relation that defines as much certain categories of consanguines as certain categories of affines, i.e. the conjugal couple and the parents-in-law. It is also applied to people who have shared breast milk and to children who live under the same roof. Moreover, siblingship comes to define the person in a relational way, as part of a set right from the very beginning of its life, i.e. during the period of gestation with the womb acting as House. In the next chapter, I show how siblingship comes to define relations between neighbours with acts of commensality and worship, making people who share the same place into people who share the same ancestors. The question of what is a House or what is siblingship needs to be approached both contextually and processually. Instead of seeking invariable and stable definitions, we would do much better if we were to concentrate on the multiple yet momentary manifestations of a relation and an institution which owe their pervasiveness to their very slipperiness and equivocation. The concept of becoming with its emphasis on processes that allow us to make the most of the House's slipperiness and omnipresence by making these aspects integral to the analysis.

The multiplicity of forms the House takes and the surplus and the excess contained therein is present in Lévi-Strauss's original formulation. In what it is a major redirection of a method that once used to privilege the assumed

---

2 A parallel development concerns a focus on the architectural characteristics of houses in Southeast Asia and on what Waterson (1990) calls the living, animate aspects of houses.

universality of binary oppositions as the stable blocks of the human mind,[3] Lévi-Strauss argues that the very distinctiveness of House societies lies in the fact that

> on all levels of social life, from the family to the state, the house is therefore an institutional creation that permits compounding forces which, everywhere else, seem only destined to mutual exclusion because of their contradictory bends. Patrilineal descent and matrilineal descent, filiation and residence, hypergamy and hypogamy, close marriage and distant marriage, heredity and election: all notions, which usually allow anthropologists to distinguish the various known types of society, are reunited in the house, as if, in the last analysis, the spirit (in the eighteenth-century sense) of this institution expressed an effort to transcend [*sic*], in all spheres of collective life, theoretically incompatible principles. By putting, so to speak, 'two in one', the houses accomplishes a sort of inside-out topological reversal, it replaces an internal duality with an external unity. (1988, 184–5)

Leaving aside Lévi-Strauss's undemonstrated and misplaced emphasis on transcendence, we can initially say that the House is characterized by a surplus of signification; it exceeds any easy and straightforward determination. In combining theoretically incompatible principles, the House is always unfolding, always becoming. The two sides of it, especially those of descent and affinity, are manifest contextually so that when one side is present the other becomes absent, receding from view. The dynamics of evincing and eclipsing that characterize its enactments make the House into an event and foreground its relational nature, compound character and unstable, dynamic spirit.

Incestuous affines

In societies like our East Javanese case, marriage is the norm both in the statistical sense and in the moral one. A person attains full adulthood only after getting married and acquiring children. Until relatively recently, in Alas Niser most marriages were arranged by the parents and most people were already married by the time they reached their mid- or late teens. Up to the 1960s, it was also common for a person to get married several times during

---

3 As Viveiros de Castro (2007) has demonstrated Lévi-Strauss's later work – from the *Mythologiques* onwards – shows a marked departure from the strict structuralism of the early period and towards the development of a 'post-structuralist subtext' that finds expression in the pursuit of transformations that occur in and between myths. His work on '*sociététes à maison*' in *The Way of the Masks* (1988) falls within the same category.

his/her lifetime. It was not unusual for someone to have four or five serial spouses (i.e. someone who marries four or five times during his/her lifetime in a monogamous fashion) as the incidence of divorce was quite high. This picture has been changing slowly as young people, especially those attending university and coming from better-off families, are increasingly choosing their own partners and getting married in their early to mid-twenties, after the approval of parents has been secured. The younger generation also contracts marriages with the explicit expectation that the union will last to the end of their days. Since the 1960s, both a heightened sense of Islamic consciousness and modern ideas of romantic love propagated in popular culture have contributed to expectations of durable unions.

Husband and wife are expected to work together for securing the economic viability of the household through the performance of complementary tasks. Among peasant households, the preparation of the soil for cultivation is a distinctively male activity, as is the transportation of the produce. Women are charged with planting, weeding and harvesting, as well as storing and selling produce in the marketplace and converting both money and produce to food for consumption. Across the class spectrum, wives are responsible for the financial running of the household. Men typically hand the largest part of their wages to their wives, keeping only a small part for daily expenses such as cigarettes and coffee.

As in other Southeast Asian societies, the relation between husband and wife is underscored by an ethos of hierarchy that finds expression in the sibling terms of address that spouses use on an every day level. This is quite a common occurrence until their first child in born. Madurophone wives address their husbands as *cacak*, while Javanophone ones call them *mas*. Both terms meaning elder brother. Similarly, a husband addresses his wife as *a'lek* (Mad.) or *adi* (Jav.), younger sister. Alternatively, husbands might address their wives by name.[4] The arrival of the first offspring marks a change in the enactment of the conjugal relation with the couple using teknonymy; he will call her *bu* (or *ibu* or *embu*), meaning mother, while she addresses him as *pak* (or *eppa* or *bapak*), meaning father. The tracing of the relation thus shifts from siblingship to co-parenthood. The child becomes the focal point in the conceptualization of conjugal connectedness. Sibling terms are also used as address terms between *bhesan* (Mad.; *bésan*, Jav.), a reciprocal term of reference marking the relation

---

4 For the modelling of married couples as siblings among the Javanese, see Geertz (1961, 137) and Koentjaraningrat (1960, 133). For the modelling among the Madurese, see Niehof (1985, 94); among the Malays, see McKinley (1981) and Carsten (1997, 92). For the way Karo Batak lovers but not married couples use sibling terms of address, see Kipp (1986).

of the two sets of parents of the married couple.[5] Male *bhesan* address each other as *cacak* or *mas* (elder brother), while the female *bhesan* address each other as *embhuk* (Mad.) or *mbaqju* (Jav.), elder sister. This arrangement attempts to give equal status to both sides, obviating the ever present hierarchy involved in all siblingship relations.

Locals of Probolinggo explain that the use of sibling terms by married couples makes the newly established union as stable and enduring as the bonds that tie together genealogical siblings. Terms of address are performative utterances in the Austian sense of semantics, i.e. ways of doing and accomplishing things (Austin 1962). In our specific instance, the aim is to bring about the longevity, harmony and happiness promised by or seen as inherent in the unity represented by the sibling set. Following this line of argumentation, I would suggest that the terminological constitution of the marital bond as genealogical siblingship is a case of metaphor. Metaphor, Lakoff and Johnson (1980) remark, is not simply about semantic transfers of meaning in which the primary referent of a concept is extended to encompass a distinct semantic field, rendering the latter in terms of the former. There are no logical grounds for assuming the primacy of any semantic field over another, they note. What metaphor actually does is to 'organise a whole system of concepts with respect to one another' (1980, 461), thereby establishing equivalences between things which in other circumstances and contexts are kept apart. Metaphor does so, their argument continues, by hiding or eclipsing those aspects of the concepts which are markedly different and emphasizing those which are similar. The equivalence thus established is not just 'a matter of language' but of thought and action as well (see also Jackson 1983).

In the case of the young couple's siblingship, the equivalence accomplished concerns a number of things: a) co-spatiality in the sense of occupying the same dwelling, b) commensality in the broad sense of producing and consuming jointly, as the idiom of eating together across Southeast Asia indexes joint ownership or joint access to the means of production (dwelling, land, labour, etc.) (see Li 1998, 681), and c) co-substantiality established through acts of food sharing. In all these respects, genealogical and affinal siblings are portrayed as being equivalent. What is eclipsed is the difference in the way that the relation is established. While in the case of full siblings, the relation is seen as based on the sharing of ancestors; in the case of affinal siblings, the relation is the outcome of a ritually sanctioned contract that demands exchange. The transformation of the affinity into genealogy is the work that

---

5 The Javanese of Central Java do the same (Koentjaraningrat 1960; Robson 1987). Carsten reports that *bisan* (Ind.) also address each other using sibling terms among the Malays of Malaysia (1997, 221).

the illocution elder brother–younger sister sets in motion. This transformation is further accomplished with the birth of children that act as nodal points for the tracing of co-substantiality among affines a generation below themselves (see McKinley 1981, 354; Carsten 1997).

The elder brother–younger sister illocutionary act invokes the incest taboo. At the same time that the sexual union of full siblings is classified as explicitly forbidden, incest's invocation is paradoxically deemed as essential to making the affinal union fertile. In this scheme of things, human reproduction is made to appear as contingent on the performance of an explicitly abject act in which transgression features as the necessary condition for the production of new life. The backdrop to the invocation of incest is, as Headley notes, mythological (2004, 91, 109–99, 136–7). The Javanese and Madurese have several mythological accounts that feature incestuous unions between full siblings (as well as between mother and son, and father and daughter). The most famous of these myths is the story of elder sister Princess Sri and younger brother Prince Sadana that narrates the strong impulse of marrying one's full sibling and the adventures that the prohibition of this marriage sets in motion for our heroes. According to some versions of the myth, the heat released by the incestuous impulse provokes the death of Sri and Sadana from whose cadavers emerge animals and plants, especially rice. According to other versions, the incestuous union is consummated indirectly by a double proxy involving Sri's and Sadana's children from separate unions. Their marriage inaugurates a line that all the future kings of Java will come from. As Heringa observes (1997), such myths are still central in regulating the ritual proscriptions regarding rice cultivation in Java that indirectly enact the sexual union of Sri and Sadana as an essential component that ensures successful and plentiful harvests.

The theme of siblingship is pertinent to the rituals surrounding marriage which, despite apparent variation, involve a plethora of conventions that act in the same way metaphors do, making siblings out of unrelated persons. What McKinley observes for the Malays is also true for Probolinggo, namely the marriage ritual itself is 'a step by step construction of the married couple [as] a superhuman person whose bodily oneness can be represented as siblingship a generation before the fact' (quoted in Kipp 1986, 638; see also McKinley 1981).

Becoming-siblings

The incest taboo separates peoples into those one is allowed to have sexual relations with, and thus marry, and those one is not. In Probolinggo, along with full siblings, prohibited unions include those between mothers and sons, fathers and daughters, grandparents and grandchildren as well as those related through the consumption of breast milk (see below). Another category of marriages are those which are strongly disapproved but can go ahead if a fine is paid and cleansing rituals are performed. Disapproved marriages include unions of first cousins, especially if they are paternal parallel cousins and/or have been brought up in the same compound (*tanean*, Mad.) or neighbourhood, and unions between consanguineal kin, wherein the groom belongs to the generational level below that of the bride (he is her nephew, for example). Sororate marriages, especially if children have been produced by the deceased relative and his spouse, as well as unions between close neighbours, are also avoided.[6]

Paternal parallel marriage (*pantjer wali*, Jav.) is problematic. In the absence of the bride's father, it is her father's brother who is to act as her guardian (*wali*) in the Islamic ceremony. The fact that it is the very same person who acts as the *wali* of the groom that cancels out the element of exchange and difference which marriage presupposes. Cross-generational marriage is problematic for another set of reasons. As Errington notes, this sort of marriage is 'ungrammatical' for societies whose kinship terminologies arrange kin into generational layers of siblings, as they create confusion with respect to the classification of people in generational layers and to the relation of authority that accrue between junior and senior generations (1987, 411–12). Sororate marriages are problematic because the children that result from the marriage of the deceased and his wife are already established in a very close degree of co-substantiality between the wife and the deceased man's brother. The latter are held to be already corporeally related through the children that marriage has already produced. Neighbours or people who are already in some relation of co-spatiality, as we will see in the next chapter, are construed as co-substantial enough to make the assertion of difference and separation difficult enough to assert.

If the incest taboo and avoidance patterns evince the absence of a necessary degree of difference for exchange to take place, the presence of too much difference between potential affines is equally thought to pose certain difficulties. In general, the discouragement of marriage between peoples belonging to adjacent genealogical layers means that spouses are sought from people who belong to same genealogical layer as oneself and one's own siblings. Chosen in this fashion, spouses are in a perfect position to act as a substitute for the full sibling one has to give up due to the incest taboo (see Errington 1987). In addition, in Probolinggo, potential affines belong more

---

6 Headley's list of prohibited marriages among the Javanese (2004, 76) is fairly similar but it also includes two other cases that concern the prohibition of further marriages between families that are already affinally related.

often than not to the category of *oreng laen* (Mad.), i.e. to 'outsiders', 'people far off', 'the ones with whom no relationship exist', 'enemies'. While it is true that marriages between relatively close relatives such as second or third cousins do occur,[7] especially among the upper strata of the local population as a strategy for the consolidation of family property, the vast majority of marriages involve previously unrelated people living in nearby or further away villages. Given the history of demographic movements that sit at the heart of the repopulation of this area of Java from the early nineteenth century onwards, the predominance of marrying *oreng laen* should not be surprising. After all, affinal relations between Madurese and Javanese, as discussed in Chapter 1, are the principal means for the creation of mixed personhood.

In the context of marriage, the degree and kind of otherness of *oreng laen* is a primary concern, as the selection of affines is a process guided by considerations of compatibility or *juddhu* (Mad., or *cocok* in Ind.). Being *juddhu* requires both the bride and the groom, and their parents, the *bhesan*, possess certain common attributes, making them compatible to each other. In this case, compatibility is seen as integral for the prosperity, stability and fertility of the union. As one person put it, 'to be *juddhu* means to be the same [*sama*, Ind.]. If the spouses are not *juddhu*, they will not walk side by side, but one will be in front and the other will be following behind.' In order to judge whether potential affines are compatible or not, a variety of means are available. The consultation of numerological divination manuals based on the five-day week of the Javanese or Madurese calendar, which are available either in bookstores or at the hands of specialists (*dhukon falak*, Mad.), is one such means. These manuals are consulted for indications as to the auspiciousness or inauspiciousness of the intended alliance (see also Jay 1969, 37, 40; Jordaan 1985, 126–37). People strongly believe that inauspicious matches result in fertility problems, financial difficulties, regular fights, illnesses and even the death of one of the two spouses. Alternatively, or in addition to manuals consultation, one can request the help of Allah in the form of a prayer (*doa*, Ind.) with the answer expected to be revealed in a dream. Divorce is often attributed to the misinterpretation of Allah's message and the miscalculation of birthdays. This approach to divorce allows affines to avoid the need to assign responsibility. Furthermore, it allows affines, especially the *bhesan*, to save face when things go wrong. Numerological incompatibility is also often used as a convenient and forceful yet polite way of turning down undesirable suitors.

Affinal compatibility is also assessed in relation to issues of status that the phrase *bebet-bobot-bibit* (Jav., descent-wealth-moral character) captures quite

---

7 This practice is referred to as *mapolong tolang* (Mad.) meaning 'to bring the bones together'.

accurately. The people of Probolinggo, as well as other parts of East Java, are broadly stratified in four different levels: the *se soghi* (Mad., the notables or important persons), comprising big landowners, rich traders and entrepreneurs, highly placed civil servants, university-educated professionals such as doctors, and *kyai* of translocal reputation; the *se andi* (Mad., the ones who have, the possessors), who are made up of small landholders, small scale traders, shop keepers, civil servants and other professionals of moderate means, and *kyai* of local magnitude; the *prakapra* (Mad., the ordinary ones), who must supplement their otherwise insufficient income through various labour tasks as and when they become available; and the *se ta andi* (Mad., the have-nots), who own nothing except for their labour. In general, most marriages take place between more or less equals, as elites rarely welcome non-elite families as their *bhesan*, although exceptionally gifted and promising sons- or daughters-in-law are allowed to move upwards.

Information regarding the *bebet-bobot-bibit* of potential affines is meticulously gathered in order to assess the probability of the first approach, usually referred to as 'asking' (*nyelabhar*, Mad.; to spread, to disperse), being positively received by the other party. *Nyelabhar* is characterized by indirectness, as the status of the family initiating contact is very much at stake. Before considerations reach this stage, however, information is gathered by peoples related to both sides, be they relatives, neighbours or friends. In the absence of such sources, a relative of the groom visits the neighbourhood of the girl's family, pretending to be a passer-by, and tries to find out as much as possible from the family's neighbours. Like in other parts of Southeast Asia, the *bhesan* are expected to be 'good people' (*oreng bhaghus*, Mad.), just like one's own family. Good people are people who are not haughty, proud, arrogant, envious, quarrelsome, spiteful or jealous. Their moral character is manifested in how well they get on with their relatives and neighbours, and whether they are polite, generous, merciful and respectful in manners. In Alas Niser, good people must ideally be pious Muslims as well, performing the five daily prayers, observing the fast and giving alms, while refraining from gossiping, gambling and drinking. Some people reported that affines should ideally subscribe to the same variant of Islam, although this was a point that others sought to de-emphasize. Political considerations also come into play at times. In the late 1990s, after the fall of Suharto and the proliferation of political parties contesting the 1999 elections, a potential *bhesan*'s political allegiances became an explicit concern for many people, as party differences were acknowledged as a potentially serious threat to the stability of the alliance. Similarly, several of my most devout Muslim informants admitted to going to great lengths to check the political biographies of prospective affines, to avoid becoming related to people who were once associated with the Partai Komunis Indonesia that was physically obliterated in the massacres of the 1960s, partly because of the atheism it allegedly promoted and partly because of its policy of land redistribution (Retsikas 2006).

Concerns over affinal selection and compatibility are important as much for the kinds of difference they address as for those differences they omit to name. One of the differences that is very much omitted from thematization is ethnic difference, save for marriages with Chinese-Indonesians. During the entire 18 months that I stayed in Probolinggo, I never heard of the difference between Madurese and Javanese being a concern or an obstacle in the establishment of affinity. Despite the fact that a pervasive hierarchy underwrites local discourses concerning Madurese–Javanese, people in Probolinggo are largely inattentive to it in matters of marriage. As such marriages between Madurese and Javanese, as well as between locals and migrants from other parts of Indonesia, are considered simple and uncomplicated affairs, as long as issues of wealth, status and religion do not stand in the way. In this sense, ethnic difference is subsumed in the alterity of *oreng laen*. On the other hand, marriages with Chinese-Indonesians (*oreng Cina*, Mad.), the majority of whom profess to follow a religion other than Islam, be it Catholicism, Protestantism, Buddhism or Confucianism, are prohibited from taking place. Such marriages are explicitly categorized as *haram* (Ind., forbidden) in the Quran, thus requiring conversion. However, conversion is a rare phenomenon in Probolinggo and an anathema both to Muslims and Christians, partly due to the strains it imposes in the performance and reproduction of kinship ties with one's family of origin. The rare occurrence of such marriages is also the result of the profound animosity and enmity that has marked the relations between *pribumi* (Ind.)[8] and Chinese-Indonesians across Indonesia at least since the beginning of the twentieth century. This phenomenon is intrinsically connected to the fact that the Chinese are 'somehow [seen] as inherently fabricated by affluence and monetary prosperity' (Siegel 2001, 98) that *pribumi* allegedly lack, and as belonging to 'imagined communities' laying beyond the territory of the Indonesian nation-state. In the case of affinity as in the case of the narratives relating to Alas Niser's establishment (see Chapter 1), Chinese-Indonesians are construed as out of place and outside

---

8 The term *pribumi* refers to those who were seen to be native to the territories of colonial Indonesia as opposed to Europeans and foreign Orientals such as Chinese and Arabs (see Suryadinata 1992). However, since the fall of Suharto, a series of legal reforms (Lindsey 2005) do away with the *pribumi*–non-*pribumi* distinction; the most important of these is a new citizenship law passed in July 2006. My retention of it here refers both to the time in which my fieldwork took place, i.e. prior to such legal amendments, and the fact that it is too early to assess the impact of this legislation on every day life.

the practices and processes of interaction that underwrite the emergence of mixed people.

Affinity, i.e. the becoming of *oreng laen* into kin, is a ritually regulated process characterized by formality and avoidance, gift exchange and asymmetry, with commensality playing a central role. The series of rituals performed aim to effect the transformation of unrelated and potentially dangerous others into kin through turning affinal relations into relationships of siblingship. The ritual turning of the bride and the groom into siblings is soon replicated in the generational level above them, with the becoming of the *bhesan* themselves into siblings. Such becomings are generative insofar as they are intimately related to the actualization of human fertility with the production of a new generation of persons, i.e. the children the wedding anticipates. However, the becoming-siblings involved is always unstable, contingent and far from complete. The respective rituals require indirect speech, careful orchestration and attention to detail. They are, moreover, haunted by claims and counter-claims to superiority and encompassment that, if left unchecked, might undermine the whole exercise.

If the *nyelabhar* inquiries receive a positive response, a more formal meeting (*menta*, Mad.; asking) is enacted through intermediaries (*pangada*, Mad.) who representing the two sides convey the wishes of the parents. In Probolinggo, they do so in careful and indirect manner but without the hyper-correct empty formalism that Geertz highlights in his account (1960, 53–4). If the girl's parents have had second thoughts, excuses will be made on their behalf of the sort that their daughter needs to finish school first or that she is too young to cope with marriage. If there is still a wish for the marriage to go ahead, the date for the betrothal will be set and this rather short and unelaborate event will be brought to an end after a meal has been shared.[9] Both the *nyelabhar* and the *menta* take place in the house of the girl with the parents of the groom and the bride-to-be herself being absent from the proceedings. As for the groom, he is usually present only in the *menta*, yet remains silent and with downcast eyes. The betrothal (*lamaran*, Mad.) is similarly marked by the activity of intermediaries in terms of speech making and the conspicuous inactivity of the two sets of *bhesan*-to-be who avoid engaging each other even if they know each other quite well. The *bhesan*-to-be maintain a subdued presence that also sets them apart from other guests attending the event who are more at ease with showing their joy. The bride and the groom-to-be avoid all direct communication even if they have been sweethearts for some time, with the

---

9 Among the Javanophone residents of Probolinggo, the *menta* (Mad.) stage is called *nontoni* (Jav.), the looking (over), as it is often the case that the girl will make a short appearance under the pretence of serving tea or coffee to the boy without speaking to him.

girl sitting with the women at the back of the house and the boy in the living room with the men.

The *lamaran* is the first occasion in which gifts are presented and reciprocated. Female relatives of the groom give the *penyengset* (Mad.) to the girl. Among wealthy families, the *penyengset* involves gold jewellery; more commonly the *penyengset* consists of a new set of clothes and cosmetics which the girl is expected to wear in the counter-visit to the boy's house a few weeks later. During this counter-visit (*belesan*, Mad; to reply, to return), the boy is presented with a new set of clothes consisting of a *kopiah* (Ind., the rimless cap), a *sarong* or a pair of trousers, a *dakwah* shirt and shoes. The asymmetry of the exchange is manifested in the bride's family taking precedence in visiting patterns and the *penyengset* being more elaborate and expensive. Here, the *penyengset* involves a tray with three kinds of flowers, a tray with delicacies made from sticky rice and a bunch of bananas of the *raja* (royal) kind, and a small tray with betel nut leaves of the *sere raddhin* (Mad., beautiful betel vine) kind which distinctive feature is that has 'its veins coming together' (*urat daunnya bertemu*, Ind.).[10] The asymmetry of gift-giving is counterbalanced by the commensality that accompanies visits, making the *bhesan*-to-be both the provider and recipient of food in alternating occasions, as well as by the exchange of rings, a recent practice which is of increasing popularity.

In Probolinggo, and across Java and Madura, marriage practices vary both in scale and mode of celebration according to the socio-economic background of the families involved. This background dictates the number of guests invited, the expense that is incurred, the conspicuousness of the feast or reception (*temu manten*, Ind.) and the overall duration of the festivities. Weddings also vary in terms of whether the candidates are marrying for the first time or not. Differences are also observed in the importance accorded to the civil registration procedure(*catatan sipil*, Ind.), as traditionalist Muslims tend to downplay its centrality and to subsume it to the *akad nikah* (Ind.) ceremony which is presided over by a *kyai* and is overtly religious. This is not so for modernist Muslims who contest the mediating role of the *kyai* and emphasize instead the equality of all believers. More secularist inclined town-dwellers are also content with making do without the blessings accrued by the *kyai*. Another difference concerns the observance of the bath. Javanophone town-dwellers in Probolinggo insist on the performance of the ceremonial bathing of the bride by senior female relatives (*siraman*, Jav.) the day before the wedding as a way of

---

10 Niehof reports that, on the island of Madura, the most important item of the *penyengset* is a *sirih* set that signifies official betrothal and femininity (1985, 119). This gesture is reciprocated with the presentation of cigarettes to the boy which are intimately associated with masculinity.

effecting ritual purity and bestowing blessings (*pangestu*, Jav.). For the most part, Madurophone residents in agricultural periphery of the city perform nothing of this sort. The precise sequence of rituals to be performed, the number of guests, the lavishness of festivities and the place of *catatan sipil* are therefore matters of negotiation between the *bhesan* through their intermediaries, and although disagreements do often occur, they are rarely allowed to become public.

In contrast to the betrothal which is mainly a female affair, the marriage (*akad nikah*, Ind.) itself is an all-male affair, with the women limited to preparing food in the enlarged kitchen at the back of the bride's house. Male kin from both sides and male neighbours sit cross-legged on colourful mats spread outside the bride's house and act as the witnesses of the bestowal of the *mahar* or *mas kawin* (Ind.) – the bridal gift – which validates and legitimizes the union in contractual fashion, according to both the precepts of Islam and the Indonesian marriage law. The *mahar* most commonly consists of small amount of money (say, 100,000 *rupiah*) or a set of items such as a Quran, a prayer dress (*mukenah*, Ind.), a ritual string (*tasbeh*, Ind.), and a prayer rug (*sajadah*, Ind.).[11] The *mahar* is passed from the groom either to a person designated as the bride's guardian (*wali*)[12] during the *akad nikah* ceremony or directly to the bride after the *akad nikah* has been completed and the civil registration papers have been signed. The bestowal of the bridal gift follows upon the *shighat* (Ind.), the obligatory speech of offer and acceptance the bride's guardian and the groom make respectively. Before it is presented to the bride herself, she kneels before the groom in an apparent gesture of submission and obeisance and kisses the groom's right hand, anticipating the acts that occur in the bridal bedroom away from the all male congregation. The ritual of *akad nikah* is concluded with the pronouncement of the boy and the girl as husband and wife, the performance of a prayer and the presentation of the guests with food arriving from the kitchen, as well as tea, coffee and cigarettes. Guests stay a while to converse and relax before making their way home with a bag filled with food and cakes as a *berkat* (Ind.), a blessing and a thanks for witnessing the event and praying for the couple.

The exchange of *mahar* for the girl marks her incorporation into the husband's family. It also establishes affinity as an asymmetrical relation, with

---

11 Geertz notes that in the 1950s the *mas kawin* amounted to five rupiah (1960, 56). Koentjaraningrat, who describes it as 'a small symbolic bride price', writes that in Central Java it consists of 'silver to the value of five Dutch florins [!] and a Qur'ān' (1989, 127).

12 The *wali* is a person acting as her father's representative. In Probolinggo, that person is usually the *kyai*, if present, or the *penghulu*.

asymmetry pertaining as much to the conjugal bond as well as to the *bhesan* relation. The hierarchy works in favour of the husband and his family who, as the receivers of the 'ultimate' gift (i.e. the bride), are superior to the gift givers (see also Bloch 1978). The asymmetry that the payment of *mahar* achieves is a redressing of the hierarchy that the bestowal of the *penyengset* set in motion during the betrothal, which as you will recall privileges the bride's family. The higher status accorded to the husband's side during the wedding is attested to by the stipulations of the marriage law that state 'although the legal rights and position of a man and a woman within the household are the same, the "husband is the family head (*kepala keluarga*) and the wife the mother of the household"' (Schrauwers 2000, 860). It also finds further support in the speeches made by the *penghulu* (Ind.), the subdistrict official of the Ministry of Religion, or the *kyai*, which remind both husband and wife of their different obligations to the union; the former is now the provider and protector, while the latter is the manager of the household. However, the hierarchy so encoded is destabilized and deterritorialized in the rituals that follow.

The next phase in the wedding process is called *temu manten* (Ind.), the meeting of the newlyweds. It begins with the husband's entourage arriving at the wife's house either later the same day or early the following morning. At the house gate, the husband is met by his wife and her parents. The husband and the wife hold a small package of betel nuts each in their hands and proceed to throw these at each other as they draw closer. The one who hits the other first is held to be bound to dominate the marriage, and wives do often win the contest. Next, the husband standing at the house gate steps on and crushes a chicken egg with his right foot which is then washed by his kneeling wife who kisses his right hand for the second time. Then, the father of the wife steps in and embraces both of them, one on each side, husband on the right, wife on the left, and wraps around them a ritual red shawl called *singep sindur* (Jav.). With the wife's mother following behind, the father leads the couple into the living room towards a sofa. If the *temu manten* takes place in the public space, the father takes the newlyweds to a plush platform (*pelaminan*, Ind.) that contains a sofa at the centre. The sofa and the *pelaminan* are decorated in the colours of royalty – red and gold. Then the father of the bride sits with the husband sitting on his right thigh and the wife on his left, right being superior to left. This stage of the ritual is called *timbangan* (Jav.) or *thembangan* (Mad), literally the weighing. The bride's mother addresses her husband, asking, 'How does it feel, father?' to which he replies, 'It feels like they are of the same weight [*prassan kule keduaqne padhe-padhe beraq*, Mad.].' The emphasis on *padhe*, the same, seeks both to minimize the asymmetry between wife and husband and to incorporate the latter into the wife's family as a son. The incorporation of the husband as a son eclipses affinity and evinces the relation as one of filiation, transforming in effect husband and wife into siblings. This eclipsing is readily acknowledged in the speeches made by representatives of the two *bhesan* towards the end of the *temu manten* ceremony with the husband's side urging the wife's side to treat the husband as an 'own or true child' (*anaq ongghuan*, Mad.) with fairness and forgiveness, which the wife's side readily accepts.

Next, a series of ritual gestures are performed. The newlyweds are 'planted' (*tamen*, Mad.) in the middle of the sofa by the wife's father, an act that is commonly construed as the establishment of the husband as 'king for a day' (*raja sehari*, Ind.).[13] The allusions to royalty refer to the fact that the newlyweds will have to stay still for the most of the proceedings, imitating the kings of the past who drew their potency from practising *tapa* (Jav., ascetic meditation) before embarking on life-threatening projects, such as going to war. Allusions to royalty also draw a parallel between the wedding guests who pay their respects and pray for the happiness of the newlyweds and the entourages that always accompanies royals and nobles in excursions. After the newlyweds are seated or enthroned, the wife's mother passes to the husband a red pouch containing coins and seeds (rice, maize, soybeans, peanuts, etc.), which he pours into his wife's hands. This overabundance of good fortune leads to the contents spilling on the wife's *sarong*, the sofa and the floor. While some people were keen to stress that the gesture portrays the husband as the source of conjugal prosperity, others insisted that it indexes his obligation to surrender his wealth to the wife for her to manage. While the two interpretations are not necessarily mutually exclusive, they fail to note that it is the parents of the bride who are evinced as the ultimate source of good fortune, while the husband acts as the recipient of the gift. This position further solidifies his role as a son, or rather a super-son since he is also a king.

The procurement of wealth is followed by the second act of commensality between husband and wife (as to the first see below). A ritual dish consisting of a layer of yellow rice sitting on top of white rice and decorated with vegetables and slices of boiled eggs makes its appearance, furnishing the occasion for the enactment of reciprocal and coeval feeding (*dulangan*, Jav.) between the newlyweds, who mark their dependence on one another by eating from the same dish at the same time.[14] As previously noted, acts of commensality are important in denoting both sibling and conjugal relations for such acts index joint ownership or joint access to the means of production spouses and sibling sets command.

---

13 Across Java, village weddings are based on the imitation of royal weddings. For the politics and histories that inform such ostensibly 'traditional' imitation, see Pemberton (1994).

14 Busby (2000) also makes the case that in India, the conjugal couple's intimacy is manifested and produced through eating food from the same plate.

Figure 5. Husband and wife feeding each other in public

The prominence accorded to commensality here is a direct consequence of the eclipsing of affinity we have seen through the incorporation of the husband into the wife's family as a son. The eclipse calls forth necessary adjustments to be made in the relation of husband and wife that is now evinced as one of siblingship.

While the husband has been ritually turned into the super-son of the bride's parents, his own parents and relatives are left waiting outside the wife's house, having witnessed none of his incorporation which amounts to their loss. Shortly after the *dulangan* has been completed, the wife's parents call on their *bhesan* and their entourage to enter the house and greet them formally. This is the first time that the two *bhesan* meet in full public view, as up to that point their relations have been characterized by avoidance and communication through intermediaries. This first meeting marks a significant moment in the unfolding of *bhesan* relations. The superiority accorded to the husband's parents as receivers of the gift of a daughter by means of the *mas kawin* has been transformed into inferiority by the actions of the wife's parents who have gained a son by means of the 'weighing', his enthronement and the provision of wealth for him to pass to his wife-sister. However, the 'female' *bhesan*'s superiority remains unacknowledged by the 'male' *bhesan* who, by being absent from the proceedings, can feign ignorance of such events ever having taken place. Their meeting at this very juncture is therefore a meeting of near equals, a summit of people who are a good match for each other. Near equality is established on the grounds of an oscillation of asymmetry; claims to superiority and hierarchical encompassment are met with counter-claims that involve a process of reverse encompassment. In the end, the two encompassments almost cancel each other out. The near equality of the *bhesan* is therefore grounded on a tense stalemate, more akin to a draw achieved after a hard-fought game or a battle that has ceased due to heavy losses on both sides.

Up to this point in the ritual sequence a series of moves and counter-moves have been made that can be summarized as follows: initially, the relation between the husband's parents and the wife has been eclipsed as one of affinity and evinced as one of descent; by means of gift of *mahar*, a new daughter has been gained. A few hours later, the same effect is achieved with regards to the affinal relation between the wife's parents and the husband; by a variety of means, a new son has been got. The eclipsing of affinity takes place in both instances in parallel to the ritual fashioning of the bride as the groom's (younger) sister and of the groom as the bride's (elder) brother. The ritually effected siblingship of the conjugal couple is the pathway that connects the codes of affinity and descent while affirming their difference. Neither exclusively a relation traced genealogically, nor entirely a relation of conjugality that is established ritually and performed in nomenclature, siblingship is situated at the very intersection of descent and affinity, ensuring their communication and entanglement. Rather than a third type of relation, siblingship is an alternative concept of the relation that succumbs neither to the logic of descent nor to logic of affinity but works so as to connect them disjunctively. As the very convergence of the two codes it transverses, siblingship has two faces: while one of these faces is eclipsed, the other is revealed. In other words, siblingship allows the foregrounding of descent to be take place while affinity is receding from view, and vice versa.

Returning to the ritual, we can see how siblingship performs this set of operations. The newlyweds have thus far in the ritual sequence been construed as siblings of two different sets of parents. The incorporating moves of the groom and bride to the families involved are enacted in an alternating and exclusive fashion. Moreover, the incorporation of the groom has not been witnessed by his family, while the transfer of the bride has been indirectly sanctioned by her father's proxy. The statements made in the ritual sequence up to this point are problematic for two reasons. Firstly, it is not possible for siblings to trace their descent to two different sets of parents simultaneously; secondly, the alternating and exclusive incorporation of bride and groom works to disconnect rather than connect their respective families. There seems to be simultaneously too many relations and too few. What happens next in the ritual is a further rearrangement of the relations at play, which make the *bhesan* into siblings and thus provide a resolution to the problems the ritual itself has posed.

Figure 6. Requesting and acquiring blessings

In full view of the gathered guests, the *bhesan* appear together on the *pelaminan*. The newlyweds take their place at the centre of the platform, flanked by the parents of the husband to the left and the parents of the wife to the right. The newlyweds then perform the *nyongkem* (Mad. or *sungkeman*, Jav.), the act of obeisance. They approach the parents of the wife and then the parents of the husband, moving from right to left, kneeling before their parents and pressing their foreheads against their knees, while the parents place their palms on top of the shoulder blades of the newlyweds. In interviews, this gesture was interpreted as one of respect and submission to the authority of the older generation. Perhaps more importantly, it was seen as a vehicle through which blessings (*doa restu*, Ind.) were transmitted from superior to inferior, parent to child. With *nyongkem* completed, the newlyweds take their seat at the centre and all three couples invite the guests to offer their congratulations forming a queue that might take a couple of hours to dissolve.

Flanked by the two sets of *bhesan*, the siblingship of the newlyweds appears as the result of the procreational efforts undertaken by a couple comprised of the senior generation. The two sets of *bhesan* stand as husband and wife to each other. At this stage of the ritual, the eclipsed and suppressed return to the scene, moving upwards and affecting the senior generation. The return of affinity redefines the *bhesan* relation as a relation of siblingship, one that has been established in the past through marriage. The present moment is by contrast one of stillness[15] and inaction, as all exchanges have ceased. Now it is the negation of exchange that takes centre stage. The picture drawn on the *pelaminan* is one of siblings (the newlyweds) who after having been created by a single set of siblings (by marriage, the *bhesan* as husband and wife, the generation above the newlyweds) embark upon the creation of siblings a generation below (the children that the ritual anticipates the newlyweds of having). These three generational layers insert cuts in the flow of time in the shape of sets of siblings. At the same time, siblingship is closely associated with human fertility and is taken to implicate the 'heat' of incest as necessary and essential for human reproduction. Within this frame of references, affinity and descent are defined as dimensions of siblingship, the first with respect to the past and the second with respect to the present. This leaves the future open and undetermined. The stillness encapsulated in the negation of exchange and the evocation of the incestuous couple of Sri and Sadana, however, does not last long. Too much heat and everybody will be dead. Exchange, movement and life reassert themselves sooner rather than later. The couple go to lead a nomadic life for the first weeks or months of their life together, spending their first week or month at the house of the wife's parents, next at the house of the husband's, before taking up permanent residence in either a new neighbourhood, an option preferred by Javanophone town-dwellers, or at the wife's compound which is the norm in the Madurophone periphery.

The 'nature' of siblingship

Marriage completes itself with the engendering of children. The birth of the first child is a special occasion for the couple, as it marks the transition of their relationship from one of siblingship to one of co-parenthood. Hereafter, husband and wife address each other as father and mother.

People in Probolinggo acknowledge what Houseman terms 'the [near] universal presumption of a sexual complementarity in the engendering' of new life (1988, 672), stressing the combined role played by both husband and wife in the production of the child. Bringing something to life is the result of a process of aggregation, activation and opening. According to local ideas, the father and the mother contribute their own distinctive substances, semen and uterine blood respectively, to the formation of the foetus. The foetus is not thought of as monad but as part of a set of siblings. According to some versions, the sibling set consists of the foetus and the placenta (*temone*, Mad.), which is the foetus's younger sibling (*a'lek*, Mad.) and is of opposite gender. According to

---

15 The association of stillness with power, potency and fertility are widespread in the archipelago, see Errington (1988) and Newberry (2006, 87).

other versions, particularly in Java as well as elsewhere in the archipelago, the set comprises of either three or five parts.[16] In the case of three, in addition to the foetus and the younger sibling placenta we encounter the elder sibling amniotic fluid. In the version of five parts, the set is made up of the foetus and the four 'birth siblings' which correspond to the amniotic fluid, the placenta, the blood and the umbilical cord. The set of five forms a single unit and is denoted as *tretan se paempa* in Madurese and *sedulur papat* in Javanese. The foetus and its sibling(s) are held to be alike (*paddhe*, Mad.), as they have been formed out of the conjunction of substances disposed of the same parental bodies. Their alikeness is further strengthened by their growing together in the womb (*rates*, Mad.), which as Headley notes is a House in the sense that it provides the dwelling for the sheltering of a sibling relation (2004, 87).

The potent conjunction of male and female body parts is anticipated in marriage rituals. Immediately after the *akad nikah* and the pronouncing of the couple as husband and wife, elder relatives of the bride present the pair with the *tajin merah poteh* (Mad.), a ritual dish which the newlyweds feed to each other. The dish consists of two halves of rice porridge: the first half, boiled with palm sugar, is coloured red to index uterine blood. The other half is boiled in coconut milk, and so is coloured white, signifying male semen. The dish which is consumed on the bridal bed carries promises of fertility and also forms an objectification of the elements making up the set of siblings that will grow in the womb.

The body of the womb-sibling(s), like that of the foetus, is held to be formed immediately after conception and to be made from a mixture in which semen (*peju*, Mad.) can no longer be differentiated from uterine blood. Thus, both father and mother not only contribute equally in the formation of siblingship but also in an indistinguishable fashion. It is thus impossible to identify which parts of the foetus came from the father and which from the mother. The foetus's skin, bones, flesh and internal organs are said to be made from this undifferentiated and internally balanced mixture, insofar as it contains both the coolness of semen and the heat of uterine blood. The characterization of the foetus as made up of distinct parental parts that are fused together leads to the understanding of children born of marriages between Madurese and Javanese as mixed (*campuran*).

The conjunction of parental body parts that produces the womb-siblings is commonly rendered as planting. The phrase *aeng lake enamen ning delem* (Mad.),

---

16 The 'four siblings' are discussed in Geertz (1960, 46), Koentjaraningrat (1960, 95) and Headley (2004, 99–129) for Java; and in Niehof (1985, 222) for Madura. See also Bowen (1993, 216–26) for Sumatra, Cedercreutz (1999); Nourse (1999) for Sulawesi; and Carsten (1997, 83–5) for Malaysia. In Bali, Hooykaas (1974, 1–4) notes that the four siblings are all elders to the foetus.

describing the male liquid (a euphemism for the semen) being planted into the inside (again a euphemism for the vagina), is used extensively by local men and women alike. The male seed is accounted for as *mandih*, potent and efficacious, as it transforms the female recipient from barren to fertile. While semen and uterine blood are distinguished in terms of potency, the womb-siblings' growth is wholly attributed to the nourishment provided exclusively by the mother who continues to contribute blood throughout the period of gestation. This female blood has a double source. The first source is menstrual blood which is retained in the uterus to feed the siblings. Uterine blood is construed to be of the same nature as the blood that runs in the mother's veins and similar to menstrual blood. The latter, however, is described as *keddhaq* (Mad. dirty, polluting). Its polluting nature is not inherent but derives from the incapacity to retain menstrual blood, indexing the failure to conceive (see Chapter 6). The second source of nourishment comes from the food the mother consumes. This food is transformed into blood by the operation of the liver (*hate*, Mad., also heart). According to local conceptions of the human body and mediaeval medical Islamic texts, the liver is of singular importance as it is the place where food is 'cooked' for the second time after it has been processed in the stomach (see Chapter 4). By means of this 'cooking', food is turned into blood, the life substance par excellence.

In contrast to other Muslim societies in which the mother's substances are de-emphasized in terms of the roles they play in the formation and growth of the foetus,[17] in Java both genders are acknowledged for the contributions they make. The father's semen, however efficacious it is held to be in the first instance, does not replenish the womb-siblings in any way after conception. This is despite the fact that sexual intercourse does not cease to take place and new semen does not stop being injected in the womb. As far as I can tell, locals do not have an explanation as what happens to the new semen deposits but readily dissociate them from playing any nourishment role.

The distinction between male and female substances that our discussion has rendered so far is, however, downplayed when approached from a different perspective. Regarding the origin of semen, some men I spoke to argued that semen is actually blood or a kind of blood that owes its distinctive white colour and thick texture to it having pass through the kidneys. Others claimed that

---

17 Delaney (1991) reports that, in Turkey, it is the male seed that is emphasized, and the child is perceived as originating from the father. Banks (1986, 67–9) also reports that for the Malays, the male substances are privileged, while the female parts are deemed as of secondary value. According to Fortier (2007), the Quran gives an exclusive role to sperm for physical reproduction. Other scriptural sources, such as the Sunna, attribute equal weight to male and female parts.

semen is actually bone marrow (*sumsum*, Ind.) and the penis is an extension of the spine (*tolang pongkor*, Mad.). Both explanations point to semen as originating from the back. This association was also attested to by other comments made by men. When men complained about suffering from sore joints and back pain, they were usually teased by friends who attributed such conditions to repeated, exhausting sexual intercourse the night before. As Fortier (2007) notes in her exploration of Islamic notions of semen, in Islam there is a close link between the back and the sperm, in which semen is thought of as emanating from the *sulb* (Arabic).

> In the Qur'an the term [*sulb*] denotes on the one hand, agnatic descent: 'Forbidden to you are … the spouses of your sons who are of your back (*aslabikum*)' [Surat An-Nisaa verse 23], and on the other hand, the part of the body from which the sperm is issued: 'So let man consider of what he was created: he was created of gushing water issuing between the back (*aslabih*) and the breast-bones' [Surat Al-Buruj verses 5–7]. (Fortier 2007, 28)

The intimate connection between semen and blood is particularly revealed in occasional references to semen as 'white blood' (*dereh poteh*, Mad.), a formulation that accords with cultural conventions of polite speech. Whether all bone marrow is of the same nature as semen or not is something that the people I interviewed were ambivalent and unsure about. The same goes for the fate of semen in the womb. Some men held that semen reverts back to its prior state, becoming blood again; others found this possibility rather absurd.

The process of producing siblings in the womb in which both male and female substances participate is not, however, enough for the creation of life. The embryo is said to grow rapidly and to require plenty of food and is conceived to form during the first four months of gestation, a thickened 'clot of blood' that comes alive only with the addition of the intangible substance of *roh* by Allah. The sparking nature of *roh* is likened to breath, life and movement. Yet its precise nature is held to be known only to Allah who plants it in *hate* (Mad., heart/liver) of the foetus. At the end of the four month period, the foetus quickens through divine intervention, an act that recalls the creation of Adam and re-establishes the connection between the divine and the human.

While in the womb, the foetus coexists with its sibling(s) forming one half of a pair or one part of a set. The relations informing the pair/set are transformed upon birth with the four siblings becoming intangible cognitive aides. After birth, the four siblings, i.e. the amniotic fluid, the placenta, the blood and the umbilical cord, are held to proceed to inhabit the seats of perception, i.e. the nose, the ears, the eyes and the mouth, activating the senses and supporting the baby's cognitive processes. While descriptions of one-to-one correspondences between the four siblings and the four organs differed from one person to the next, what is important to stress here is the intimate association drawn between the four-plus-one womb-siblings and the five senses. The five senses people in Probolinggo recognize, as well as elsewhere in Java, are sight, smell, hearing, talking and *rasa* (Ind., taste, touch and feelings) (see Chapter 5). The transformation of the sibling relation from one of growth in the womb to one of growth in the world is ritually marked. The ritual deals with the handling of the tangible aspects of the younger sibling placenta. The placenta is placed inside an earthenware pot and buried at the back of the house – to the right if the baby is a boy or to the left if it is a girl – with a candle lit on top for 40 consecutive days.

In general, gestation is construed by locals as a process of becoming. This becoming implicates a relation, i.e. siblingship. The convergence of the two gendered substances in the womb and their intersection with the divine *roh* creates a person. The person in question is not the foetus, however, but the relationships in which it is embedded. In other words, the person is the set of siblings, a pair/whole made up of parts, a compound consisting of heterogeneous members. These members/parts are intensively connected through mutual dependence and support, on the one hand; and through the distinctions their arrangement into elder and younger establish, on the other. The relations the relationship of siblingship registers are therefore disjunctive, bifurcated and split; the hierarchical tensions and agreeable co-operation subsist and inhere in the very same person.

It is important to stress here that the nature/culture distinction is wholly alien to our setting (Retsikas 2010a). In Java, the social is not the antithesis of the natural. Procreation rests on the actualization of relations of three different orders. The first order is the convergence of detachable body parts the parents' sexual intercourse brings about. The second order involves relations with the sacred which are signalled by the arrival of *roh* Allah has dispatched. According to Sunni jurists and locals of Probolinggo, *roh* qualifies the pair/set as human (Fortier 2007, 32). The third order of relations involves the relation of siblingship pertaining to the 'contents' of the womb. The similitude of womb-siblings is indicated by their sharing of the same parents, dwelling in the same place, feeding and growing together. Difference is indexed by the division of the set into younger/junior and elder/senior members. It is also indexed by means of gender; younger sibling placenta is thought to be of the opposite sex to the foetus, which underscores the pair's, and thus the person's, androgynous character.[18] The differences that make up one dimension of siblingship should caution us against treating the set as a seamless, faultless, tightly integrated

---

18 The concept of androgyny is explored more fully in Chapter 6.

unity. Pairs/sets are amenable to processes of disaggregation and deassembly. The operation of the incest taboo requires the parting of siblings, setting in motion the substitution of one sibling for another by means of marriage and demanding that a pair/set is dissolved so that another is formed. These are the becomings siblingship traces. The differences that make up sibling sets should also caution us against equating sibling similitude with siblingship as identity. As I have shown, siblings both differ from and resemble one another. The disjunctive character of siblingship means that it is disinterested in observing identity, as it is a process that knows of only pauses and rests rather than end points.

Neither birth nor marriage alters the fundamentals of the person as a relation. The fundamental importance of siblingship remains unchanged and the person continues to be composed of relations. What changes are the parts related, not the way they relate to each other. The transformation of womb-siblings into cognitive aides instigates a new becoming, making space for one's womb-siblings to be replaced with a new set of siblings located outside the womb. Such siblings have already been produced by prior acts of procreation undertaken by one's parents or have yet to arrive. In turn, marriage marks the beginning of further becoming. It effects the substitution of consanguineal siblings that must be parted because of the incest taboo with a spouse who is also conceived as a sibling.

Outside the womb, the child is a member of a sibling set that contains the sisters and brothers the parents have given it. Genealogical siblings are co-substantial for they have been produced by the convergence of the very same parental substances and have shared the same sources of growth. This food often comes from the fields the parents cultivate. The food gets transformed into blood in the *hati*. Food is consumed by siblings in the same dwelling. The fields and the house(s) are the joint property of siblings insofar as they stand to inherit from it, if not necessarily in an equal manner.[19]

---

19 Inheritance patterns are quite complex. Javanophone town-dwellers divide property equally between bothers and sisters. Madurophone villagers usually privilege daughters, especially with regards to the inheritance of the house. Islamic law favours male children, awarding them double of what is given to female children. However, in practice, inheritance patterns display extreme fluidity. Issues relating to who looks after the parents in their old age, who is earning more and how much, as well as who can rely on the support of parents-in-law, are crucial considerations in property division. In addition, such divisions take a long time to be completed, usually starting with the marriage of one of the children. Sometimes they are concluded several years after the death of both parents. In the intervening years, pragmatic considerations continue to influence the allocation of property with plenty of negotiation taking place among siblings.

Concurrently, birth order differentiates siblings into seniors and juniors;[20] gender plays an additional, although less emphatic role in differentiation. People in Alas Niser describe relations between consanguineal siblings as permeated by harmony, trust, solidarity and co-operation. Much is made of feelings of mutual affection (*rasa tretan*, Mad.) that underlie sibling relations. On the whole, such harmony and trust is based on the protection senior siblings must provide their juniors and the respect and obedience juniors must show to their elder siblings. At the same time, people in Probolinggo are very attentive to the rivalries and animosities that permeate sibling relations, especially between brothers, as they can sometimes give the impression of being cautious and cagey towards relatives, including siblings. Richer villagers would thus not refrain from complaining about their less affluent siblings, who they describe as a constant source of nuisance, needing loans, help with getting a job, etc. In the same vein, gossip about next-door neighbours' family histories often centres on conflicts between siblings over money and the division of property, as well as educational and professional attainments.

The relative fragility of consanguineal siblingship is closely related to the relative endurance of bonds between affinal siblings, i.e. the conjugal pair, the parents. Their relation of siblingship established through marriage and enacted through their addressing each other as younger sister/elder brother is reconfigured with the birth of the first child. The importance of children for connecting anew persons is well attested by Errington, who notes that:

> In kinship theory, we usually think of a 'cognatic stock' of people as linked by a common apical forebearer of whom they trace themselves. Something similar like this process happens retroactively in the exogamic societies of the Centrist Archipelago, where the birth of children links people in the generational levels above. Even with the birth of their children, spouses remain non-kin to each other [*sic*] …, but they are linked by a common kinsperson in the generational level below themselves. I like to say that affines in such societies are linked by 'apical children', a phrase that captures succinctly, even though the image is upside-down, the process I have just described. (1989, 420)

As I have discussed, the arrival of 'apical children', or more accurately of siblings a generation below, transforms the relation of husband and wife from

---

20 The hierarchy of siblingship permeates both Madurese and Javanese. Cousins are distinguished into senior and junior. Senior cousins are the children of a parent's elder siblings; junior cousins are the children of a parent's younger siblings. Senior cousins are addressed as *cacak* if male or *iyu* if female, and junior cousins as *a'lek*. Birth-order distinctions among ascending generations are therefore manifested in the generations below.

one based on affinal siblingship into one of co-parenthood. Siblings a generation below furnish new nodal points for the tracing of connections between people of ascending generations, providing material or corporeal evidence of their connection. The prevailing practice of conjugal couples addressing each other as father and mother highlights the emphasis placed on downward, future-looking siblingship. The production of siblings a generation below allows for connections to be read backwards as well as forwards, i.e. connections flow as much from the future to the past as from the past to the future.[21]

People in Alas Niser point out that, even if a marriage dissolves through death or divorce, the relation between ex-husbands and ex-wives, as well as that between the *bhesan*, should ideally be preserved, especially if the alliance has born fruit. When the rather short marriage of Rahma ended abruptly with the death of her husband, Yusuf, in an accident, Rahma's parents-in-law claimed the body of the deceased for burial in their compound (*tanean*, see Chapter 4). However, when during the following year, Rahma wanted to remarry, her parents visited Yusuf's parents to notify them of Rahma's intention. They justified this act on the grounds of being simply good manners. Despite the fact that a lot of divorce cases involve acrimonious conflicts, there is still an emphasis put on the relationships enduring through and for the benefit of the children. In another case, the marriage of Halima and Sughi had produced two children but ended in divorce after Sughi was found to be having an affair with another woman. However, the two *bhesan* kept up visiting each other, exchanging gifts and labour services. Part of the reason had to do with the grandchildren, who were residing with Halima's parents after Halima migrated to Surabaya to look for work. Sughi's parents made substantial contributions to the education of their grandchildren. The children were also spending short periods in the new house their father had established through his new marriage.

Moving parts

The becoming-siblings we have seen so far have dealt with the detaching of parts of persons (semen and uterine blood) in sexual reproduction and the detaching of persons as parts from pairs that are made up of consanguineal siblings and their subsequent attachment into other equivalent pairs consisting of affinal siblings. However, the means through which siblingship is constituted is not limited to these. The sharing of breast milk and the transferring of children correspond to additional technologies for the social production of sibling relations.

---

21 On children, teknonymy and future-looking kinship on Bali, see also Geertz and Geertz (1964); and Carsten (1997), on Malaysia.

In Probolinggo, people explicitly referred to matrimonial prohibitions between people who have shared breast milk. These people are designated as *tretan sosso* (Mad. milk siblings) or *nunggal suson* (Jav., fed from the same breasts). Marriage between them is considered incestuous and is thus explicitly prohibited. The same goes for unions between the provider of breast milk and the recipient. The connections that flows of breast milk create are often phrased in terms of descent (*toronan*, Mad.). This is in turn related to the legal importance Islam affords to breastfeeding and local theories of human physiology that describe breast milk as blood.

Following childbirth women in Probolinggo consume herbal medicines (*jamo*, Mad.) that they either prepare themselves or buy in an industrially processed form. Each *jamo* is endowed with a specific efficacy. *Jamo sere*, for example, cleanses the womb from unwanted gestation and childbirth leftovers; *jamo kepuh* (Pangium Edule) contributes to the generation of large qualities of breast milk. The most important *jamo*, however, is *jamo pejjeen*. This *jamo* consists of a variety of ingredients, in particular, *temo labek* (Mad.; *Curcuma Xanthorrhiza*, Lat.), *temo ereng* (Mad.; *Curcuma Aeruginasa*, Lat.), *temo jrengok, temo konceh* (Mad.; *Gastrochilus Pandurata*, Lat.), leaves of the *me'beh* tree (Mad.; *Endospermum Malaccense*, Lat.), tamarind and salt. This strong, dark-coloured, thick potion is consumed three times a day throughout the first 40 days after delivery. Interviewees claimed that *jamo pejjeen* turns the mother's blood into breast milk, making it appropriate for baby food. *Ebbu* Salmah, a mother of five and a midwife, put it most succinctly: 'Breast milk is blood … the breast milk that [resides] inside the mother is blood but [because of the medicine] it comes out white' (*aeng sosso reah, dereh…aeng sosso ning delem bu dereh tape kalowar poteh*, Mad). The idea that breast milk is actually transmuted blood helps explain both the avoidance of breastfeeding babies other than one's own and the prohibition of marrying one's *tretan sosso*. This prohibition is explicitly established in the Quran. A local Islamic scholar translated the relevant section (verse 23 of Surat An-Nisa) pertaining to the forbiddance of marriages between 'you and the woman who gave you her breast to suck' (*kakeh ban binne se berriq aeng sosso*, Mad.) for 'such a woman is like a mother to you' (*binne reah pada ban bu kakeh*, Mad.), noting that the prohibition covers also the relation between 'you and your breast suckling sister' (*kakeh ban a'lek binne aeng sosso*, Mad.).[22]

---

22 On milk siblings in Java, see Geertz (1961, 59) and Headly (2004, 76). For the role of breast milk in other Muslim societies, see Altorki (1988); Eickelman (1984); Parkes (2005); Rao (2000). Fortier (2007) notes that Islamic jurisprudence recognizes a kin relation between the child and the wet nurse's husband whose semen is considered to be at the origin of her breast milk. However, I have not come across a similar belief linking the husband's semen with breast milk in my area of research.

While milk siblings are equivalent to consanguineal siblings in terms of incest prohibitions, other criteria clearly set the two categories apart. The most important consideration to this effect is the fact that milk kinship is neither legally recognized in Islam nor in local practice as creating rights to inheritance from the milk mother. However, in all four cases of milk siblingship I encountered during fieldwork, *tretan sosso* made extensive use of sibling terms (elder/younger brother/sister) with the question of seniority settled through reference to the slot the milk child occupied in the overall order of children the milk mother had given birth and raised.

Along with the circulation of milk, transfers of children often take place with close relatives and neighbors entitled to claim a child on the grounds of either being childless or requiring a child to look after them in their old age.[23] Foster children are referred to as *anaq ngalak*, a raised or taken child, in Madurese, or an *anak akon*, a recognized or claimed child, in Javanese. Claims to children are made as early as possible, sometimes during pregnancy, with the transfer usually taking place before the baby reaches 40 days old. The actual transfer is validated during the *tasmian* (Ind.) ritual held at the foster parents' house with the child receiving a name and having his/her hair treated amid Quranic recitations and Allah-glorifying exhortations by the gathered witnesses, who are mostly relatives, neighbours and friends of the foster parents. Although Islam does not recognize rights of inheritance to foster children and limits the obligation foster parents have to the provision of education, people in Probolinggo utilize the Islamic ritual of *tasmian* with its communitarian emphasis to validate claims to foster children. According to local practice, *anaq ngalak* enjoy the same rights of inheritance as the *anaq kandung* (Mad.), 'the children of the womb'. Moreover marriages between *anaq ngalak* and *anaq kandung* are considered abhorrent, despite Islamic rules allowing for such unions to take place. In matters of incest and inheritance, foster siblingship is equivalent to consanguineal siblingship.

A manifold of manifestations

I started this chapter with a consideration of Lévi-Strauss's notion of the House as he was the first to note that House societies' distinctive feature centres on their tendency to combine 'theoretically incompatible principles' (1988, 184). I have argued that the House, as articulated in East Java, manages to connect

23 Jay (1969, 72) points out that in Java siblings have rights to each other's children. Beatty concurs, writing that 'the exclusiveness of the maternal tie is neither encouraged nor defended: rather everything seems to conspire against the idea of maternity as a fact of nature' (2002, 476).

descent with affinity in dynamic fashion for in certain contexts and respects the House is evinced through relations of descent, and in others through relations of affinity. In concert with a series of anthropologists working on Southeast Asia, I concentrated my attention on the relation of siblingship and argued that siblingship plays a central role in effecting this always-tense connecting to come about. This accomplishment is intimately related to siblingship's circulation both in relations of descent and in relations of affinity with newlyweds and the respective parents-in-law, the *bhesan*, addressing each other in sibling terms. Through its participation in both codes, siblingship ensures their partial communication and asymptomatic entanglements. In other words, siblingship's centrality is directly attributable to the connections it affords to be drawn between relationships of descent and relationships of affinity. These connections make descent and affinity neither identical nor indistinguishable, as siblingship connects them disjunctively, i.e. through affirming their difference. The differences in question relate to the means through which consanguineal and affinal modes of siblingship are established. While consanguineal siblingship rests on the sharing of the same parents, along with the sharing of the same dwelling, food and property up to a certain point in time, affinal siblingship requires ritual action, i.e. the rites sanctioning marriage, before the sharing of the same dwelling, food and property become possible for the conjugal couple.

The relation of siblingship and the institution of the House with which it is co-extensive form the manifestations of the figure of the *diaphoron* person in the plateau of East Javanese kinship. In the first instance, the *diaphoron* person corresponds to the disjunctive synthesis of the codes of descent and affinity in the institution of the House.

A further, second instance of the *diaphoron* person has to do with the incest taboo. In contrast to Lévi-Strauss's reading of the situation in terms of transcendence, my reading of the *diaphoron* person stresses immanence, especially the immanence of affinity in descent. This is clear enough in myth of Sri and Sadana, which portrays one's full sibling as the ideal marriage partner. Such narratives recognize the desire for sex with one's full sibling as integral to the accomplishment of fertility and abundance of plants, harvests and humans, and the inception of order in the form of royal governance. However strong the desire, such unions are nevertheless prohibited. The prohibition of full siblings unions sets in motion a process that will substitute the sibling one has given up for another person with whom marriage is allowed. However, the incest taboo in Java works in a most paradoxical way. The purificatory effect, in the Latourian (1993) sense that the taboo has in terms of setting up distinctions that separate people into those one can marry and those one cannot, is dislocated and displaced almost instantly by a reverse process that takes place during weddings and which converts the person one marries into one's sibling. The incest taboo, taken together then with statements made during the wedding and the nomenclature that applies to newlyweds, set up the paradox of impossible relations becoming possible. The *diaphoron* person in this instance manifests itself as the pair of newlyweds with the latter forming a paradoxical 'entity' that almost realizes in a most normative manner everything that is axiomatically prohibited.

The third manifestation of the *diaphoron* person in the plateau of kinship relates to similitude and hierarchy being reciprocally presupposed and implicated in relations of siblingship. I have argued that in East Java the person is not conceived of as indivisible and monadic, a subject equivalent to Western images of the unique individual. Rather, the person is thought of and enacted as part of a sibling pair/set. In this sense, the person is composed of the relationships connecting the parts, the circuits that hold them together. These relationships and circuits involve both similitude, with siblings said to be alike in certain respects, and hierarchy, with siblings said to be markedly different from each other. This difference is commonly patterned in terms of elder and younger pairs.

The conception of the person as an assemblage made of parts allows for the possibility of parts to be detached with the purpose of being reattached into another pair/set, forming in the process a new assemblage. This is the fourth manifestation of the *diaphoron* person discussed in this chapter and is intimately related to processes of becoming. I have traced the becomings in question to the person's treble articulation. The first articulation is an event that takes place in the womb with the assembly of the foetus and its four siblings. This set is destined to be dissolved upon birth, with the four womb-siblings transforming themselves into intangible aides that inhabit the baby's outer centres of perception. The deterritorialization of the relationships formed in the womb is accompanied by a new territorialization that involves the baby's insertion into another yet equivalent sibling set. This set consists of the children that the baby's parents have already created or are going to create, in addition to those that they have fostered or are going to foster and those that the mother has breastfed or is going to breastfeed. The second articulation takes place in the parents' house or its vicinity and is marked in most cases by the shared consumption of food that the parents provide. Sooner or later, however, this set will dissolve as well, with the process set in motion by marriage. As a result, the siblings will move out of the house; the property they have had joint access to up to this point will be divided; conflicts might surface; the parents will surely grow older and die. The third articulation of the person as a detachable part of a pair/set is activated by the incest taboo surrounding full siblings that demands their parting and involves encountering a new sibling at the very edge of kinship.

In the following chapter, I explore further the dynamic and paradoxical character of siblingship through a consideration of the circulation of food, prayer and ancestors that takes place at the level of the neighbourhood and argue that the neighbourhood is in effect set up as a House. The chapter that follows sheds light on the avoidance of marrying one's close neighbours, as we have already noted, and takes us right into the heart of the enactment of sociality in East Java. However, the processes of becoming-siblings as it is discussed in the following chapter should not be taken as the final word on the subject, as neighbourhood sociality will be revisited in the last chapter of the book when its 'dark' side will come into full view through a consideration of the practice of sorcery.

Chapter 4

MATTERS OF SCALE:
FEEDING, PRAYING, SHARING

A topography of relations

Neither siblingship nor the House are limited to wombs and dwellings. The present chapter charts the becoming-siblings involved in the enactment of relations among neighbours (*tetenggha*, Mad.). Of primary importance in this becoming is the circulation of detachable parts of personhood occurring in ritual occasions. The circulation of food, potent speech and ancestors within the frame of communal rice meals conceals the difference that marks the persons of neighbours as separate and distinct. Ritual circulations therefore correspond to a specific technology for the momentary eclipsing of difference and act to establish the neighbourhood as a House of a higher scale. The neighbourhood (*kampong*, Mad.) is made manifest as a worship community whose members relate to each other as siblings: in the process of ritual participation they come to share not only the same space but also the same ancestors and the same food.

In topographical terms, Alas Niser is comprised of single houses and larger compounds, connected with an array of narrow streets leading to front porches and a multitude of paths that spring out of kitchens located at the back. Both single houses and compounds designated by the term *tanean* (Mad., yard, also homestead)[1] are Houses in that they register relations of siblingship. As we have seen in the previous chapter, single houses encompass two distinct kinds of siblings. The first is the married couple, which address each other as elder brother/younger sister for the period immediately following their marriage, until the arrival of the first offspring. From then on, they address each other as father and mother. The second form of siblingship Houses contain relates to the couple's descendants, a relationship also marked by a hierarchy based on birth order. Compounds are also Houses. In this case, what is manifested and realized spatially are degrees of siblingship that are more distant than that of a set of full siblings.

Compounds or *tanean* are made up of people whose ancestors, being full siblings, shared a common house in the past. That house, designated by the term

---

1 *Tanean* are significant socio-spatial units in Madurese society (see de Jonge 1989 and Niehof 1985).

patobin (Mad.) and normally situated at the northern side of the yard, along with the *langgar* (Ind.), the small prayer house, and the cemetery, where the *tanean*'s ancestors are buried, form the focal points of the residential cluster. A *tanean* consists of several houses, inhabited by the female offspring of that initial set of full siblings. As a result, all the houses comprising a *tanean* are related through women, as it is usually women who inherit them. Further dwellings are located both to the west and to the east of the *patobin*, as well as opposite to it, forming another, parallel line. These two parallel lines of houses are 'joined' at the top of the *tanean*, designated by the *langgar*'s position, where men perform their daily prayers. In contrast to the Houses of second order, that is the single houses, the *tanean* does not hold material or immaterial wealth in common, with the exception of the cemetery. Both the physical structure of houses and the land comprising the *tanean* are owned by single houses, since divisions of property follow shortly after marriage, while the *langgar* is the inherited property of the couple that resides at the *patobin*. The cemetery, however, remains collective property. The cemetery and the compound as a whole encircled as it is by a low bamboo fence form the spatial manifestation of memories of siblingship which are traced back to the very first set of siblings who founded the compound.

Food sharing plays much less of a role in the constitution of *tanean* kinship. Locals often stress the need for the autonomy of each separate house. This is marked by the separate kitchen and/or hearth each house has and by members of each house eating separately on an every day level. However, food sharing and ancestor sharing are enacted with particular intensity during an array of rituals that form the basis of the spatial constitution of the neighbourhood. The neighbourhood is thus a House in its own terms, produced through a scheme of ritual praxis that reaggregates and redistributes two of the most important elements in the production of siblingship, namely ancestors and food. In this regard, ritual activity allows for the articulation of place and the production of personhood through processes of deterritorialization and reterritorialization similar to those discussed in the previous chapter. During ritual exchanges, food, ancestors and prayers are assembled in new configurations which make possible for the characterization of neighbours as siblings.

Vitality for the living

In Alas Niser, as elsewhere in Java and Madura, *slametan* (Jav.) or *konjengen* (Mad.)[2] feasts are a neighbourhood affair, involving either male or female

---

2 While the Javanese term *slametan* refers to the achievement of *slamet* (well-being), the Madurese term *konjengen* refers to a gathering, from *konjeng*, meaning to visit, call on, meet and attend.

representatives of nearby houses, although mixed gender feasts are also sometimes held. The people invited are all close neighbours. 'The basis of selection', as Geertz writes, 'is entirely territorial: relative or not, friend or not, anyone who lives within a short distance from one's own house in any direction must be invited and must come' (1960, 12). Invitations are delivered orally. Usually one of the children of the host family goes around neighbouring houses early in the morning or the previous night to make the call. This casual event is coupled with the ordinary way guests are dressed, especially in male gatherings, appearing in every day *sarong* combined with a T-shirt (or a shirt) and a *kopiah*, the rimless black velvet cap. The informality of the proceedings is also stressed in the small talk guests engage in, in the living room of the host's house and the relaxed atmosphere that prevails.

The guests sit in a circle. The centre of the circle is defined by the collection of foods that the women have prepared. Depending on whether the feast is small or large, the women in charge of cooking extend from those residing in the host house to other kin and neighbours. The food prepared for *slametan* is different from that consumed on an every day basis. Despite the fact that the type of food varies from occasion to occasion, it most often comprises of a large cone of yellow rice set on a bamboo tray and decorated with coconut leaves. Javanophone locals refer to this as *tumpeng robyong*, literally meaning the 'mound of approval'. Madurophones call it *rasol*, as it is similar to that included in the celebration of Prophet Mohammed's birthday. Festive food also involves a whole roasted chicken buried under another mound of rice, side dishes of various vegetables, parcels of sticky rice wrapped in banana leaves, several fruits like bananas, mangoes, Nephelium and Zalacca tree fruits and home-made cakes (*jhajhan*, Mad.) of seven colours (*joh pettoh*, Mad.).

The food is served to the participants towards the end of the ritual by one or more of the guests and certainly not by the host. Those serving will move to the centre of the circle, fill the dishes with generous portions and present them to their fellow guests. At the same time, hot tea will be brought from the kitchen, located at the back. This is the place where the women are gathered while the all male *konjengen* takes place. The women will not enter the living room but will pass the tea on trays to male kin for them to distribute. After the guests have finished eating, something that is done quietly and somewhat hurriedly, they receive clove cigarettes. More food wrapped in black plastic bags arrives soon afterwards from the kitchen. This food, which is designated as *berkat*, literally meaning blessing (from the Arabic word *baraka*) is taken home to be eaten by the guests' wives and children, i.e. those neighbours who did not attend the *slametan* in person. The *berkat* is usually made of white rice, noodles and pieces of chicken; sometimes home-made cakes are also included. The *berkat* differs from every day dishes usually consisting of rice mixed with corn as well as vegetables and small pieces of meat or fish.

The communal meal forms the culmination point of the ceremony which opens with a speech delivered by either a relative of the host or neighbour who acts as his representative. While both Beatty (1999) and Geertz (1960) note that in their respective areas the speech is delivered in very formal high Javanese, in Alas Niser it is in low Madurese. In the Javanophone neighbourhoods of downtown Probolinggo, the speech is delivered in Javanese *ngoko*, although Indonesian is sometimes used especially in *slametan* dominated by civil servants. This choice of language level is necessitated by the fact that the vast majority of people in Probolinggo are fluent neither in high Javanese nor high Madurese. While both Geertz and Beatty argue that the use of high Javanese marks the occasion with a certain formality, the employment of the *kasar* language level in Probolinggo suits the casual and ordinary character of the whole affair, indexing both the intimacy and relative equality of neighbours.

The speech begins by stating the purpose of the ceremony. *Konjengen* are usually given for a variety of reasons, most commonly associated with life-cycle stages, agricultural tasks or other more mundane activities. Thus the purpose stated can vary from the celebration of the host's daughter's seventh month of pregnancy, the inauguration of harvest, the move to a new house or the acquisition of a new motorcycle. The speaker expresses the sincerity and purity of the host's intentions and the host's wish for the participants to act as witnesses both to the host's intentions and the life event. The representative also expresses the host's gratitude to the guests for attending. According to the traditionalist variant of Islam that is dominant in Alas Niser, the guests' collective prayers are instrumental in contributing to the host family's achievement of the state of *slamet*, meaning secure, content and in good health, because they increase the likelihood of the host's intentions (or wishes, *hajat*, Ind.) being granted by Allah. Unlike elsewhere in Java, the speaker petitions no spirits, either village, ancestral or those dating back to conception. He also makes no references to and gives no explanation of the symbolic foods such as the five-coloured rice porridge (*tajin lemah berna*, Mad.; *jenang manca warna*, Jav.) or the glass with the three-coloured flowers. Such foods are nevertheless laid on the mat next to the rice cone. The speaker only mentions the names of the Prophet and Allah in closing his speech.

People in Alas Niser are quite wary of the *syirik* connotations of certain of their ritual activities and extreme care is taken to avoid committing sins. *Syirik* stands for the contravention of the central Muslim precept of monotheism and accrues from actions that can be interpreted as attributing divinity to entities besides Allah. The pre-occupation of locals with *syirik* was described to me as of recent origin, dating back to the early 1950s, a period when the divergence between traditionalist and modernist understandings of the faith became very pronounced and was explicitly politicized.[3] Most people remembered their forebearers placating village spirits, making long references to the symbolism of the five-coloured porridge and, in cases of ritual meals held for dead ancestors, of seeking to attract ancestral souls through the presentation of personal belongings and incense burning. As a response to modernist critiques, certain practices have been eradicated while others have been reframed. Today, the burning of incense is understood as a visualization of the ascent of prayers to the sky. At the same time, there has been an elimination of all ritual references to the rice goddess, Dewi Sri, who was once held as the ultimate supernatural owner of rice fields and the very source of fertility and placated during agricultural *konjengen*.

Parallel to these changes, there has been a renewed emphasis on accommodating different religious viewpoints. The few modernists found in Alas Niser, mainly educated newcomers from other places in Java, avoid being vocal about their doctrinal opposition to *slametan*. By taking a scripturalist position that holds only the Quran and the Hadith as the absolute authorities in matters of religious orthodoxy and orthopraxy, Islamic modernism has long called for the purification of the faith from historical accretions, including the *slametan* feasts which are construed as remnants of Java's Hindu-Buddhist past.[4] Despite such polemical pronouncements, more recently modernists in Probolinggo and elsewhere have sought to carve a more accommodating

---

3 The modernist vs. traditionalist distinction goes back to at least the late nineteenth century, which saw the disintegration of what Ricklefs (2007) calls the 'mystic synthesis' and the polarization of Javanese society along the religious categories that Geertz's (1960) famous study somewhat took for granted. For the rapid Islamization of Java from the 1970s onwards, see Hefner (1987). For more information on Islam in Java, see Chapter 5.

4 One of the recurrent themes of such differentiation is that traditionalist Islam recognizes the authority of ancestral custom (*adat*) and the authority of the Islamic legal schools, particularly the Shafiite one, in defining Islamic practice and belief in addition to the Quran and the Hadith. In contrast, the modernist position is strictly scripturalist in the sense that it relies only on the Quran and the Hadith, denying absolute authority both to other written texts and to ancestors. It is on this basis that modernists call for the purification of the faith from historical innovations. Moreover, modernists espouse an understanding of the scriptures based on the exercise of reason, emphasizing the translation of the scriptures into local vernaculars. In contrast, traditionalists focus on religious experience and the performance of religious rituals that are held to generate merit and blessings. The relation between the varieties of religious understanding and practice in Java has culminated in the debate between Geertz (1960) and Beatty (1999), on the one hand, and Woodward (1989), on the other. For a more recent study, see Daniels (2009). On the varieties of Islam elsewhere in Indonesia, see Bowen (1993) and Telle (2000). For a comprehensive study of the politics of Islam, see Hefner (2000).

position. As both Beatty (1999) and Bowen (1993) have showed, downplaying doctrinal differences in every day life is intimately related to the avoidance of public criticism of the meaning of *slametan* feasts. This avoidance is often coupled with 'a compartmentalization of the ritual [that] allows people to acknowledge some of its components and ignore others' (Bowen 1993, 241) as well as the redesignation of such feasts as *sedhekah*, an alms-giving rite that draws explicitly upon the Islamic value of charity. As a result of these accommodations, some modernists in Probolinggo do give *slametan* and participate in other peoples' celebrations. Yet some of the more scripturally inclined avoid giving themselves any but are happy to attend feasts given by others. Both kinds of modernists underscore their attitudes through appeal to the value of *rukun* (Ind., harmony) that ideally regulates relations between neighbours.[5]

The second part of the ritual is dominated by the recitation of prayers. In Alas Niser, unlike other places in Java, all *konjengen* necessitate the presence of a *kyai* who leads the recitation. The *kyai* begins with a recitation of *Surah Al-Fatihah* which is the opening part of Quran and is held to provide an alternative to the confession of the faith. The recitation is in solemn and clear voice and is followed by the recitation of other parts (*surah*) of the Quran, this time in unison by all the participants. Although the majority of the guests have only a vague understanding of Arabic, they are able reciters as they have spent their childhood afternoons learning to read Arabic in classes held in mosques or *pesantren* (Islamic boarding schools). The recitation of Quranic verses is followed by a collective *dikir* with the *kyai* leading. The *dikir* or *dhikr* (Arabic) practice comprises of a collection of specific formulaic utterances that mention the divine names with which Allah is described in the Quran, the most usual being *la ilah illa Allah* (Arabic, there is no deity but God).

The glorifying utterances are recited rhythmically and in unison by the participants who move their heads backwards and forwards looking increasingly withdrawn. It is often the case that *dikir* sessions are followed by *salawat* prayers, especially if the host has a reputation for being a pious Muslim. The *salawat* session is addressed to the Prophet Mohammed and most commonly comprises of Quranic verses dedicated to him, although non-Quranic praises to the Prophet, available in books included in the *pesantren* curriculum and sold at book shops, can be readily incorporated. After the *dikir* and *salawat* sessions end, the *kyai* proceeds to recite the final prayer. The prayer

---

5 This accommodating stance towards *slametan* feasts is absent from the developments that Guinness (2009) charts in an urban neighbourhood in Yogyakarta where *slametan* disappeared altogether from communal life in the early 2000s and was substituted with more overtly Islamic rituals such as *sembahyang* (prayer) sessions.

is in Arabic and despite the fact that there are special prayers to fit all occasions the most generally recited prayer is *doa selamat* (the prayer of well-being). The *kyai* petitions Allah to provide the host and his family with good health and prosperity, as well as to show mercy when the day of Judgement comes. While the *kyai* prays, the participants sit with their palms turned upward towards the sky, their eyes closed, occasionally bringing their palms to their faces and uttering *amin* in every pause of the *kyai*'s recitation.

Among traditionalists the presence of a *kyai* in *konjengen* feasts is instrumental for the ritual to achieve its full efficacy. The *kyai* possesses the expert knowledge of the occasion-specific prayer; he is the one who understands the prayers' lexical meaning and knows the appropriate way of its recitation in Arabic. A *kyai* comes to acquire such expertise through long-term education in Islamic schools. The occasion-specific prayers are included in the *al-kitab* (Arabic, religious books) taught in these schools. Prayers are also handed down orally by charismatic teachers to their trusted students and partake in the sacredness with which such bonds are imbued in the mystical traditions of the faith (see Schimmel 1975). According to these traditions, the *kyai* is also a potent person who, by virtue of his knowledge and publicly performed piety, stands closer to Allah, acting thus as an intermediary. All three elements, i.e. the purity and potency of the reciter, the intrinsic power of Arabic language and its correct recitation, form part of the prayer's efficacy (see also Bowen 1993, 98–102). When one of the three is lacking, villagers are quick to point out that the prayer will not reach Allah (*tidak sampai Allah*, Ind.) but will stop halfway to heaven. As a result, the collective petition will not be granted.

The prayer recited by the *kyai* forms the peak of the collective recitation preceding it. The collective recitation of Quranic verses and the *dikir* session are understood as further instances of potent speech that has intrinsic powers in and of itself. All around the Muslim world, certain verses of the Quran are considered to be imbued with special efficacy and are used in specific contexts and for specific purposes. Moreover, it is held that the recitation of any portion of the Quran entices Allah to grant favours to the petitioners. This is so for the Quran is the word of Allah. Traditionalist Muslims hold that every time Allah hears somebody uttering His word and chanting praises of Him, He becomes emotionally moved and takes a liking to that person. People in Alas Niser read the Quran in private as much as the fulfilment of a religious obligation as a way of enticing Allah to notice them. Such practice is believed to produce specific results for the reciter, namely the generation of merit (*pahala*, Ind.) one stores for the day of Judgement. Quranic recitation often accompanies private prayers and is said to contribute to the latter being fulfilled. In the context of public gatherings such as *konjengen*, the participants' collective recitation is performed partly for the benefit of the host. Although the *pahala* generated remains tied to the individual reciter, collective recitation presents Allah with a more powerful request since it is supported by a multitude of people, thus increasing the possibility that the host's wishes will be granted. The strength of numbers is often cited by traditionalists as the very explanation for *konjengen*'s collective character. As one person put it, 'If a person recites the Quran [*ngaji*, Ind.] by himself, his request may or may not reach Allah, hence ... may or may not be fulfilled but if all his relatives and neighbours and friends gather and *ngaji* together then I am sure that he is to receive what he asked for, God willing.'

Konjengen feasts provide occasions in which neighbours participate in the most important moments of each others' lives. All major life-cycle and agricultural stages are marked by invitations for participating and witnessing events related to growth. These gatherings not only celebrate vitality but in effect generate it. Food and prayers are the primary sources of well-being, as well as objects of transaction among neighbours. The *konjengen* participants contribute their prayers, performing ritual work for the benefit of the host family. Their labour is reciprocated immediately with food. The equivalence of food and potent speech is based the fact that they are intricately associated with growth and proliferation, the promotion and extension of life. In this regard, neighbourhood sociality is predicated on exchanges that sponsor and encourage the life process.

Neighbourhood exchanges are based on the delineation of the host's and the participants' houses as separate and distinct. This separation is intrinsic to the event in the sense that it allows for exchange to take place, parting donors from recipients at the very moment of their interaction (Strathern 1988). In addition, the difference between hosts and participants is instantiated in their differentiated contributions. Participating houses offer potent speech; the house of the host reciprocates with food. The relation between food and prayers is asymmetrical. Although speech and food are equivalent in the sense that they both promote growth, they are not equal. Prayers rank higher for the vitality they ensure is immaterial, invisible and *halus* in nature, originating from a divine source. In contrast, the more *kasar* qualities of food render it material and visible, originating from human sources. The asymmetry registers the host who receives the *halus* gift as superior to participants who labour for the host's well-being. However, as we shall see shortly, the asymmetry and the sharp differentiation of participants into donors and recipients that the event of exchange necessitates is a valid description of sociality only when *konjengen* feasts are analyzed from the perspective of the single houses participating. The picture changes dramatically when the analysis moves a scale upwards and proceeds from the perspective of the *kampung*. This changing of scale and perspective evinces the *kampong* as an undifferentiated unit, making the separation of and the difference between houses to disappear from view.

Vitality for the dead

In Probolinggo, the terms *slametan* and *kongengen* are reserved for neighbourhood feasts focusing on the living. Such feasts are thought of as separate to those given for the benefit of the dead, despite similarities in structure and attendants. Feasts for the dead are differentiated into *tahlilan* and *yasinan*. *Tahlilan* mark the recent departure of a deceased at stipulated intervals while *yasinan* form the basis of associations which convene on a rotating basis weekly or bi-weekly. The difference between feasts for the living and the dead is moreover marked by the absence of the *tumpeng robyong*, the whole roasted chicken, and the five-coloured rice porridge from rice meals dedicated to the dead. The food for these occasions consists simply of rice and small portions of meat as well as vegetable sidedishes.

According to all variants of Javanese Islam, the commemoration of the dead forms a central obligation for all Muslims. However, the variations that do exist relate to disagreements regarding whose obligation it is and the obligation's overall purpose. According to traditionalists, the obligation to remember the dead falls upon both the direct descendants of the deceased and his/her neighbours. Modernists maintain that that it is only the children of the deceased that are allowed to pray for their dead parents. For modernists, praying for the dead is also limited in terms of the efficacy of the act. Traditionalists hold that commemorative practices can act on the posthumous fate of the deceased. Modernists object to the holding of ritual meals for the benefit of the dead on the grounds that the idea that the living are able to assist and aid the dead contravenes the basic precepts of Islam. As Bowen (1993, 269) observes for the Gayo and Telle (2000) for the Sasak, the very idea of producing merit for the dead radically undermines the individual's moral accountability to God that Muslim puritans stress. Despite the modernist argument that death severs all ties between the living and the dead, modernists in Alas Niser and Probolinggo do participate in rites of commemoration (*tahlilan*) given by their neighbours. However, they deny that such rites have any bearing upon the deceased. Modernists also refrain from giving themselves any such rituals.

Among traditionalists, two types of rice meals for the dead are normally held. As in the rest of Java and indeed in other parts of the Islamic world, *tahlilan* gatherings mark the recent departure of the deceased on the first, third or seventh, forty-forth and hundredth evenings after death. In other parts of Java, the final *tahlilan* that completes the rites is held on the thousandth day after death (Geertz 1960; Koentjaraningrat 1989). From then on, the grave of the deceased is visited on various occasions with decreased frequency as time passes by. However, in Probolinggo, caring for the dead continues after such dates and is institutionalized in the form of *yasinan* associations.

Yasinan associations are formed on the basis of common residence, with neighbours praying for each other's dead. Despite its assumed voluntary character, membership of such associations is gender-exclusive and all houses are expected to send a male or female representative. Omission to fulfil this obligation is accompanied by accusations of arrogance and undue pride. *Yasinan*, and other similar associations such as *salawatan*[6] and *khataman*,[7] have a formal structure with an elected chairman, secretary and treasurer, attendance lists and records of the members' financial contributions. Such associations have at their disposal electronic sound equipment, musical instruments such as tambourines, and mats. Part of the financial contributions collected is used to purchase this equipment and in the late 1990s contributions amounted to 2,000 rupiah per member house per meeting. Another part of contributions is offered to the host house as compensation for the expenses it incurs. In this case, the amount did not normally exceed that of one thousand rupiah per member house per meeting. In general, meetings are held on a rotating basis determined by the drawing of a lottery. When each member house has had its turn, the *yasinan* association temporarily disbands, although in most cases it will soon start up again.

As in rituals for the benefit of the living, the *yasinan* opens with a short speech delivered by the *kyai*. The speech states the purpose of the meeting and gives the names of the dead ancestors to whom the ritual is dedicated. The dead ancestors are those of the house in which the *yasinan* is held and they are designated as the sole beneficiaries of the merit (*pahala*) that the collective recitation of *Surah Yasin* (chapter 37 of the Quran) and *dikir* will generate. In contrast to *konjengen*, the neighbours neither pray for the benefit of the host nor do they retain ownership of the *pahala* they produce. Rather, they forfeit such ownership, transferring the merit (*pahala*) to the host's dead ancestors in a manner similar to the Gayo of Sumatra (see Bowen 1993, 266–7). The request recited by the *kyai* petitions Allah to show mercy by reducing the punishment ancestors receive in the afterlife. For traditionalists, dead ancestors who have received large quantities of merit are thought to have most of their sins remitted and thus to be relatively free from punishment, awaiting peacefully the Day of Judgement. The production and transfer of merit is followed immediately by the serving of food, principally rice, and the offering of tea and cigarettes.

---

6 *Salawatan* associations are dedicated to the chanting of Quranic and non-Quranic verses in praise of Prophet Mohammed. Such verses also commemorate Mohammed's return to Mecca after his flight to Medina, a major event in Islamic history.

7 *Khataman* association meetings revolve around the recitation of the Quran from beginning to end, completing a full reading in every meeting. The Quran is divided into 30 parts (*juz*). Each member is allocated a specific part and all members recite their different parts synchronically.

Figure 7. Generating merit for the dead

Along with *slametan*, *yasinan* associations reveal the spatial limits of neighbourhoods, not in the sense of establishing a perimeter, but in a positive sense of allowing the neighbourhood to establish its presence. Place emerges out of *yasinan* associations, which in turn engage neighbours in exchanges. The *yasinan* generates place through the unfolding of a series of relations that revolve around a rotating mode of exchange and the manifestations of care which neighbours are expected to show for each other's dead.

Unlike other parts of Java, in Probolinggo there are no ambilineal ancestor orientated kin groups of the kind that Koentjaraningrat (1989) calls *alur waris* and Sairin (1982) calls *trah*. These groups, which emerged mainly as a result of the reorganization of aristocratic Javanese society during the period of high colonialism, are formed around a single apical ancestor of a certain import. They are also characterized by optional and despatialized membership that includes both local kin and kin living further away. However, there are some strong similarities between *trah* groupings and *yasinan* gatherings. *Trah* form worship communities too, focusing on tending the grave of the apical ancestor and giving ritual rice meals. In the case of Muslim *trah* (see Headley 1997), this apical ancestor is intimately related to demographic mobility, forest clearing, Islamization and the establishment of a locality. Here once again, narratives of origin merge with topostories through the medium of ritual commemoration. But whereas in Central Java, *trah* seem to provide an alternative to neighbourhood sociality founded on networks spanning across localities, in Alas Niser neighbourhood and genealogy are made to temporarily collapse into each other through the commemoration not of a single ancestor but of their multitude.

In line with the rather unfortunately named trend towards 'genealogical amnesia' observed in Java and other parts of the archipelago, the ancestors commemorated in *yasinan* usually reach only the third or fourth generation above that of the host. However, as among aristocratic Javanese and pious Muslims in Central Java (see Headley 1997; Sairin 1982), there are a few cases such as that of the descendants of the 'first people' (see Chapter 1) whose memories ascend back six or seven generations. The dead in question include relatives from both the father's and mother's side, as well as that of the spouse. Furthermore, these ancestors are usually lineal. Collaterals such as dead uncles or aunts are rarely mentioned. A pervading characteristic of *yasinan* is thus its constant evocation of ancestors who originated from other places and whose identities, while alive, were distinct from those of their descendants, i.e. these ancestors were Javanese or Madurese, but not mixed. In numerous cases, memories of migration constitute a rather sharp break in people's genealogies which stop short of incorporating those ancestors who never came to live in Alas Niser. Many locals confessed themselves ignorant of the names of those remote ancestors of theirs who belonged to ascending generations of their more recent ancestors who migrated to Alas Niser. In other words, the *yasinan* ritual is permeated with a sense of a genealogy starting from the zero point of migration. This was more pronounced among people who were third-generation migrants. In their case, memory depth was circumscribed by demographic mobility, rendering kinship connections with people in Madura and ancestral origin places in Java out of memory's reach. While they all presumed that their migrating ancestors had ancestors, they felt no obligation towards commemorating them. This was coupled with a certain indifference they exhibited towards tracing and maintaining kinship with people in Madura and Java through visiting and exchanging gifts.[8]

In *yasinan* as in *konjengen*, the circulation of food is articulated with that of potent speech. In general, words and things are considered as interdependent and equivalent as they move in opposite directions. This movement separates the exchanging parties from each other, manifesting their boundaries. The boundaries of the parties involved in the exchanges do not coincide with the skin boundaries of individuals for it is not 'individuals' who are involved in

---

8 This does not of course apply to newcomers who do maintain such links. However, such links tend to thin out and are reproduced with lesser intensity by the newcomers' descendants, i.e. second-generation migrants.

such rites but persons who act in their capacity as representatives of houses. The locus of agency tends therefore not to be the individual but the house that acts via a particular member, male or female. Analytically speaking, houses are made up of relations of siblingship. As a result it is the set of siblings making up a house that provides the locus of its agency. However, in the context of exchanges considered here and which take place between houses, the relations houses consist of are eclipsed and concealed from view with the consequence that the exchanging parties are made to appear as singular rather than plural. In other words, during *slametan* and *yasinan*, houses are evinced as internally undifferentiated entities devoid of relations that hold together parts. For the purposes of engaging in relations with other similarly constituted units, houses manifest themselves as undifferentiated and singular as a matter of necessity.

The separation of houses that exchange causes to take place is underwritten by the hierarchy marking the relation of sacred words and food. In contrast to *konjengen*, the vitality that sacred words produce is geared towards contributing to the posthumous well-being of dead ancestors, ensuring a state of tranquillity and serenity and carrying promises of compassionate and merciful judgment. The production of *pahala* is compensated immediately with the gift of food, a gift appropriate to the living. As Strathern (1988) reminds us, in the absence of a universal medium of ritual exchange, the value of the differentiated gifts can be judged with regards to their relational contrast, i.e. the differential value to each other (see also Foster 1990). Potent speech far exceeds the conventional attributes of food, as it is indifferent to the boundary between life and death through its conversion into merit; merit is of value both to the dead and the living. In addition to being invisible and thus more *halus*, potent speech is not subject to scarcity and finitude through consumption (see Keane 1994). Its relative abundance and durability strengthens in turn the words' capacity for overflowing boundaries. Although traditionalist Muslims believe that the production of merit can be calculated with some degree of certainty depending on the number of recitations completed and the number of people participating in the recitation, gifts of food are easier to quantify. This is partly because food bears economic properties as well entering into other spheres of exchange as a commodity with a market-specified value. It is very much against the possibility of construing food as a commodity for sale that neighbour feasting practices are articulated. The withholding of food from market transactions elevates food contextually to an equivalent though unequal partner of sacred words. The unmarketable quality of sacred speech displaces momentarily the commodity aspect of food. The appropriation of the higher gift of efficacious speech by the host house manifests its superiority *vis-à-vis* the rest of the participants who labour for the benefit of the host's ancestors. Here as in marriage transactions (see Chapter 3), the recipient of the more valued gift stands higher than the donor.

The hierarchy between houses that *yasinan* exchanges herald is provisional. The interchangeability and alternativity in the assumption of the positions of the sacred words' provider and recipient, which is in-built in the rotating mode of holding meetings, introduces a range of further complexities and dynamics that will be analysed shortly. Before that, however, I will go on to describe a third case of ritual transactions that takes place during the holy month of Ramadan.

Sound and sentiment

Fasting during the ninth month of the lunar year is prescribed as one of the five pillars of the faith. In Java, the fast marks a certain reversal in the rhythms of every day life as early mornings and late evenings become the focus of activity with people busying themselves with food preparation and consumption before the day breaks, something which is repeated after dusk, with the addition of the performance of non-obligatory prayers. The period of fast also coincides with the intensification of neighbour transactions, especially those surrounding food and potent speech. This time the food concerned appears both in mediated, cooked, and unmediated, raw, form; while the merit that Quranic recitation generates affects both reciters and listeners.

All Muslims in Alas Niser see fasting as more than a simple obligation. It is primarily construed as a test for their religiosity. One often hears the *kyai* extolling the prophets and the saints for the patience and strength they showed when Allah put their faith to test. Fasting is also conceived as a practice that develops the 'feelings of care' (*rasa kepedulian*, Ind.) towards the needy and deprived, instilling in the believer the capacity to empathize with their troubles and the will to act so as to alleviate them. The payment of *zakat fitrah*, the religious tax that takes place towards the end of Ramadan, exemplifies this point. Moreover, the performance of the non-obligatory evening prayers (*taraweh*, Ind.), and the group recitation of the Quran (*tedarus*, Ind.) are some of the main activities through which one can accumulate *pahala* and avoid heavy punishment in the afterlife. However, the main meaning locals attribute to fasting has to do with its purificatory effect. This internal catharsis is often phrased in terms of a born-again idiom since traditionalists maintain that after the Ramadan one is as pure and free of sins as a newborn baby.

Both the start and the end of the fasting month are marked by food prestations. In the evening that opens the fast, women cook a special cake (*kue apem*, Jav.), the cake of forgiveness. The cake, which is distributed to and eaten by one's neighbours, is held to petition Allah to show mercy and give strength to the cake-giver so that he/she is able to withstand the test of fasting. The cake also anticipates the asking for forgiveness enacted among relatives, neighbours and friends during *Lebaran*, the feast that concludes the month long fast. Similarly, the evening that marks the arrival of *Lebaran* involves food transactions with dishes of yellow rice, noodles and chicken circulating among neighbours. These exchanges take place at the same time that *takbiran* (Ind.)[9] celebrations are held, with youths chanting in Arabic on top of trucks and motorcycles, beating drums and carrying torches and banners, to announce the end of the fast.

The last ten days of Ramadan involve the holding of *konjengen maleman* – from *malem* (Mad., evening). Since eating is forbidden from dawn to dusk, *konjengen maleman* takes place right after the performance of *sholat maghrib*, early in the evening. Although no gatherings are held, dishes of glutinous rice circulate between neighbouring houses. These prestations take place on odd-numbered dates.[10] Female heads of houses meet beforehand and organize the exchange of gifts by dividing the *kampong* into different groups. Each group is responsible for cooking and distributing food to the rest of the groups on a specific date, with the cooking done on a house rather than group basis. In this way, neighbours exchange symmetrically, assuming alternately the role of gift-giver and gift-receiver.

The interdependence of food and prayers is emphasized during the fast. The performance of *taraweh* prayers held every evening during Ramadan just after *sholat isyah*, the final prayer of the day, is accompanied by the consumption of coffee or tea and cakes. These are provided once again on a rotating basis. Despite the fact that formally speaking *taraweh* prayers are not obligatory (*wajib*) but rather optional yet meritorious (*sunnah*, Ind.), in Probolinggo they have assumed the status of an obligatory ritual with the vast majority of men rushing to *langgar* and mosques to perform them at the prescribed time. Women, who customarily pray neither in *langgar* nor mosques except for special occasions such as the day after the end of Ramadan (*sholat Idul Fitri*), perform *taraweh* in a room inside their own house. These women are responsible for the provision of the materials of men's public commensality. Men's gatherings in *langgar* and mosques manifest the *kampong* as a worship community that generates merit and consumes food collectively. The separate houses that make up the *kampong* are informed days earlier by the caretakers

---

9 From *takbir*, the proclamation of *Allahu akbar*, 'God is great'.
10 One of these odd numbered dates is the 'Night of Power', i.e. the night on which the Holy Book is believed to have descended from the highest to the lowest heaven. Reciting Quranic verses and performing good deeds on that night is held to result to special blessings.

of the *langgar* and mosques about which dates they have to provide drinks and cakes. This is done either through the compilation and distribution of lists of names or by word of mouth.[11]

Taraweh is followed on a daily basis by *tedarus*, the group recitation of the Quran. Javanese Muslims recite the Quran throughout the year. During Ramadan, there is an intensification of this practice with the emphasis now placed on the complete recitation of the book from beginning to end. The recitation is accomplished by *tedarus* groups which are gender exclusive; men hold *tedarus* recitations in *langgar* and mosques, while women gather in the living room of a different house in the neighbourhood every night. Both groups recite the Quran with the participants taking turns, i.e. succeeding each other rather than reciting at the same time.

Neighbours' chanting dominates the evening aural environment. The chanting sometimes lasts for a few hours. It can also last for the whole night from around eight o'clock until just before dawn. The recitation is conceived as generating merit (*pahala*) both for those who recite and for those who listen. *Tedarus'* recitation is therefore dedicated neither to the event's host as in *konjengen*, nor to the host's dead ancestors as in *yasinan*. As the place in which the recitation is held is a public one (the rotating basis of female gatherings transforms houses into public spaces) the merit produced is disseminated to the neighbourhood as a whole. The neighbourhood comes to be defined as a place animated by and filled with the purposeful chanting and the attentive listening of sacred words. Chanting and listening allows for the bringing forth of the neighbourhood. The recitations are transmitted through several loudspeakers, placed on the roof of the *langgar* and mosques which transfer the merit produced around the neighbourhood. It is through the collective, rotating chanting that the neighbourhood seeks to secure visions of Paradise for the afterlife of all the persons it envelops and sustains.

The production and circulation of merit is underlined and reinforced by commensality. Every time the *tedarus* neighbourhood group completes a full reading of the Quran, achieving therefore a *khataman*, a *konjengen* is held to celebrate the event. These *konjengen* are special in two ways. Firstly, there is

11 Traditionalists and modernists differ in terms of *taraweh* prayers as well. In Probolinggo, unlike other places in Java, such differences do not escalate in public confrontations (see Möller 2005, 298–300). Rather, traditionalists and modernists in Probolinggo often share the same worship places. Their differences have to do with the number of *rakaat* (Ind.essential units of all prayers, consisting of bows and prostrations) each variant deems appropriate: traditionalists perform twenty *rakaat* of *taraweh* plus another three designated as *witir*, modernists perform eight plus three. In traditionalist-dominated Alas Niser, modernists would often leave after eight *rakaat* to perform *witir* at their home, often returning to the mosque for the drinks, the cakes and conversations.

Figure 8. Celebrating a complete reading of the Quran

pooling of resources. A collection of raw foodstuffs occurs the previous day, with each house contributing an equal amount of raw rice (*berras*, Mad.), raw pieces of chicken, vegetables, spices, sugar etc. The female members of each house organize both the collection and the transformation of raw food into cooked food. Secondly, cooking is a collective effort undertaken in the same hearth. Usually one of the neighbourhood's kitchens becomes the focus of activity. This kitchen is extended through the addition of temporary hearths, each dedicated to the production of a specific component of festive food. Although any house can qualify for this function, it is commonly richer households that volunteer, thus augmenting their status in the locality. In the process of cooking, the raw materials pooled are mixed together. Their mixing severs the identification of particular items from particular donors and inflects the neighbourhood as a unit. This unity is manifested as much in the pooling and mixing of raw materials as in the collective labour of women who convert them into consumable, nourishing substances. The finished product of this process is transferred from the kitchen to the *langgar* and placed in the centre of the gathered males. There the food is distributed to all participants who will eat as much as they desire and take portions of the remaining food back to their houses for the women and children to eat.

Tedarus konjengen take place more than once during Ramadan with their frequency depending on the pace of Quranic recitation. Some *tedarus* groups operate by reciting one *juz* (Ind., section) of the Quran every evening.

This allows for the achievement of a single complete reading during the fast. Such groups hold only one *konjengen*. Most neighbourhoods, however, opt to recite three *juz* a night. These neighbourhoods hold three *konjengen* during Ramadan, once every ten days, since the total number of *juz* – 30 in total – corresponds roughly to the total number of days of the fasting month. In the case of my own neighbourhood, the *tedarus* group had opted for a 24-hour non-stop recitation. This meant that the group completed a full reading every two and half days. All in all, eleven *konjengen* were held for the fasting month of 1999. The emphasis on the intensification of Quranic recitation rests on the belief that the total amount of *pahala* generated depends on the number of complete readings; the higher the number of *khataman* the more *pahala* the neighbourhood produces and shares. These calculations often form the basis of competition between neighbourhoods since *tedarus* amounts to a public performance of collective piety. The larger the number of *tedarus konjengen* the more pious the neighbourhood presents itself in the eyes of other neighbourhoods.

Ex-changing scales

So far, three types of neighbourhood transactions have been considered. In comparing these three types it becomes apparent that while in the first two cases, *konjengen* and *yasinan*, the unequal value of the things exchanged separates the participating houses into low-status donors and higher-status recipients, in the third case relating to Ramadan activities, there is a pooling of words and food at the level of the *kampong* that breaks down the boundaries between the houses and mitigates the dissolution of hierarchy. Transactions of the third type emphasize the indistinguishability of neighbouring houses in the production of vitality for this life and for the afterlife with this non-differentiation permeated by the principle of sharing.

The contrast this comparison creates between *yasinan* and *konjengen*, on the one hand, and Ramadan transactions, on the other, is misleading. The transactions of the first type can be said to foster difference and separation only if the variable of time is suppressed from our considerations. The reintroduction of time into the analysis reveals that *yasinan* and *konjengen* transactions implicate reversals in the flow of goods and the assumption of alternate positions by the people involved. As all present transactions always evoke past flows of goods and anticipate or even enforce new ones to be undertaken in the future, the difference and hierarchy between neighbouring houses are eclipsed by an indeterminate sense of sharing. The scale in which this eclipsing is registered spatially as well as socially involves the *kampong*. Both the importance of time and scale make imperative a change of perspective in our analysis of transactions. Formally speaking, exchange entails the adoption of the perspective of the house as a constitutive unit of sociality and foregrounds the house's separation from others. This renders the *kampong* as a mere collection of parts (houses) related through processes of reciprocity. In contrast, sharing as the excess and the surplus – the incessant, uninterrupted and perpetual transacting generates – pertains to the perspective of the *kampong*. This excess makes the distinctiveness of houses recede from view and foregrounds the neighbourhood as a single and indivisible whole.

The reversibility of flows and the ability of positions to alternate that characterize transactions, as seen from the eyes of the *kampong* as it were, acquire their particular dynamic from a rotating mode of transacting. Rotation permeates both *konjengen* life-cycle rituals and rites of ancestor commemoration, ensuring the delayed exchange of identical goods.

Both *konjengen* and *yasinan* rituals are held on a rotating basis. They are, thus, similar in form to the rotating credit associations (*aresan*, Mad.) described by Geertz (1962). Rotation is more obvious in the case of *yasinan* since the structure of the meetings is predicated on the members taking turns praying for each others' dead ancestors and offering and receiving food. In *yasinan*, the immediate reciprocation of merit with food is a valid description of what is involved only if we see such gatherings as discontinuous events, i.e. as events located outside the logic of rotation. Seen within this logic, food and prayers do not form a dyad of gift and counter-gift. Rather, the obligation to attend *yasinan* is embedded within the obligation to hold a *yasinan* when one's turn is due. Rotation ensures alternativity and reversal: the previous gathering's host will be transformed at a later date into a guest who will pray for the dead ancestors of the new host and will receive food similar to that he has himself offered previously. Rotation also guarantees that prayers and food move between neighbours in such manner, whereby like goods are exchanged for like.

The rotating basis of *konjengen* is not as straightforward; the reason for this is that the time span within which the delayed exchange of identical goods occurs can extend over years instead of weeks or months. Since all members of a *kampong* are expected to hold *slametan* for most if not all life-cycle events, *konjengen* transactions demand their continuous perpetuation. Within a time period that knows no determinate bounds and in which exchanges do not necessarily balance out perfectly, all *kampong* houses are expected to take turns holding feasts to celebrate a daughter's wedding or a son's circumcision. In this case, rotation depends not on the drawing of a lottery but on the domestic cycles.

Rotation, alternativity and reversal, constitute the *kampong* as a distinct domain and scale of sociality. The transactions realized therein amount to the 'denial' of reciprocity in the strict sense of the term. This 'denial' is contingent on the encompassment of dyadic exchanges between houses within a redistributive frame that has no precise and discernible centre. The hierarchy that dyadic exchanges set in motion is embedded within a rotational mode of transacting that allows neighbours to take turns claiming higher status. It also ensures that like goods are exchanged for like. The end result of rotational transacting is that the *kampong* emerges as a status flat yet tense arena characterized by equivalent claims neighbours have on each others' capacities for potent speech and food. The equivalence of such claims guarantees that speech and food are shared among the residents of the *kampong*. The transactions of the third type that occur during the Ramadan are the most dramatic effect of this sharing. Sharing of either the rotating or the pooling variety corresponds to the primary means of the *kampong* coming into being. This involves the eclipsing of houses as separate and distinct units engaged in dyadic exchanges and necessitates the evincing of the very same transactions as founded on sharing. Furthermore, this evincing wholly partakes of the perspective of the *kampong* as it allows the *kampong* to make itself manifest as an internally undifferentiated and smooth space that knows no internal fissures and has no lines of interior demarcation.

The sharing that constitutes the *kampong* in East Java is quite different from the one Gibson (1985, 1986) privileges in his account of the Buid, a highland group of shifting cultivators in the Philippines. Buid sociality is permeated by enactments stressing companionship, individual autonomy and equality at the expense of the values of kinship. There is an astonishing ease in the initiation and termination of social relationships which is directly dependant on the dissociation of the obligation to provide a feast, food or labour from the obligation to attend and to receive from those sponsored by others. Dyadic exchanges are avoided for they are seen as competitive and unequal. Among the Buid, Gibson claims, giving is not directed to specific persons from whom one expects a return but to an undifferentiated community made up of those present. In Probolinggo, by contrast, there is no dissociation of giving from receiving; entitlements to gifts do depend on past donations and the values of kinship are treasured. In Probolinggo, therefore, sharing does not result in the avoidance of dyadic exchanges but is the product of the contextual eclipsing of reciprocity by rotation and pooling. It is also the result of the operation of different scales with reciprocity pertaining to the scale of the house, while rotation and pooling effect the scale of the *kampong*. In other words, sharing is a *within* relation at the level of the *kampong* that conceals the operation of reciprocity as a *between* relation at the level of houses.

Rotational sharing does not conform either to Sahlins' (1972) famous tripartite division of modes of reciprocity and the latter's distinction from redistribution. Sahlins associates sharing with 'generalized reciprocity', the free or pure gift generously and disinterestedly offered. The stipulation of a return is vague and the latter's timing is not immediate but deferred. As a result, there is a non-overt reckoning of debts. Sahlins also argues for an overall distinction between reciprocity and redistribution or pooling on the grounds that while reciprocity requires social duality, building upon the pre-existing separateness of the exchanging units, redistribution 'stipulates a social centre where goods meet and thence flow outwards' (1972, 189). Such a centre is provided, for example, by the institution of the chief in Polynesian polities.

Rotational sharing is unlike generalized reciprocity as there is a strong emphasis on the obligation of an identical return. On the other hand, rotational sharing is similar to generalized reciprocity insofar as the time that elapses between prestation and counter-prestation is not an immediate and pressing concern. In *yasinan*, the time lag depends on the lottery; in *slametan*, on domestic cycles; in certain Ramadan exchanges, on preferences relating to the calendar. In all three cases, the return is not immediate but delayed. The delayed exchange of identical goods that underpins rotational sharing is also different from Sahlins' category of balanced reciprocity. Balanced reciprocity and rotational sharing are similar in terms of the stress placed on the overt reckoning of debts and the requirement of an equivalent return. However, the operation of different time scales dictating the delayed nature of the return underscores rotational sharing's distinctiveness. In addition, the return does not take place within a finite and narrow period, but is sometimes deferred until some remote point in the future.

The material presented here also raises serious doubts about Sahlins' method of arriving at an unambiguous delineation of redistribution from reciprocity. Rotational transactions and Ramadan pooling do correspond to mechanisms of redistribution. In the Javanese case, however, there is no centre equivalent to the rank of the chief that works towards the collection and subsequent dissemination of the resources it has managed to extract. *Kampong* sharing is acephalous; it knows of no centre or authority. Furthermore, the social duality with which Sahlins associates reciprocity is equally problematic as it is taken for granted. In contrast, I have argued that the positions of donor and recipient are the effect of exchange, not the exchange's *a priori* cause. Moreover, social dualities of this sort are established in Java at a specific scale in the enactment of sociality. The scale in question pertains to houses that become separate and distinct in the course of exchanges. The houses' distinctiveness, however, is eclipsed when transactions are seen from the perspective of the neighbourhood that privileges construing transactions as based on rotation and pooling. Houses and *kampong*, reciprocity and rotation/ pooling, are entangled in a tense relation of mutual implication and reciprocal presupposition. This reciprocal presupposition entails dynamic processes of eclipsing and evincing. The evincing of the neighbourhood demands the eclipsing of the house, and vice versa. Similarly, the evincing of rotation and pooling requires the eclipsing of exchanges based on social dualities, and vice versa. Moreover, the evincing of rotation and pooling is directly related to the establishment of the *kampong* as a higher order House in its own right.

Digesting the multitude

In the previous chapter, I argued that siblingship is contingent on transfers of detachable parts of personhood. The circulation of body parts in the form of semen, blood and breast milk and the circulation of persons in the form of spouses and children as parts of sets are instrumental to the establishment of Houses and of relations of siblingship of which Houses are made up. The circulation of potent speech, food and ancestors performed at the level of the neighbourhood during ritual occasions has similar effects.

In Alas Niser as in other places in Java, there is a widely acknowledged avoidance of marrying one's neighbours (see Chapter 3). When asked about the reason for this, people would only comment that it is preferable (*lebbi bhegus*, Mad.) that people who live in the same *kampong* refrain from marrying each other, noting that the strains and tensions involved in relations between affines are inappropriate for neighbours. This avoidance, which has no basis in Islamic stipulations, is observed quite faithfully. Indeed, the only case I know of a marriage between neighbours (*tetenggha*, Mad.), involved the son of a newcomer family with the daughter of a long-term resident. In this case, the difference as to origin places was deemed adequate enough for the marriage to take place. Avoidance is, of course, not as strong as incest prohibitions; yet the strong aversion towards reconstituting *tettengha* as affines is a reliable indicator of the near equivalence people in Probolinggo strive to establish between the categories of neighbours and genealogical siblings.

Genealogical siblingship is related to the co-substantiality that the convergence of parental substances creates. This in turn guarantees that siblings share the same ancestors. Genealogical siblingship is also established by means of co-spatiality, i.e. growing up in the same house, and of every day commensality. There is also the joint access to means of production. What neighbourhood transactions endeavour to achieve is the replication of such sharing on a higher scale.

Sharing ancestors among neighbours is the outcome of *yasinan* rituals. What the activity of commemoration accomplishes is a firstly, a reversal in the flow of genealogical connectedness and secondly, an extension and a replenishment of the person of participants in terms of its sources of growth. The reversal is embedded within the traditionalist variant of Islam that sees prayers as means of affecting changes in the posthumous condition of the dead. In the same way that prayers ensure the well-being of the dead in the afterlife, they refashion relations between the dead and living, creating connections that move from the present towards the past. From the perspective of each separate direct descendant, transacting with the dead involves the generation and transfer of merit as a return for the gift of life, nurture, knowledge and property, with which ancestors have furnished their offspring. From the perspective of the neighbourhood, *yasinan* implicate neighbours with genealogically unrelated dead. Neighbours pray and generate merit for each other's dead in the same way that an ancestor's direct descendants are required to do. In the process, neighbours treat one another's dead as their own, appropriating what is other and alien and turning it into a dimension of the self. Prayer-reciters and prayer-receivers, the dead and the unrelated living, become connected through the merit the living are capable of generating for the benefit of the dead. The transfer of merit flows in the reverse direction to that of semen and blood. The transfer of semen and blood designates past and future generations as genealogically related. In *yasinan*, the verticality of the connection is maintained but it travels in the opposite direction and is established through the generation and transfer of merit.

Transactions with the dead have fundamental consequences for the projection of the spatiality of the *kampong* onto temporality. *Yasinan* gatherings articulate a vision of the neighbourhood as having sprung from a multitude. At the remote end of a *kampong*'s history, *yasinan* postulates neither a single apical ancestor nor a set of siblings, but a multitude, affirming the heterogeneity of ancestors that make up the neighbourhood, with their differences related to the diversity of places they are from (see Chapter 1). The reversibility of time allows for genealogy to be articulated on a non-exclusive basis and promotes the diversification and multiplication of the origins of the participants. The end result of this spreadout-ness is the expansion of the range of dead that a person treats as one's own and a consequent replenishment of his/her sources. As genealogies are tirelessly redrawn, disseminated and shared, the *kampung*'s spatiality is made to coincide with temporality. In other words, place and genealogy become conjoined through ritual actions the purpose of which is as much to create place as it is to create specific kinds of persons in that place.

The assertion the peoples of Probolinggo make about being mixed persons is partly founded on the rituals of commemoration that cultivate and instil a sense of sharing the same yet multiple ancestors. In this respect, ritual makes neighbours into people marked by co-substantiality. This sense is reinforced by ritual acts of commensality. Whereas genealogical siblings and affinal siblings practice commensality on a daily basis, by preparing and consuming ordinary meals together, neighbours share more lavish meals during ritual occasions. Food is directly related to vitality and growth. Ritual occasions are accompanied by collective acts of commensality. This ritual commensality multiplies and expands any given person's sources of growth through the appropriation and corporeal incorporation of the food presented as a gift. Due to the reciprocal nature of feasting and the alternativity of the positions of food-provider and food-receiver, the incorporation of a multitude of others into one's self is intrinsically coupled to the demand to disperse and scatter one's self into many directions. In the process, the boundaries between self and other, as far as neighbours are concerned, are broken down with the *kampong* emerging as an undifferentiated entity that comprises of multiple sources of origin and growth that are shared equally among the people inhabiting it.

For my interlocutors, food is of special significance for it is construed as a transubstantiation of blood. The transformation of food into blood is performed by the *hati*. In addition to being the seat of *roh* and the primary centre of perception, the *hati* in its association with the liver rather than the heart occupies a definitive place in human physiology as conceived by locals. Several of the people I interviewed, including those conversant in Sufism and other, less pious Muslims, conceive the *hati* as a clot of blood (*sekumpul darah*, Ind.) that produces blood from the juices of digested food. According to their understanding of the functioning of the human body, food is cooked in the stomach in the first round of digestion. It is then thought to proceed to the *hati* in liquid form; there it is cooked for the second time (*massaqan keduaq*, Mad.) and converted into blood. The blood so produced proceeds to the heart, which works as a blood pump (*pompa darah*, Ind.). Due to its systolic and diastolic movements, blood reaches all parts of the human body by way of the veins.[12]

We can think of food transactions as blood transfusions. The bodies people in Probolinggo are endowed with are fluid and alterable in the sense that the blood of which they are composed is neither fixed nor simply given at birth. Blood circulates in the shape of food and its circulation is particularly intensive among neighbours. Those that partake in ritual commensality have bodies that become; this becoming allows neighbourhood sociality to be registered corporeally through the mediation of food.[13] Thus, people embody sociality

---

12 Ullmann (1978) notes that for the great doctors of mediaeval Islam the liver was of particular importance, firstly, as the seat of the natural faculties – those of conception, growth, and nourishment – and secondly, as the blood-producing organ. On the associations among digestion, the senses and perception in Hindu India, see Pinard (1991). The idea that blood comes from the transformation of food is also found among the Malays of Langkawi (see Carsten 1997, 109–15).

13 Fajans summarizing work on food in Melanesia, writes that food is not simply transformed, i.e. from raw to cooked, but is primarily transformative: 'it acts as a transformative agent, constructing or changing the entities between which it mediates' (1988, 145).

in a literal rather than metaphorical fashion, as their bodies consist of the very relationships that contribute to their growth. The consumption of food that originates in the productive capacities and activities of other people turns their very otherness into an intimate part of the self. The circulation of food on the basis of a rotational mode of exchange, and food's prominent place in pooling arrangements, guarantees that blood circulates incessantly between neighbours whose bodies depend on access to each other's sources of growth.

Food, and particularly rice, is intricately associated with land as its product and extension. The fields in which rice is grown are themselves closely related to particular ancestors through the acts of forest clearing and cultivation which the latter have performed. Such fields form part of the inheritance bequeathed to future generations, manifesting relations of genealogical connectedness. The access to multiple origin points produced by *yasinan* rituals is conjoined with access to multiple sources of consequent growth through food transfers. Food transfers also make possible for neighbours to access each other's means of production, primarily agricultural fields and labour. This access is not of a proprietarial nature as ownership claims is not what is at stake here. The appropriating impulse in operation, rather, is similar to the one articulated in ritual claims to multiple ancestors. Both appropriations work in tandem to accentuate the upscaling of siblingship at the level of the neighbourhood.

The *kampong*

Writings on Javanese sociality have long been heavily influenced by the Geertz's descriptions of Javanese society as a mere mathematical aggregate of nuclear families. Clifford Geertz's aphorism that 'there is no organic religious community, strictly speaking, … There is only a set of separate households geared into one another like so many windowless monads' (1960, 128) is echoed by Hildred Geertz's view that 'kinship, with its inflexible, particularistic, ascriptive social ties, plays only a secondary part in Javanese social structure as a whole' (1961, 2). The effort to go beyond such overly familiar renditions of Javanese society as a random collection of discrete units which are given by the 'facts' of biological procreation has been recently taken up by both Beatty (2005) and Newberry (2006), who propose an anthropology of emotions and an anthropology of models and copies respectively.

For Beatty (2005) what is going on between households is as significant as what goes on within them. As Beatty rightly argues, informal visiting, child borrowing, an ethic of mutuality and, most importantly, rituals of commensality engender a broader, indeterminate and unbounded social field: the *kampong*. Social behaviour within the neighbourhood is guided, he argues, by particular ways of feeling. Emotions such as respect, reluctance and shame both actualize

and constitute *kampong* social relations. Despite the obvious advantage that
this approach has in deprivatizing emotion by giving it social currency, it
remains problematic because it does not appropriately disentangle *emic* from
etic definitions of emotion, paying insufficient attention to the particularities of
what the Javanese call *rasa*, a term which cannot be easily translated as emotion
as it also involves the senses and the whole process of cognition (see Chapter 5;
Retsikas 2007b). Furthermore, this approach paints too cosy and pleasant a
picture of the *kampong* which is certainly at odds with other aspects of local life
involving everything from low-level animosity to violence (see Chapter 6).

Newberry's (2006) work in Central Java builds upon Carsten's work on the
Malays of Langkawi and focuses on the exchanges that connect houses and the
work that women perform to this end. For Newberry as for Carsten, the house
(i.e. dwelling) is primary and as such provides the model the neighbourhood
strives to imitate. In particular, Carsten argues that during feasts similar to the
ones described in this chapter, 'the community represents itself … in the idiom
of the house. Villagers say that the house "surrenders" to the community, which
then takes over the function of food-sharing' (1997, 183). This mirroring effect
is, however, circumscribed by a crucial difference that separates the house as
the model from the *kampong* as the copy: while relations internal to the house
are permeated by generalized reciprocity and hierarchy, relations within the
community are based on balanced and symmetrical reciprocity underscoring
an ethic of equalitarianism.

My approach to *kampong* sociality departs significantly from both these
approaches in that it does not accord any epistemological primacy to emotions,
nor does it privilege the ontological priority of the dwelling. Indeed I have
laboured to show that the parallel constitution of the *kampong* and the dwelling
is not the result of the appropriation of a function but rather the outcome
of the operation of different scales; such scales are themselves related to the
perspective one is to adopt when viewing transactions. From the perspective of
the dwelling, the circulation of potent speech and food can best be described
through the lens of reciprocity with houses asserting their separation from
each other by engaging in dyadic exchanges that distribute them in unequal
yet reversible positions as donors and recipients. However, these very same
transactions when viewed from the perspective of the *kampong* acquire a different
character. Thus, I have argued that the dynamics unleashed by rotating modes
of transacting and Ramadan pooling contribute to the exceeding of dwellings
and the denial of the logic of reciprocity as the connective tissue. This excess
brings the *kampong* into being as a House in its own right and heralds the
becoming-siblings of neighbours. The siblingship in question is established
through processes of disaggregation that tore houses open, disentangling the
parts houses have been made of, sending such parts off to separate directions

and down along different trajectories. Such processes entail subsequent moves towards reaggregation, i.e. the reattaching of the parts which have been temporarily 'freed' into new combinations. The latter processes amount to nothing more and nothing less than the production of new sets of siblings. The parts dwellings consist of, namely ancestors and food, are ritually detached from the house and reattached to the *kampong* in such a way that all *kampong* residents have claims to them. Neighbours, in other words, are constituted as siblings, as they are able to trace their origin to the same set of ancestors and attribute their growth to the food circulating in the *kampong*. Ancestors and food are appropriated as common 'property' and this in turn instantiates the *kampong* as a decentred and undifferentiated unit whose members are similar to each other. The precise relation of the dwelling to the *kampong* can therefore be said to be one in which the house does not exist in a transcendental sense of the term as always already given. Rather the house is to be thought of as subsisting and insisting in the *kampong* as the exceeded and the eclipsed.

The identity of the neighbours as siblings is derivative of the difference the *kampong* affirms. This affirmation finds its clearest expression in the multitude of ancestors commemorated in *yasinan* associations and the practice of taking turns in affecting their posthumous fate by means of potent speech. It is also manifested in the amassing of large amounts of raw foodstuffs for the staging of ritual meals during Ramadan that come from a multitude of directions. The gathering of ancestors and the gathering of foodstuffs underscores the mutuality of the lives neighbours lead and allows for the *kampong* to make itself present as an unstable, contingent 'oneness' founded on a multiplicity of sources of origin and growth. This 'oneness' necessitates the undertaking of ritual work with ritual being responsible for the disaggregation of the sibling relations of which houses are composed and the reconfiguration of siblingship in the spatial register of the *kampong*.

The becoming-siblings of neighbours examined so far, however, has addressed only one side of the relationships that are constitutive of *kampong* sociality. In the previous chapter, my argument was that the relation of siblingship is two-headed, pointing in two opposing directions at once. In this vein, I argued that the importance of siblingship is directly related to the connections it affords between descent and affinity without reducing one to the other. I also argued that siblings are connected as much by similitude as by hierarchical difference. What is missing from the picture of *kampong* sociality drawn so far is precisely this other side, this opposite yet equally important direction.

The becoming-siblings of ritual transactions emphasizes an aesthetic and ethic of convivial intimacy, mutual dependency and sharing. This conviviality is, however, haunted by competition, strife, conflict and sometimes outright aggression. The processes of becoming-enemy as an inherent dimension of *kampong* sociality are explored in Chapter 6. For present purposes, it is important for me to note that potent speech and food share the dual nature of siblingship. In Java, as in other parts of the world (Fischler 1988; Eves 1995), the very things that promote vitality and well-being are suspected of harbouring harm and death. Thus sharing food is also thought to be a potentially dangerous activity, as food can be adulterated and used for the purposes of sorcery. Similarly, potent words can encompass spells that can be fatal to those whom they are directed against. Sociality is a risky affair, the outcomes of which are far from determined. Before I venture into an exploration of this darker side of neighbourhood sociality, however, I must concentrate on another sort of becomings. These becomings centre round human contact with the sacred and involve the interaction of Muslim human subjects with Allah, his intermediaries and the spirits. The becomings that sorcery effects can only be fully understood when the processes involved in becoming-sacred have been discussed.

Chapter 5

A PULSATING UNIVERSE:
ANNIHILATING, ENHANCING,
MAGNIFYING

Intimate contractions

> One is too few, and two is only one possibility.
> (Haraway 1991, 180)

In his introduction to the influential *Fragments for a History of the Human Body*, Michael Feher raises a question that is the key pre-occupation of the present chapter: what kind of body do people 'endow themselves with – or attempt to acquire – given the power they attribute to the divine? A practical question, since it amounts to asking oneself what exercises to do to resemble a god physically or to commune sensually with him' (1989, 13).

The importance of the question for my purposes arises partly from the discussion of the preceding chapter which focused on the becoming of the neighbourhood into a House. As we have already seen, this process takes place within a ritual framework of exchanges with meals of commensality working towards the eclipsing of separation and the eliciting of non-distinction among a multitude of neighbours who proceed to act as one. These processes of becoming-kin involve interactions as much among the living as between the living and the dead, as genealogically separate ancestors are recast as shared. However, cosmological themes remained in the background of discussions in the previous chapters. The current chapter aims to make explicit the kinds of relations that people in Probolinggo entertain with the populations of *alam ghaib* (Ind.), the unseen and immaterial world that consists of a bewildering multiplicity of beings inclusive of Allah, the angels, *jin* (Ind.) and the dead. I aim to bring the sociality that becoming-kin entails, as outlined in Chapters 3 and 4, into dialogue using processes and practices of interaction involving humans and non-humans. Such interactions entail processes of becoming-sacred. The second reason I find Feher's question of great significance is because it reminds us that any attempt to arrive at an explanation of what it means to be a person depends ultimately on the ways the distinction between the human and the divine is foregrounded.

In the Quran, the dimensions of the distinction between man and Allah are set out. The Throne Verse, which adorns many living rooms in Probolinggo with calligraphic displays of piety, defines Allah as ultimately beyond the grasp of human perception: 'He knows what is before them and what is behind them, and they cannot comprehend anything out of His knowledge except what He pleases' (*Al-Baqarah*, 2:255).[1] To be human is based on negativity: on the negation of the possibility of knowing with certainty Allah who as the creator of life and death exceeds them both. As the outcome of creation, humans are bound by processes of growth, maturation and ultimately decay. Certain Quranic passages, however, provide affirmative descriptions or approximations of God's nature, listing His attributes as the one, the most merciful, the most compassionate, the eternal, the supreme, etc. Muslims all over the world chant the names of God over and over again, either in solitude or in public, a key practice called *dhikr* (Ind.), meaning recollection. The Islamic concept of monotheism (*tawhid*, Ind.), i.e. Allah has no partner but is indivisibly one and complete, adds a further dimension in the difference between humans and the divine. Humans are both numerous, having partners and associates, and divisible, i.e. they consist of an assortment of elements that Allah brought together in the process of man's creation (see below). Furthermore, the immateriality of God solidifies the distinction: He does not exist in a body, He is neither created nor limited in any way. Islam means submission to the commandments of Allah as set out in the scripture and this in turn defines humanity as bound with the obligation to obey them.

Yet, as Ernst notes, 'another theme that attracts close scrutiny [by the faithful] is the intimate relation of closeness that can exist between God and humanity. "We created man, and we know what his soul whispers to him, for we are nearer to him than the jugular vain" ([Surah] 50, 16)' (1997, 41). This closeness between creator and created, this drawing near of the human and the divine, is communicated within Islam in a series of themes such as those of sharing intimacy with God, the human longing for union and the human annihilation in divine presence. All of these themes are distinctly developed within the traditions of *tasawwuf* (Ind.), literally meaning the process of becoming-Sufi (Schimmel 1975).

Building on Chittick's definition of Sufism as the 'interiorization and intensification of Islamic faith and practice' (1995, 102), Julia Howell, in a groundbreaking article on Sufism's revival in Indonesia, shows how this broad

---

1 The Holy Quran, trans. Mohammad Habib Shakir. http://hemaidy.zoomshare.com/files/english-quran-shakir-wb.pdf (accessed 29 March 2012).

definition allows us to recognize a number of things: firstly, 'that devotional practices and religious concepts associated with Sufi traditions are often employed by Muslims as spiritual enhancements of their everyday lives, even when they are not undertaking a mystical path of dramatic personal transformation in the hope of direct experience of the divine', and secondly, and consequently, that the study of Sufism as a study of a specific stream of devotion within rather than outside Islam should 'encompass Sufi mystics independent of Sufi orders (*tarekat*) as well as those practicing within them' (2001, 702, n.2; see also 2005).

The diffusion of key Sufi concerns and practices in the social milieu of the faithful in Java are examined in this chapter through a consideration of the experiences of two people in Alas Niser who are renowned for their capacities as healers. Their narratives chart significant events in their lives that have brought about profound transformations in their personhood. These narratives emphasize a series of important themes. Firstly, they draw attention to the fact that the space occupied by the distinction between the human and the divine is imagined as being subject to fluctuation. The distance that separates believers from Allah is conceived thus as subject to processes of contraction and subsequent expansion. Secondly, the narratives also highlight the force that makes such contractions possible. The force lies in the undertaking of religious regimes of ascetic practice which culminate in the bestowal of healing capacities as attachments to the make-up of healers' embodied existence. In what follows I also discuss the often objectionable bodies with which such people endow themselves, while highlighting the dangers that are associated with ascetic practices , and the moral ambivalences that surround those equipped with healing powers. The desire of our protagonists to achieve intimacy with the divine, I argue, is mediated by the experience of a certain kind of death that results in the annihilation and subsequent empowerment of the human. The acquisition of the capacity to heal, the process of becoming-sacred, is contingent upon the contraction of the space that separates humanity from divinity and the achievement of an amplified degree of agency and control over the forces at play in the world.

Taken as a whole, regarding the acquisition of the power to heal, personal narratives evince the miraculous powers of the divine in this world. They also demonstrate the extraordinary character of healers who, as a result of having achieved contact with the divine and the sacred, are equipped with super-human capacities (see also Werbner and Basu 1998). The excess that healers embody, however, does not displace the distinction between the human and the divine. This contrasts with the scripturalist position which in all parts of the Muslim world, including Indonesia, conceives such practices as tantamount to contravening the doctrine of *tawhid*. Through emphasizing that their capacities are given from God and that He works through them, the healers of our case, along with others in different parts of the Islamic world (see Rasanayagam 2006), shift the dimensions of the distinction between the human and the divine from the fixity of an insurmountable ontological difference into a fluid, inchoate and indeterminate intimacy that allows for divine otherness to be experienced within the human self. Indeed, this whole process of the intensification of religious practice and transformative empowerment is built around a concerted effort to make such a shift of dimensions possible.

The processes of becoming-sacred are located within the orthodox (*mu'tabar*, Arabic) al-Ghazalian perspective of Sufism that consciously dissociates the possibility of humans achieving temporary communion with the sacred from a position that assumes such communion as leading to their fusion and eventual identity.[2] As Howell writes, 'latent within Sufism has always been the possibility that the Lord's "servant", in rapturous communion with the Lord, would lose all awareness of self and Other and experience identity with the Divine. Giving voice to such an experience, the tenth-century Persian mystic al-Hallaj declared, "I am God"' (2001, 706–7; see also Ernst 1997, 117–19). Both al-Hallaj and the Javanese mystic Seh Siti Jenar, one of the nine saints (*wali*) who spread Islam in Java and who made similar pronouncements in the fifteenth and sixteenth centuries, were put on trial and subsequently executed for contravening *tawhid* and denouncing the normative piety of the *syariah* (the Islamic law). The story of Jenar, which is a well-known in contemporary Java and whose grave is still visited by some Muslims, circumscribes the borders of traditionalist religious orthodoxy on one side. The other side is circumscribed by scripturalist interpretations of the faith that emphasize a return to pristine Islam; this side both calls for the elimination of mystic practices often construed as un-Islamic, and is overly concerned with legal formalism.[3] The space in which our East Javanese healers' narratives are located is undeniably a space of struggle and contestation over Islamic orthodoxy and orthopraxy. In the present study, however, I am not concerned with mapping these struggles and showing their relation to the history of Islam in Java and to the politics of Indonesian society. While every effort is made to historicize and contextualize

---

2 For an informed account of al-Ghazali's mysticism, see Elkaisy-Friemuth (2006, 119–51).

3 The situation is, of course, much more complex than this contrast indicates. Certain *tarekat*, such as *Tijaniyah*, are part of the wider reformist movement of the nineteenth century and are explicitly against saint cults and ecstatic practices. At the same time, the modernist rejection of Sufism has been undergoing modification since the 1980s. In an effort to supplant formalism with emotional content, certain Sufi emphases and practices have been reassessed as permissible by many modernists in Indonesia as well as elsewhere.

the practices of the people I interviewed within the overcrowded religious landscape of Java, the task of providing a full account of this diversity and its evolving trajectories falls outside the purpose of this study. My pre-occupations are different and have to do with charting the becomings that *tassawuf* allows for, and with exploring the ontological consequences that the breaching of boundaries between humanity and divinity brings about. At the same time, I am setting out to elaborate further on the concept of the *diaphoron* person as a site of difference rather than identity. The *diaphoron* person emerges out of intense processes of sociality between human and non-human as a composite figure, an unstable compound made of several elements, an uneven assemblage of parts which, although separate and distinct, manage to work well together due to the circuits of connections passing through them. In this chapter, the *diaphoron* person emerges as a process of assembly and connectivity through a careful and detailed consideration of narratives relating to the acquisition of the capacity to heal, as well as an in depth examination of local ideas that portray the human person as constituted by multiple sets of four.

The enlightenment of the enchanted

When I first met Kyai Salahuddin in 1998, he was a 48-year-old father of three, and an Islamic scholar offering instruction to the basics of the faith to neighbourhood kids. He was tall and thin, his head always adorned with a *kopiah*. He had a striking, almost towering presence, something his almost permanent smile did much to soften. In the course of my fieldwork, Kyai Salahuddin renovated his house, making it into a beautiful white-washed and spacious structure. He also added a small mosque with the traditional three-tiered roof. His plans for the immediate future included the establishment of a *pondok pesantren*, an Islamic boarding school, to cater for the educational needs of his expanding following. A plot of land had already been purchased for this purpose with the actual building scheduled to take place after his performance of the *haj* (Ind.). The very month I left Java for Europe (March 2000), the *kyai* left the village together with his wife for Mecca.

Kyai Salahuddin was a relatively young upstart in the religious elite of the area, as he was neither a descendant of a *kyai* nor married into the family of one. His father, a farmer, had died before he was born, leaving his mother with the difficult task of raising him on her own. His current prosperity and the respect he commanded locally were based on his religious knowledge (literacy in Arabic and ability to understand and explain the Quran and other scriptures), personal virtues (piety, generosity, politeness, lack of self-interest and indifference towards wealth), as well as on his capacity to heal. Every day from early in the evening until the early hours of the morning people from as far as Malang and Lumajang would gather in his living room in search for a solution to their troubles and a cure to their ailments. An assortment of conditions required his constant and immediate attention, leaving him with little time for rest. The conditions ranged from marital problems, such as infertility and regular arguments, parental concerns with a son who had gone astray or a daughter's refusal to marry the man her parents had chosen, and professional troubles, such as being bypassed for promotion or not getting on with one's superior, to minor and major illnesses such as stones in the kidneys and the bladder, diabetes and cancer that biomedical doctors had already diagnosed.

Kyai Salahuddin's capacity to deal with troubles and illnesses effectively was related to events that had taken place two decades ago. These events were marked by the suffusion of his heart with divine light. This is how he himself narrated these events to me:

> When I was still young, studying Islam at the *pondok pesantren* in Sidogiri [in neighbouring Pasuruan], I became aware of my desire to acquire *elmo* [Mad. mystical power/knowledge], which is blessed and useful. My aim was to put it to good use, to the service of the nation and the people, to enhance people's Islamic consciousness, to make them pious, calm their turbulent hearts, turn them from hot to cold. I did not intend to become a *kyai*. One cannot decide such things himself, for it is Allah the one who regulates human affairs. But my desire was sincere [*ikhlas*, Ind.]. I wanted to solve people's problems, ease their difficulties. It was during one night that *elmo* came to me. It came by itself. It wasn't bestowed to me [by a human]. It arrived the time I was performing *sholat tahajjud* [Ind., the supererogatory late night prayer] at the small prayer house … I was deep into praying when suddenly, it came. … It entered me. … The *elmo* entered here [he put his hand on his chest]. … *nddhuuk*! It came. I was praying to Allah and Allah sent His light [*senar*, Mad.] … my *batin* [Mad., inner self; he put his hand on his chest] became the receptacle of His light, fulfilling my wish. Several days after, a villager arrived at the *pesantren* asking for my help and calling me *kyai*. I was not a *kyai*, I was merely a teacher [*guru*, Ind.] at the *pesantren*. His boy was sick, some kind of high fever. … Suddenly, I realized that at the time of *sholat tahajjud*, it had come … that a *becaan* [Mad. incantation, formula, prayer] had entered me. So, I took some water and I recited the *becaan* over it [the water], breathing out onto the water and calling Allah's name; Allah is the one who cures, I am the one who strives. The boy drank the water and recovered immediately.

Some years after these events had taken place, Kyai Salahuddin returned to Alas Niser. With this education completed, he went back to his mother's home and soon afterwards was married and had two children. In Alas Niser, he used to spend his time teaching the children of the neighbourhood to recite the Quran while fasting and praying regularly. From time to time, he would receive requests for healing. This was when a second more dramatic event took place.

> My name then was Yatim. I had few visitors unlike now. Back then [in 1991], I was tortured for 99 days. That happened when I was already married for nine years. The torture involved my *batin*. My *batin* did not recognize my wife, my parents or children. I became oblivious of the world, feeling as if I was to die the very next moment. All I did for 99 days was to stay indoors, being quiet and reciting Allah's name. I was bathing seventeen times a day and feeding myself with leaves throughout that period. In my *batin*, nothing except Allah mattered and His name was active/moving [*bergerak*, Ind.]. I had forgotten all about my wife and parents. In my *hate* [Mad., heart], I could see the way that leads to Allah. ... I could see all the people. It was then that the light struck me again ... *struum*! Like an electric current ... it entered me. ... My *batin* became full with understanding and *elmo*. Later on, a lot of people who did not understand what had happened to me paid me a visit. I engaged them in conversation and their difficulties immediately entered me. ... In my *batin*, I could sense [*rasa*, taste/touch/feel] the difficulties they were facing. Their difficulties were there, in my heart. That was because of the *elmo*. This *elmo* is called *elmo mahrifat*. It allows me to see their *batin* ... to see if they are good, pious people or evil, to see their intentions, their thoughts, their character ... immediately ... *shreed*! ... enters here [he pointed to his chest].

Nddhuuk, *struum* and *shreed* are the sounds he used to mark the reception of the sacred into the human. This reception is the means by which the human person is enhanced, his agency augmented. The gift of divine grace is transferred via a beam of light, itself originating from Allah. In penetrating the confines of the human body, it reaches deep into the body's innermost recess, the heart and the *batin*. The beam of light carries *elmo*, the power to heal, the capacity for knowing other people's thoughts and feelings. Nothing is secret any more to the recipient of divine light. Kyai Salahuddin could *rasa* (taste/touch/feel) 'the way that leads to Allah' and 'all the people'. He claimed to having attained the highest station of Sufi traditions that of *mahrifat* or gnosis.

The reception of *elmo* tormented the recipient with spasms and loss of consciousness. Forces similar to electric currents penetrated his body. We can imagine it shaking and tightening as it became the receptacle of a divine in source incantation. The body was transformed at that very moment. Yatim felt like dying. His body became the meeting place of the human and the non-human. It was taken over by a potency that radiated outwards, that was abler to 'make [people] pious, calm their turbulent hearts', bless marriages and *padi* fields, generate fertility and prosperity. The original person was no more; Yatim became Salahuddin; Salahuddin was and was not Yatim.

Kyai Salahuddin's narration of the conditions that allowed for the bestowal of the gift of performing miracles rests on the evocation of central tenets of *tasawwuf* that he studied both as a senior *santri* in *pesantren* in Pasuruan and Madura, and later on, as an initiate and subsequent deputy of a specific brotherhood, the *tarekat Qadiriyah wa Naqsyabandiyah*.[4] These conditions are at the heart of traditionalist Islam in Java, the variant that Geertz (1960) calls *santri* Islam.

Santri piety is intimately related to the recognition of the *syariah*, and especially those aspects that concern worship and family law, as the basis of Islam. This basis is often considered to be the minimum requirement on behalf of the faithful, and thus inadequate in and of itself as a vehicle for the full realization of personal devotion. The extensive complex of supererogatory devotion as the necessary supplant to the *syariah* is provided by *tassawuf* itself defined both as a distinct philosophical tradition and a set of popular practices. Dhofier (1980) refers to the popular aspect of *tasawwuf* in Java as the *zuhud* complex. It consists of an intensification of religious practice beyond the obligatory and the formal that finds expression in the frequent recitation of the Quran, participation in *pengajian* (study groups), the performance of recommended prayers and recommended fasting, the practice of *dhikir* and pilgrimage to the graves of saints.[5] As Woodward argues, for those willing to dwell further into the faith, joining a Sufi brotherhood and undertaking a series of more intense austerities and particular intellectual training is the next step along a continuum whose ultimate aim is the achievement of closeness with Allah (1989, 117).

Progression along the path of supererogatory devotion provides a broad outline of a sacred hierarchy. The upper limit of this hierarchy is sealed by the Prophet Muhammad, the Perfect Man. As proof of Muhammad's perfection, villagers in Alas Niser often mention not only his selection as the messenger, but also his miraculous ascension to heaven. There the Prophet is said to have

---

4 Prominent among the objects decorating Kyai Salahuddin's living room were portraits of his teachers. These were arranged in two separate lines: one line related to the pesantren of Sidogiri, and the other to the *tarekat*. Such portraits furnished the always necessary proof of his spiritual genealogy (*silsilah*), authorizing the authenticity of his religious knowledge via the establishment of legitimate links of transmission. For more details of Qadiriyah wa Naqsyabandiyah's presence in Madura and East Java, see Van Bruinessen (1995).

5 Modernists object to the *zuhud* complex on two counts: firstly, because in their opinion, it is supported by 'weak' *hadith*, and secondly, because it detracts attention from one's duties to this life as it is overly pre-occupied with afterlife and blessings.

conversed with the other prophets, as well as with Allah who dictated the forms of the five daily prayers to him. The attribution of purity to the Prophet is related also to a story according to which prior to his ascension to heaven, Muhammad's chest was cut open, his heart cleansed with water taken from a famous well located near the Kabah in Mecca, and then filled with faith and knowledge by angel Gabriel.

Muslims, the world over, hold that the emulation of the Prophet's ways provides the most certain path towards salvation. The development of *hadith* literature aims to furnish concrete examples of the Prophet's life and deeds for such a purpose. However, while the Prophet can be emulated, his purity cannot be surpassed. As a result, the state of sainthood ranks lower to prophethood. In Java, the most revered saints are the nine *wali* who are said to have propagated Islam to the island. Such figures are the subject of extensive hagiographic literature and their tombs are still visited by many people, some of which are in search for blessings (*barokah*, Ind.), while others construe the pilgrimage as an act of faith (*ibadah*, Ind.).

Kyai Salahuddin's claim to having achieved *mahrifat*, the highest station of Sufism, brings him into the fold of sainthood and several people in his entourage certainly saw him in this way, often describing him as 'a friend of Allah' and a 'specialist in mysticism'. *Mahrifat*, the *kyai* explained to me in a subsequent conversation, is the fourth and final station for every Sufi (see also Schimmel 1975, 98–9). The first station is *syariah* which traditionalist Muslims in Java take to be the outer or external (*lahir*) manifestation of the faith. The second station is called *tarekat* as it opens the path towards the inner realization of Islam. As such, he said, *tarekat* corresponds to Islam's *batin* (the inner core). At this point the *kyai* felt compelled to make the necessary distinction between *tasawwuf* and *ilmu kebatinan* (Ind.) which permeates both anthropological and local accounts of religious diversity in the island. In contemporary Java, *ilmu kebatinan* refers to modern mystical cults that are often seen by traditionalist Muslims as lying outside Islam for they openly denounce organized religion and mix and match elements taken from diverse religious traditions, including Islam, Christianity and Hindu-Buddhism. In contrast, the *kyai* reiterated, *tarekat* is within the fold of Islam and corresponds to traditions of mysticism as developed over the centuries by pious Muslim mystics. To successfully walk the path requires adhering to ascetic regimes which are geared towards the cleansing of the soul, so that it can be drawn nearer to Allah. Further progression along the path *tarekat* has opened up brings one into the third level, *hakekat*. *Hakekat*, Kyai Salahuddin explained, reveals the ultimate reality and the real objective for every aspirant. The ultimate reality is that only Allah exists; one's actions must therefore be motivated by sincere love for Him. The fourth station, *mahrifat* is to bring the path to a conclusion, to realize the objective; it means 'to vanish' (*hilang*, Ind.)

or 'die' (*meninggal dunia*, Ind.), and through one's death 'to approach' (*mendekati*, Ind.) or 'unify' with Allah (*menyatu sama Allah*, Ind.).

The theme of temporary death as integral to achieving unification with Allah is central in al-Ghazali's (1058–1111) work. One of the greatest jurists, theologians and mystics of Islam, whose texts are widely used in Javanese Islamic boarding schools (see Dhofier 1982, 149), al-Ghazali defined the orthodox way of reaching unification with Allah as resting on self-annihilation (*fana*, Arabic), 'the nullification of the mystic in divine presence' (Schimmel 1975, 144). Self-annihilation is the result of steadfastness in orientation and commitment to the divine:

> Whoever looks at the world because it is God's work, and knows it because it is God's work, and loves it because it is God's work, does not look save to God and does not know save God, and does not love save God, and he is the true unifier (*muwahhid*) who does not see anything but God, nay who does not even look at himself for his own sake but because he is God's servant – and of such a person it is said that he is annihilated in unification and that he is annihilated from himself. (al-Ghazali, quoted in Schimmel 1975, 146)

As Zoetmulder (1995) argues with respect to al-Ghazali's works, this unification is neither thought of as the permanent merging of God and human into a third, hybrid entity nor understood as an event partaking to beings that already belong to the same ontological plane. Rather, annihilation occurs in a space marked by ontological difference and as an experience is limited to the human person. Annihilation necessitates a voluntary self-emptying and self-concealing, i.e. a temporary eclipsing of the human achieved through careful supererogatory devotion, painful ascetic discipline and deep reflective concentration. The eclipsing of the human allows for the evincing of the divine, a miraculous arrival that more often than not takes the form of a beam of light descending upon the faithful. In this regard, it is important to stress that neither for Kyai Salahuddin nor for al-Ghazali does annihilation result in the human becoming identical or equal to the divine, as annihilation is held to be incapable of transcending the distinction between the creator and the created, the being by itself and the being by another.[6]

For al-Ghazali, as for lots of other Sufis, Allah is the origin of the light descending upon the mystic. The passing of the light is instrumental in his

---

6 The same distinction is also central to al-Junayd's thought. His works, which are also widely known and respected in the *pesantren* tradition, emphasize that the purpose of Sufi practice is 'the destruction of human attributes and a return to a state in which one is an idea in the mind of Allah' (Woodward 1989, 130).

thought in establishing both the separation and intimacy between Allah and the seeker of knowledge. In another passage, the theologian thus writes:

> Comparing the one from whom [light] is borrowed with the borrower is just using a metaphor. ... Well then, the True Light is He who has the power to create and to command, by Whom illumination is imparted and maintained. No-one shares this name with Him in reality or can claim a right to it alongside Him, except insofar as He Himself deigns to give this name, as a master does with his servant when he donates possessions to the latter and even calls him master. (al-Ghazali, quoted in Zoetmulder 1995, 24)

Kyai Salahuddin's annihilation can be conceived as taking place in a universe of flexible dimensions, a pulsating universe whose outer limits contract and then expand in oscillatory fashion and in perpetuity. The shifting nature of the universe means that centripetal movements of contraction succeed centrifugal ones of expansion, and vice versa. Yet such ebbs and flows do not cancel the universe's dimensions and proportionality. The alternating contractions and expansions which the universe undergoes allow us to think of the space occupied by the distinction between the human and the divine as being subject to similar fluctuations of expanse. The point zero of human–divine distance corresponds to self-annihilation with the contraction having been brought about by the intentions and actions of both the knowledge seeker and Allah.

The dynamics of such shifting, pulsating universe are partly to be found in the *kyai*'s account of his 99 days of torture. Although Allah is mentioned in the Quran with several names, traditionalist accounts count his attributes by limiting the number of His names to 99. Each one of the days making up Kyai Salahuddin's torture is therefore a case of a profound meditation on every single one of Allah's attributes and a calling for Him to come, to draw nearer. At the same time, Kyai Salahuddin portrays himself as quite passive during the same period, and it is clear that he conceives of his experiences as a test of devotion orchestrated by Allah. On the other hand, the effort to get close to Allah is singularly propelled by his own desire for knowledge and by the state of his intentions. *Ikhlas* (Ind.) means sincere and in a religious context, its significance rests on the distinction between *muslim* and *mukmin*. *Muslim* is someone who submits to Allah's commandments in an outward fashion with the performance, e.g. of *sholat* being restricted to the required bodily movements and the utterance of the set formula. *Mukmin* is the person whose devotion is true to the eyes of Allah rather than to other humans. The state of *mukmin* is a state of sincerity for worship stems from a heart that is pure and unadulterated by earthly desires for praise by others, wealth or status. The reward for *ikhlas*, for knowing what to desire and for desiring in the correct register, is the gift of light, the gift of knowledge.

The metaphor of the path has over the centuries led to a growing repertoire among the traditions of *tasawwuf* that relate to the states and stations that the God-seeker is supposed to traverse. On the human side are specific stations (*maqam*) one has to go through; on the divine side are states (*hal*). *Maqam* refers to the ethical qualities the Sufi must cultivate along the path so as to progress further. *Hal* refers to the 'gifts from God that overtake the wayfarer involuntarily; they are essentially beyond the control of the individual' (Ernst 1997, 102). In those moments when stations converge perfectly with states, there is annihilation and temporary unity through the contraction of the dimensions of a fluctuating universe.

Contraction seems to elude time altogether; it can be said to be momentary and fleeting. It is always succeeded by expansion as annihilation gives way to a rebirth. Despite eluding time, contraction leaves behind traces of its achievement, as well as evidences of the existence of the divine and its profound care for human welfare. One such trace is the capacity to heal. Kyai Salahuddin, as well as other healers in Probolinggo, were clear that such traces should not be mistaken for evidences.

> People come here because they are suffering. [Whether they are healed or not] does not depend on me. It depends on Allah. If Allah wishes for them to be healed, they will be. If He does not, they won't. I am just putting in the effort, the one who determines [the outcome] is Allah. Lots are those who are cured. But I cannot say I did it myself. If someone says that he does it himself, it means that that person has not become one with Allah. One can only put in an effort; the effort is the one that brings about unity [with Allah]. *Dukun* say that they did it themselves and ask for money. I only accept what I am given. If I am given something, that's fine; if nothing, that's fine too.

The re-evincing of the difference between the human and the divine that was temporarily eclipsed during the non-time of contraction, as that between the Lord who determines and the potent man who strives, means that annihilation does not annul the ontological distinction between man and God. Kyai Salahuddin's version of *tasawwuf* is part of what Bousfield (1983) terms as the 'unity of witness' (*wahdah al-shudud*, Arabic) thesis which is quite distinct from the doctrine of the 'unity of being' (*wahdah al-wujud*, Arabic). These two quite distinct schools were prevalent in Javanese mysticism during the nineteenth century and their differences led to bitter controversies. As Woodward has convincingly showed, due to a series of changes that took place from the late nineteenth century onwards, some of which brought Javanese Muslims into more intense communication with theological ideas that were dominant over the same period in the Middle East, the 'unity of witness' school came to achieve supremacy over time in Java (1989, 134–5).

While the differences between the two schools are subtle, they are of immediate importance. Simply put, the 'unity of being' takes the view that God is immanently present in humanity. This view finds its most eloquent expression in the doctrine of the emanation (*martabat*, Jav.) taught by Sufi masters such as Fadl Allah and the Sumatran Hamzah Fansuri. According to the Javanese version found in the *suluk* literature (see Zoetmulder 1995), the world is thought to have come about through a process of seven successive divine emanations or dispersions of divine essence.[7] Man is the lowest and final of such emanations; yet, he remains one with Allah, forming part of Him, containing within him fragments of divine essence. The mystical path Hamzah Fansuri taught is based on this type of ontological similitude of man and God where the goal is for the mystic to transverse the order of emanations backwards so that a return to perfect oneness with God can be reinstated. According to Bowen, the doctrine of emanation is still echoed in the practices of many contemporary healers in the Gayo highlands of Sumatra (1993, 106–18). However, in contemporary Java, neither I nor Woodward (1989) encountered any *santri* who accepted the emanation thesis. In contrast, the al-Ghazalian thesis of unification through annihilation, the 'unity of witness', is widely accepted. Having said this, I should add that a series of modern mystical cults, several of which have branches in downtown Probolinggo where they draw their rather limited membership primarily from civil servants and some middle-class professionals, make extensive use of the principle of monism, emphasizing the indwelling God present in every man.

Mystical cults are part of the *kejawen* religious orientation and their members, to quote Beatty, 'are those people who stress the Javanese part of their cultural inheritance and who regard their Muslim affiliation [the *syariah*] as secondary' (1997, 158). Often some do openly renounce the *syariah* altogether as an empty vessel full of unnecessary formalisms, cutting all ties to organized religion. While both Geertz's (1960) classic study and Beatty's (1997) more recent one treat *kejawen* as a distinct religious orientation on the outside of Islam, Woodward (1989) is at pains to show how *kejawen* is a variant of Islam. Key conceptual vehicles such as the microcosm–macrocosm distinction, the emphasis placed on *rasa* and potency, and a relation between man and God as premised on intimacy are, for Woodward, shared by both *santri* and *kejawen* Javanese, albeit with some significant degrees of difference. Such differences

---

7   The emanation thesis was also a key resource in the central Javanese royal courts' claims to legitimacy in the eighteenth and nineteenth centuries, see Jacques (2006).

are differences within Islam rather than between Islam and non-Islam (see also Woodward 1988).

The imagining of *santri* and *kejawen* as the exclusive and formally opposed categories that Geertz (1960) elaborated on has deep historical roots. According to Ricklefs (2007), these have to do with the impact of colonialism and the coming of reformist Islam to the island in the late nineteenth century. Prior to this period, the Islamic courts of Java had achieved a synthesis of Javanese understandings of Sufism with an acceptance of local, pre-Islamic beliefs. In this synthesis, a sense of an Islamic identity and the fulfilment of the basic rituals of the faith were of integral importance. However, from the late nineteenth century, the synthesis was shattered in ways that allowed for the imagining of being Javanese as separate from being Muslim and for the forgetting of their previous inextricable connections. The disempowerment of the indigenous courts, the new forms of economic extraction and the new system of education, with its emphasis on secular modernity and the sciences the Dutch put in place, worked in tandem with the often vociferous critiques of newly arrived reformists who had studied extensively in the Middle East and castigated a whole range of practices as non-Islamic. According to Ricklefs, the birth of *kejawen* was a response to the reformist critique through its internalization and to the profound political economic changes Javanese society was undergoing. Colonialism and Islamic reformism thus stimulated a desperate search for a Javanese past, free from Islam which glory carried promises of future reincarnation. In the course of the twentieth century, the opposition between *kejawen* and *santri* reached an apogee with its politicization of the associated identities and their enmeshment with mass organizations, processes which reached new heights with the communist massacres of 1965–66.

Ambiguous animals

In Probolinggo as in the rest of Southeast Asia people who have the capacity to heal are treated with suspicion. This has to do with the fact that the potency that derives from intimate connections with the beings that populate the *alam ghaib* is seen as inherently morally neutral. In addition, the power of the Quran is conceived to be able to harm as much as to heal others. *Elmo* is generally considered to be a kind of knowledge and a substantive power that is not intrinsically bound to and limited by morality; and people who are effective as healers are often said to dabble in sorcery (Anderson 1990; Bowen 1993). The moral ambiguity of potency makes it all the more necessary for those who have the capacity to heal to distance themselves from morally suspect activities by distinguishing themselves as good

Muslims. In this respect, *kyai*-ship with its high degree of Islamic learning and the cultivation of the corresponding ethnical character provides some assurances as to the benevolence of the capacities at play. However, as I have shown elsewhere (Retsikas 2006), a *kyai* can be and is often accused for acting selfishly and immorally. The importance accorded to the personal piety of the healer is coupled with a stress on ascertaining the origins of his/her power. While potency coming from Allah and the angels is seen as relatively, if not inherently, safe, much depends on the intentions of the recipient. The kinds of *elmo* associated with a healer's contact with capricious and ambivalent *jinn* are less so. The same goes for *elmo* originating from dead persons. Finally, *elmo* coming from association with *setan* is entirely fraught with danger, as these beings are wholly inimical to humanity's welfare.

While the followers and students of Kyai Salahuddin described his potency as coming directly from God, others in the locality criticized him for being a *dukun*, a mere healer, expressing scepticism about the depth of his religious knowledge and the extent of his piety. His critics were members of long-established *kyai* families who felt their authority undermined by the young man's expanding following and would often bring attention to the fact he did not descend from a *kyai* and to his relatively rapid prosperity. The former accusation sought to cast doubts over the authenticity and legitimacy of Kyai Salahuddin's knowledge, as people believe that descendants of *kyais* transmit their knowledge through bodily substance and that such knowledge (*elmo laduni*, Mad.) is by far superior to any acquired or achieved *elmo*. The second accusation involved the implication that at the centre of his prosperity was Kyai Salahuddin's readiness to work for money, putting his power at the disposal of evil people for the accomplishment of evil deeds. As a response to the moral ambiguities surrounding potency, any *kyai* claiming to possess healing powers and other *dukun* were eager to demonstrate their religious devotion, personal qualities such as generosity, kindness and disinterest in earthly possessions, and most importantly, emphasize that their capacities were, if not a direct gift from God, then at least part of dealings with morally sound ethereal beings, such as angels, Muslim *jinn* and benevolent dead.

Pak Uddin was a part-time farmer and part-time *dukun* who was renowned in the locality for his ability to heal any kind of illness related to blood circulation problems, ranging from regular headaches and bad backs to arteriosclerosis, through performing massage (*pejet*, Mad). Pak Uddin was in his late-40s and owned a couple of *sawah* plots which he cultivated with the help of his wife and his only child, a relatively young widow with two children of her own. Their property, which included a modest dwelling, had been purchased relatively recently with funds coming from his successes as a healer.

On a hot midsummer evening Pak Uddin offered me the following narrative of how he came to acquire his capacity for massage:

> In the past, I was making a living through collecting recycled materials and reselling them. I was praying to Allah to help me to find a way to earn a living. I was praying night and day, wondering whether something would change or not. It was a very hard time for me; there were times I would continue working long after *sholat maghrib* [sunset prayer] or would be caught in the rain and fall sick for several days. I would cry often in my prayers wondering whether my life would always be like this. Then, someone responded … a voice coming from the shadows answered back saying that it would change my situation provided that I would choose between open eyes [*melak mata*, Mad.] and an open *hate* [*melak hate*, Mad.]. Where are the eyes? Where is the *hate*? I said that I choose an open *hate*. The eyes are above; they are the sun and the moon. The *hate* is the earth; the earth is the navel [*bujhel*, Mad.]; the navel is the *hate*. I checked to see where the voice was coming from. There were no humans around. The voice was sent by Allah. That took place when I was performing *sholat isya* [the evening prayer] at eleven o'clock. I went back to my bedroom but it wasn't long before I heard a rustle coming from outside. As there were a lot of thieves at that period in the neighbourhood I went out to see what it was. Nothing … I couldn't see anything. So I went back to my bed. There it went again. I went out and I saw a shadow [*bejengan*, Mad.]. I immediately recited a *shalawat* [a verse in praise of the Prophet] but the shadow moved towards me and sat in a chair right beside me. I asked it who it was and the shadow replied, 'If you are me, I am you' [*mon engkok kakeh, kakeh engkok*, Mad.]. Then it asked, 'Do you want me to give you something?' I replied I did and the shadow disappeared for the second time. The following Thursday night, it came back saying that it was going to fulfil its promise but before that, it said it had to beat me. 'If you feel pain, I will be feeling it too; if you do not, I won't.' These were its words. Then, it started beating me on my back, on my arms and legs, everywhere. I was in great pain but I didn't scream. It reappeared the following week, on Thursday night. It said that this time I should prove myself strong. I was put into the sleeping position and I was massaged by the shadow. After massaging me, it asked me whether I wanted its *elmo*. I replied that I did. It also asked me if I remembered the way it had massaged me, to which I also said I did. It wasn't difficult to remember, I could repeat it easily. Before it disappeared, it gave me a *becaan* [Mad., incantation] and it told me to recite it 200 times every time I prayed and to accompany my prayers with reciting *Surat Fatir* and *Surat Rahman* twice. *Surat Fatir* is about *rezeki* [Ind., prosperity, blessings] while *Surat Rahman* is about compassion. All these are branches and the tree is Allah. So I was instructed to recite His name 200 times after each of the daily prayers. I had to perform all these without taking any break, non-stop. I was also told that I had to abstain from eating for 40 consecutive days. The shadow revisited me for

the last time 99 days later. It was then that I was given a snake [*olar*, Mad.]. The shadow asked me, 'Are you brave enough to receive a long animal? If you are sick, I am sick; if you are bitten, I am bitten.' 'I do accept it,' I said. After a while, I saw a very long snake coming towards me. I was scared. I said to the snake, 'Hey, snake! If you are good, please enter [*tore masok*, Mad.].' The snake came closer and wrapped itself around my body. I felt I was dying for its grip was tightening. At that time, a black cat passed by and the snake set me free. It then moved to my belly … from my belly, it entered me. The whole snake entered my belly from my navel and disappeared, entering inside me. Next day, I went to a *kyai* to ask him what it all meant. 'Yesterday, I saw a cat and a snake. What's the meaning of it all?' 'The snake is *elmo* … it entered your body. It is already inside you. The cat is the Prophet's favourite animal. You have to show respect. Do not worry. It was a trial [*ojian*, Mad.] until all the *elmo* was given to you,' the *kyai* replied.

Several themes we have already discussed in the previous case reappear here. Becoming equipped with an extraordinary capacity is the result of a process of bodily penetration that heralds an ontological transformation. This transformation is the result of an addition and a surplus to the ordinariness of being solely human. The process begins with the right set of intentions: the intention for personal improvement realized within the context of religious devotion that authorizes it as legitimate. It also demands a trial, a test of one's faith. Pak Uddin's trial involved him visited by a being of shifting forms and multiple appearances.

His purity of intentions was challenged by the posing of a dilemma between 'open eyes' and an 'open *hate*'. Open eyes index a burning and uncontrolled desire for earthly possessions; an open heart indicates sincerity and the will to knowledge. Having passed the first hurdle, Pak Uddin's test continued with the multiplication of ascetic regimes, the successful undertaking of which provided further evidence of his worthiness for becoming the recipient of the gift. Succumbing to higher authority willingly and without fear, receiving beatings without complaint, withstanding pain without screaming, fasting for 40 consecutive days and engaging in intensive and tiresome Quranic recitations that went beyond the obligatory: these were all techniques for the opening up of the path, the opening of the *hate*. This opening instigates new forms of sociality; this time one deals and communes with non-humans. The intensity of these dealings creates the contraction of the space that the distinction between the human and the non-human occupies, bringing about an intimacy which seizes the human with the tightness of the grip of a snake. There is annihilation coming. Pak Uddin in a similar fashion to *kyai* Salahuddin felt close to or like dying. This death is marked by the diffusion of divine light into the deepest recesses of the human, in one case, and by the penetration of an animal in form entity into the human body through the belly button. The light and the snake are sacred additions to the human make-up that is replenished and constituted anew by the light and the snake becoming an integral part of a new being that is part human, part non-human.

The contraction of the distinction between the human and the non-human, and the crossing of the boundaries involved is fraught with danger. The recitation of a *shalawat* provided some assurances as to the benevolence of the shadow, as malevolent beings are held to disappear once confronted with Arabic words. The appearance of the shadow on Thursday evenings was also a good sign as according to Javanese beliefs Thursday evenings fall within the time frame of the day of Friday, the most sacred day of the week. Furthermore, the invitation to the snake to enter his body only if it was good worked to reassure Pak Uddin's imagined audience of the auspiciousness of the interaction. Pak Uddin remained nevertheless uncertain about the moral constitution of the *elmo* even after he had been penetrated. The assumption of the form of a snake by the shadow encoded the moral ambiguity of potency, an ambiguity which was subsequently resolved by the appearance of a cat and the reassuring words of the *kyai* that the cat is the Prophet's favourite animal.

In Islamic cosmology, the snake is intimately associated with the devil, and the story of the snake which allowed the devil to sit between its teeth so he could enter Paradise and thus bring about the downfall of the first humans is well known in Java. Locals also hold that the punishment the snake met for his association with the devil was its transformation from a beautiful quadruped to a creature forced to crawl upon its belly. On the other hand, in the Quran the snake is also associated with Moses' rod (see *Surah Ta-Ha*). On the occasion of Allah's manifestation in the fire, Moses' rod assumes the form of snake and it is the same rod that was later instrumental in the performance of miracles such as the making of water flow from rock, the production of milk and honey, and the passage across the Red Sea. In Pak Uddin's narrative, an association between the snake and the rod is implicitly drawn in the beatings he received by a stick of some kind.

The appearance of the cat has a major cathartic effect. The Prophet's fondness for cats is well attested to in the *hadith* literature and there are plenty of stories about Muhammad's favourite cat, Muezza. In one such story it is told that when Muhammad was called to prayer he found Muezza asleep on the sleeve of his robe and that he preferred to cut off the sleeve rather than disturb his cat. In general, Schimmel notes that in Islam

the cat is a clean animal, her presence does not annul ritual prayer, and the water from which she drank can still be used for ablution. There are variants of the story of how Abu Hurayra's cat, which he always carried in his bag, saved the Prophet from an obnoxious snake, whereupon the Prophet petted her so that the mark of his fingers is still visible in the four dark lines on most cat's foreheads, and, because the Prophet's hand stroked her back, cats never fall on their backs. (1994, 23)

The snake and the devil, Moses and the rod, the cat and the Prophet not only place Pak Uddin's experiences of becoming-sacred within a recognized genre of the hagiographic and the miraculous, but effectively recast religious symbols from historically and culturally arbitrary signs into active figures in the unfolding of his person. His person can thus be seen as an assemblage of human and non-human parts and materials. The non-human that initially assumed the form of an immaterial shadow, and then of a potent animal consequently became a constitutive part of Pak Uddin's ontological make-up.

The composite, compound character of healers' persons carries certain parallelisms with Haraway's (1991) notion of the cyborg. For Haraway, cyborgs are cybernetic entities, part machine, part human organism, with the former acting as 'prosthetic devices, intimate components, friendly selves' (1991, 178) that extend human capacities beyond the ordinary. Their constitution rests on contradictions and tensions; cyborgs populate technologically advanced worlds in which the tightly organized domains the project of Enlightenment established have given way to multiple and unstable connections across divides. At the heart of Haraway's conceptualization lies an understanding of the postmodern subject as posthuman and of the relation as the primary and minimal unit of analysis.[8] Being neither simply machines nor solely human, cyborgs correspond to assemblages that allow Haraway to foreground difference as the condition of possibility of the subject. In other words, Haraway's cyborg is an instance of what I call the *diaphoron* person. Cyborgs as future *diaphoron* persons allow us to privilege difference at the expense of postulates of unitary identity and 'partial connections' as the constitutive relations that bring the parts together (Strathern 1991, 36–41).

---

8 More recently, Harraway (2003, 2008) has applied much of the same line of thinking to human–animal relations, challenging conventional biological wisdom and demonstrating that the human and canine are companion species, which have emerged and co-evolved along each other in the transversal domain of 'natureculture'. The becomings such companion species are involved in do not cancel out their contingent differences, but rather amplify them through the various claims humans and dogs make on each other. She is quite critical of a conception of animal rights as the generous extension of human rights to non-human animals, asserting that 'in a relationship, dog and humans construct "rights" in each other. ... Possession – property – is about reciprocity and rights of access. If I have a dog, my dog has a human' (2003, 53–4).

Haraway's cyborg is a figure good to think with as it overcomes a series of familiar dualisms that animate much of Western metaphysics (nature and culture, non-human and human, body and mind, woman and man). A cyborg is neither part of culture nor of nature, neither of the body nor of the mind. Instead, it is permeated by internal division and external irony. 'Irony is about contradictions that do not resolve into larger wholes, even dialectically, about the tension of holding incompatible things together because both or all are necessary and true' (Haraway 1991, 149). New possibilities open up for cyborgs, built on the grounds of establishing and maintaining connections between parts which, despite remaining distinct in terms of their ontology, manage to work well together.

The extension of the machine through its coupling with the human, and the augmentation of the human through its pairing with the machine result in an expanded set of capacities. The powers of the cyborg are comparable yet not commensurate to the powers of East Javanese healers. The contraction of space of the distinction between the human and the non-human furnishes for healers new parts, and with them an ability to do things the singularly human cannot achieve. The attachment of the other on the self makes the other into a dimension of the self without denying its separateness. The human self and the non-human other are connected through a multiplicity of circuits which must be maintained in good working condition to be effective. The contingency of these circuits, the fragility of the relations making up the *diaphoron* person of the healers and of cyborgs, displaces the urgency for identity totalization and favours unstable becoming-other.

When I asked Pak Uddin how he managed to identify which part of the patient's body was sick, he replied that he started looking for the sickness through touching the patient's body with his fingers. He would start from the lower part of the body moving upwards, waiting for his 'fingers to know'. When the fingers 'met' the sickness, he said that he would be overtaken by a sensation akin to being stricken by an electric current. 'It is the *elmo* that drives my fingers to meet the sickness and to perform massage,' he claimed. 'The *elmo* is in my *hate* and from there it flows [*aghili*, Mad.] all over my body, to my head and fingers. I cannot explain it to you. Everything happens because the snake is in my body. It is as it said: "You are me, I am you".' Similarly, Kyai Salahuddin's gazing capacity rested on the combination of ordinary, human eyes able to discern material objects, figures, colours, etc. with the eyes of *elmo* that are sensitive to feelings and thoughts of other humans and can see into *alam ghaib*, rendering the invisible visible. When I asked him about how he managed to 'see' into another person's *batin*, Kyai Salahuddin replied that it happens 'by itself', 'automatically' (*dengan sendirinya*, Ind.), i.e. with the same degree of awareness and amount of effort that is required in breathing, digesting or moving one's feet.

Yet Pak Uddin's *elmo* was capable of detachment and reattachment into new bodies. As such, it maintained a certain degree of separation from him. His powers, however embodied and sacred, could depart and circulate both through commoditization and inheritance. Some years ago, Pak Uddin had been approached by neighbour of his who was interested in learning to perform massage. Pak Uddin accepted him as an apprentice in exchange for a substantial amount of money. The apprentice spent several months observing Pak Uddin massaging his clients, subjecting himself to the same regiment of fasting and praying that the master healer maintained. In the end, he did learn how to massage but, in Pak Uddin's words, 'he could not heal people … his massage was not as efficacious as it should have been.' This was not so much for lack of diligence on the part of the apprentice, as for certain constraints involved in training as an educational technique. 'It is nearly impossible to be taught *elmo*. *Elmo* is in the body and his body did not know *elmo*,' Pak Uddin explained.

Bodies that already share certain parts with those of healers are in prime position to be *elmo*'s future recipients. In this instance, the separation of *elmo* from the healer is anticipated to be realized within the moral realm of kinship. The passing of *elmo* to one's descendants qualifies it as a form of inheritance (*pusaka*, Ind.) with the actual transfer taking place at the very moment of the healer's death. In this regard, the *elmo* is often imagined as detaching itself from the healer's body together with, or through, his very last breath. The willing offspring in Pak Uddin's case is his only child, a daughter; she is expected to receive the *elmo* through inhaling her dying father's last breath. Their relation as being of 'one blood' (*situng dereh*, Mad.) is construed as a condition that is both necessary and sufficient for *elmo* to work well in the new recipient, i.e. with the same degree of efficacy as before, provided of course that the purity of the daughter's intentions and depth of religious devotion is at least equal if not greater than her father's.

Sets of four

For some of the healers (*dukun*) I got to know intimately, *elmo* was not permanently affixed to their bodies. Rather it took the form of friendly 'instruments' that could be temporarily attached to their persons so as to expand their capacities. These were mainly people who had come to own (*endik*, Mad.) spirits, mainly jinn, through the successful completion of trials under the supervision of a senior guide, another *dukun* under whom they had once apprenticed. Relations with spirit aides on the whole were conceptualized as based on hierarchy with spirits acting as the healer's servants or even slaves, responding to his summons and requests and offering him privileged access to knowledge unavailable to others. Such hierarchies are nevertheless unstable and subject to inversion with the healer expected to become the spirit's servant after death. While alive, however, healer and spirit are often described as forming a pair that works together and with great efficiency for solving other's people troubles, often for a set fee. One such healer, Pak Sukoco, claimed to own 40 spirit aides. He often asserted that spirits revealed the cause of sickness by whispering in his ear and declared that his intimacy with one of them, a female spirit called Aisha, involved sexual relations as well.

In general, the breaching of boundaries between human and non-human, the experience of intimacy and the subsequent extension of human capacities are processes made possible and facilitated by a specific component of the human person. This locals refer to as *roh*, from the Arabic *ruh*. *Roh* is one of the constituent parts of very human person and forms a critical link and a decisive pathway in the communication of human with non-humans, allowing for connections to develop and attachments to grow. The *roh* of human beings shares a certain affinity and likeness with the ethereal beings populating *alam ghaib*, the unseen world. The link *roh* forms is also believed to become particularly active under certain conditions some of which involve the undertaking of ascetic regimes, as we have already seen instrumental in the becoming-sacred of our previous two cases.

In what follows, I seek to discuss local ideas about the component parts that make up the human person and chart the relations parts entertain with one another and with non-human beings. These ideas draw inevitably upon Islamic notions found across the Muslim world yet are also embedded within distinctive archipelagic, 'Indonesian' frameworks that organize the human into sets of four (see Errington 1988; Bowen 1991, 115). In the course of the discussion, it will become clear that human persons are conceived of not as finished wholes but as assemblages, i.e. systemic aggregates of closely connected yet clearly differentiated parts which despite been engaged in complex circuits of co-operation retain nevertheless a high degree of autonomy. The four parts human persons consist of are: the *roh*, the corporeal or substantive body itself consisting of four elements, the four drives and the four plus one senses.

For humans, the process of coming into being entails practices of aggregation and alignment. The combination of uterine blood and semen is seen to provide the material basis for the foetus. However, its formation involves a process of animation, something that takes place during the fourth month of pregnancy or thereabouts and is marked by the coming of *roh*. Informants stress that *roh* comes from Allah and liken the animation of foetus to the creation of Adam who was brought to life by God breathing into his body. At the same time locals took pains to emphasize that *roh* is not identical with Allah (*bukan Allah*, Ind.), insisting that the precise nature of *roh* is beyond human comprehension. However, *roh* is held as entertaining an undetermined yet close connection with the God, due to having been sent by Him.

Generally, *roh* is conceived as an ethereal, incorporeal, immaterial kind of body, and is referred to as *badan rohani* (Ind.), the spirit body. Despite being intangible, *badan rohani* is both sensate and sensible. When humans fall asleep, *roh* is said to separate itself from *badan jasmani*, the corporeal body, leaving behind its abode in the *hati* (heart/liver), flowing out through the nose; it is then able to travel autonomously. Its wanderings produce dreams which consist of the *roh*'s encounters with the dead, spirits and angels, as well as the *roh* of other living human beings while asleep. Communication with non-human beings is possible, several people asserted, for their constitution is approximate to that of *roh*, all being equally intangible, immaterial yet affective.

Roh is generally held to be the human element that survives death. In death, like in sleep, the *roh* of the deceased interact freely; they are said to talk, move around, eat, drink and even have sex, while still maintaining some loose connection with the body, or what remains of it, in the grave. Traditionalist Muslims in Java, as well as other parts of the Islamic world, hold that a deceased person's *roh* watches his relatives bathing the corpse from above, listening to their speech and feeling empathy for them. A dead kinsperson's *roh* does sometime visit his relatives in dreams, to inform them of happenings in *alam kubur* (the realm of the grave, also *barzakah*, Ind.) so that they act piously to avoid punishments in the afterlife (see Smith 1980; Smith and Haddad 1981, 121). The relative separation of *rohani* from *jasmani* that death causes to take place, however, is not held by Muslims as final. Their connection is to be renewed on the Day of Judgement. While people in Probolinggo were far from certain about the precise nature of the events of the Day of Judgement, the majority of them understood the relevant Quranic passages to guarantee the resurrection of the corporeal body and its realignment with the deceased's *roh* so that the human being that once was will return to life in its original earthly form.[9] Others, however, were more sceptical, allowing for the possibility that

---

9 Modernist Muslims in Java as elsewhere are far less concerned with *alam kubur* than traditionalists, delving into the Quran with a pragmatic attitude that emphasizes human accountability and responsibility in this life rather than the possible awards, pleasures and punishments of the afterlife (see also Woodward 1989, 122–3). In addition, modernists emphasize that it is the *roh* only that receives punishment in the realm of the dead, something that differentiates them clearly from traditionalists who hold that both the *rohani* and the *jasmani* get to be punished. The negation of the possibility of the living interacting with the dead also means that in modernist funerals the *talkin* (Ind., instructions to the dead) is not performed. In general, modernists have historically been quite hostile to practices of communication with spirits and on the whole prefer to entrust their health to modern biomedical practices though they do sometimes visit *dukun* seeking advice and help.

the resurrected body might not be entirely identical with the earthly body but
of a different kind that human intellect cannot grasp fully.

In general, *rohani* and *jasmani* are believed to share the same form, to have the
same appearance. The corporeal and the incorporeal bodies of human persons
are connected by means of iconicity as they are held to strongly resemble each
other, forming mirror images. The symmetry iconicity guarantees means that
in sleep as well as in the afterlife, the living and the dead are distinguished from
one another on the basis of their facial characteristics, their dress preferences,
language and speech styles, and ways of moving. The same holds true for *jinn*
that are subject to similar processes of recognition. As one person put it, *jinn*
are 'like humans: they too are divided into female and male, are human-like
in terms of shape and clothing, have lots of different nations, and each nation
has its own country'.

The *badan rohani* is a sentient and sensible body endowed with agentive
and affective capacities. These characteristics it shares with *badan jasmani*,
the corporeal body (see Chapter 2). Moreover, the two closely resemble one
another. The spirit body can thus be productively theorized as the presencing
and instantiation of the human person in the realm of the grave (*alam kubur*),
and the realm of the unseen (*alam ghaib*). This presencing takes place in the
context of specific kinds of relations. In its dealings with the dead, the *jinn*,
the angels and Allah, the human person appears (or is made to appear) as
rohani. In these particular realms and in reference to these relations, what is
or what used to be a living human person is evinced through only one of its
parts becoming actualized. In other words, in sleep as well as in death the
corporeal body is eclipsed, receding from view, becoming virtual. In contrast,
in this world of materiality and coarse visibility (*alam dunia*, Ind.) it is the *roh*
that is concealed from view, residing deep into the heart/liver. In reference
to the relations human beings entertain with other living humans, it is the
substantive, material body that actualizes (or is made to actualize) the person.

The corporeal body itself is a composite. Its materiality is referred to as clay,
which locals hold to consist of four different elements (*anasir*, Ind.): soil, water,
fire and air. Allah is said to have chosen these elements because they are 'a
good match for each other', as the properties assigned to them cover the whole
spectrum of attributes locals assign to physical objects. These properties are:
hot for fire, cool for water, dry for air or wind and wet for soil. The condition
of being human is intimately related to the make-up of *badan jasmani*. As one
person put it, 'without each one of these [elements], [the being] is not perfect,
is not human'. Animals, plants and spirits have been created either from one
of these elements – the *setan*, for example, are made of pure fire – or from
combinations of elements totalling less than four – fish, for example, are taken
to consist of soil and water.

The third component of human persons is also arranged as a set of four. This component is referred to as *nafsu* and is usually translated as both soul and desire. Writing with respect to Sufism, Sviri argues that the relevant Islamic literature is permeated by 'two contrasting meanings of *nafs* [*nafsu* in Arabic]'; one associates the *nafs* with a vital energy residing in the body and the other designates the *nafs* as 'a negative, earth-bound fiery entity that needs to be constantly condemned and watched over' (2002, 13; see also Chapter 6). However, even when the *nafs* are understood as desire they also seen as capable of transformation from negative to positive by a concerted human effort requiring ascetic exercises and sincere religious devotion. When this is achieved man is ennobled and perfected.

The people I interviewed were equally ambivalent regarding the *nafsu*, considering them both necessary for life yet dangerous if left unchecked. Each of them emphasized the necessity of bringing them under conscious control. Pak Herianto, a middle-aged civil servant, healer and member of the Naqsyabandiyah brotherhood,[10] enlisted the four *nafsu* as: *nafsu aluamah*, indexing the excessive and rapacious desire for wealth, status and possessions; *nafsu amarah*, indicating the anger and belligerence aroused when extreme feelings of displeasure take hold; *nafsu mutma'inah*, referring to the propensity for conforming to religious precepts and doing good; and *nafsu sufyah*, indicating the quest for inner serenity that originates in one being close to Allah. The task of every human, he continued, is a struggle for moral perfection, realized through limiting the influence of *nafsu aluamah* and *amarah*, and extending the scope of operation of *nasfu mutma'inah* and *sufyah*. Responsibility therefore arises out of the morally neutral constitution of humanity with accountability relating to the necessity of asserting control over both good and evil. Success in this endeavour, Pak Herianto continued, makes man's status rank higher than that of angels as the latter are made of pure light, knowing thus little of temptation and repentance.

Roh and *nafsu* are intimately related. While *roh* resides in the *hati* (heart/liver), the *nafsu* are said to be located in the *hati*'s vicinity, although some people pointed to the lungs. Their spatial intimacy means that *roh* is directly affected by the *nafsu*. This much is apparent in ideas regarding the colouring the *hati* acquires during a person's life course; the *hati* of saints is said to have become white, while those of evil people of having gone black. The connective circuits of affect the tie *roh* and *nafsu* together are also attested in another way yet. Despite the fact that *nafsu* do not survive death, they nevertheless exercise a profound influence on *roh*, as the latter's posthumous fate in relation to the distribution of awards and punishments in *alam kubur* is determined by a man's relative success and failure in controlling the *nafsu* while alive.

---

10 On the history of this brotherhood in Indonesia, see Van Bruinessen (1994).

Roh, jasmani and *nafsu* are connected in complex ways to the senses as well. The senses are organized into a set of four plus one. In Chapter 3, I discussed the foetus's siblings and their transformation into cognitive aides that inhabit the outer seats of perception, i.e. the nose, the ears, the eyes and the mouth. These aides activate the senses, allowing for communication and understanding to proceed. The four senses locals recognize – sight, smell, hearing, talking – are complemented by a fifth sense that of *rasa* which plays an important role and which often indexes the person as a whole in its association with the *hati*.

The primacy of *rasa* and the *hati* is well-documented in the ethnography of Java. Building on the insights of Gonda (1973) who comments that the Javanese combined the original Sanskrit meanings of *rasa* as 'taste', 'tactile perception' and 'inward feeling' with the concept of *rahasya* (i.e. 'secret' and 'hidden significance'), Clifford Geertz writes that *rasa* has two primary meanings. In the first place, it is taste-touch-feeling as 'it includes within itself three aspects of "feeling" that our view of the senses separates: taste on the tongue, touch on the body, and emotional "feeling" within the "heart"' (1960, 238). Secondly, it is truth. Geertz writes: 'as the first, or sensationalist, definition of rasa indicates both feeling from without (taste, touch) and from within (emotional), so *rasa* in its second or semantic sense, indicates both the meaning of events in the … external behavioural world of sound, shape, and gesture, and in the far more mysterious … [internal world], the fluid inner world of life' (1960, 239).

These rather abstract formulations have a series of very important implications. Javanese metaphysics displace two distinctions: firstly, the distinction between tactile and gustatory sensation, and secondly, the distinction between sensation and emotional experience. In other words, the taste of things is taken to be barely distinguishable from the emotions formed in one's *hati*. Emotional and sensory engagements with the world amount to the same process. Furthermore, these feelings and sensory engagements are taken to reveal the 'essence' of everything apprehended. It is in this way that *rasa* derives its meaning as 'hidden significance': truth stems from experience which is at once sensual and emotional.

As Stange's (1984) work makes clear, *rasa* and the *hati* are at the centre of the systems of knowledge of many *kejawen* associations and Sufi brotherhoods in Java. These systems exhibit certain divergences – some of the former construe, for example, the *hati* as the esoteric locus of Vishnu; while some of the latter as the place where Allah and his 'servant' meet. It was within the context of dissociating Sufism from *kejawen* practices – the latter 'mixes elements from Buddhism, Hinduism, Islam and Christianity' – that Pak Herianto explained to me the significance of *rasa*. 'Human beings [are] composites of many elements ... *roh* and *jasad* [the corporeal body]. ... *Roh* is everywhere, given by Allah, but is not Allah ... only Allah knows the nature of *roh*. *Roh* resides in the *hati*; *jasad* is *roh*'s equipment in this world [*alam dunia*, Ind.].'

According to Pak Herianto, the *hati* is divided into two parts. The upper part or *sirri* (from the Arabic *sir*, meaning secret or mystery) is located two fingers distance above the left nipple. *Sirri* is the centre of feelings. The lower part or *kolbih* (from the Sufi term *qulb* meaning the inner heart) is the centre of morality and decision making. Together with the third centre, the *fikroh* which is located in the head and holds the capacity for reason (also *akal* from *'aql* in Arabic), they comprise the human cognitive system. Pak Herianto explained the functioning of the human cognition in terms of circuits of connections, automatisms and transformational capacities. *Fikroh* receives all the 'stimuli' one receives through the sensory organs, processes them by way of reasoning and sends them to *sirri*. *Sirri* transforms thoughts into feelings by means of isolating, discerning and differentiating the qualities of the things apprehended as emotions. Finally, *kolbih*, the locus of morality, works like a filter to form judgements by subjecting the emotions it receives from *sirri* to moral scrutiny. It then makes decisions about the appropriate response and course of action. The decision taken is transmitted back to *fikroh* which, in turn, makes the *jasmani*, the corporeal body, act accordingly. By means of these circuits, Pak Herianto, along with many others, claimed that the *hati* and not the mind is the ruler of the person.[11]

This account of human cognitive processes has very little in common with either the intellectualist or the empiricist theses which are common in the Euro-American world. Whereas Cartesian intellectualism attributes cognition to the *a priori* existence of transcendental consciousness and envisions the world as the product of mind's representations, empiricism envisions a passive subject who simply registers the stimuli the world holds for it. In other words, whereas intellectualism assumes the existence of subjects and ends up with the discovery of quasi-objects, empiricism takes the existence of objects for granted and along the way detects quasi-subjects. The metaphysics of the people I worked with break clear from the dilemma of prioritizing subject or object, for they foreground the relation between the subject and the world differently. This relation is foregrounded as one of reciprocal constitution and co-extension achieved through the digestive capacities of the *hati*.

---

11 This account both differs from and echoes other Naqshbandi accounts regarding the centres that make up the human person. Ernst notes that a typical Naqshbandi account recognizes six subtle centres rather than the three (plus the fourth, i.e. the *jasmani*) acknowledged here (see 1997, 107–8). Webner's Naqshbandi informant, Hajji Karim, speaks of seven centres which allow for the entry of divine light into the human body (2003, 183–4) with five of them being located in the chest.

The process of cognition Pak Herianto described is directly related to digestion because the *hati* also has a certain role to play in human physiology. In its association with liver rather than the heart, the *hati* is the only organ capable of producing the most fundamental substance for the inception and perpetuation of life: blood. As noted in Chapter 4, the *hati* produces blood from the juices of digested food. According to local ideas about the functioning of the human body which have a wide currency in the Islamic world, food is transformed into blood during what's called 'second cooking' in the liver. The liver (also known as *lever*, Ind.) and the heart (also known as *jantung*, Ind.) are held to co-operate closely. After blood has been produced in the liver, it is sent to the heart and from there to the whole of the body via the veins. By means of its circulation, blood acts not only to nourish the body but also to facilitate the interactions of *sirri*, *kolbih* and *fikroh*, and the flows of thoughts, emotions and decisions around the person.

Rasa as taste/touch/feeling and the *hati* as both liver and heart define cognition as the outcome of swallowing of the world; the world is incorporated, internalized and dissolved into the subject (see Borthwick 2000). The boundaries of person and the world, the self and the other, are constantly broken down by tactile enfoldment, the action of the teeth, the work of the saliva, the digestive functions of the liver. Concurrently, thoughts, emotions and decisions arise; the world becomes deliberated as feelings, subjected to moral scrutiny, acted upon. Persons are thus literally made of the world for the world has become them.

Reciprocal motions

Becoming-sacred is about the ascetic and meditative practices involved in the fluctuations characterizing the distinction between the human and the divine. Although the distinction itself cannot be transcended according to orthodox Sufi practices prevalent in Java, it is nevertheless subject to contractions (and expansions) with the space separating humanity from divinity becoming progressively reduced to zero. The zero of supererogatory practices of religious devotion and sincere desire for perfection enunciate human self-annihilation and announce the evincing of the divine. At the end of the process, a new person emerges that combines both human and non-human parts and members, equipped with the capacity to perform extraordinary, often miraculous deeds. To elaborate further, the process of becoming-sacred examined in this chapter effects the *diaphoron* person, a person that is constituted in and through difference. The *diaphoron* person is a multiplicity and an assemblage of attributes and capacities which are both human and non-human. The mode of being the *diaphoron* person instantiates is neither about seamless totality nor about singular identity. The human and the non-human subsist and inhere in its constitution and are intensively connected through circuits of relations that regimes of religious devotion foster and maintain.

It is only on account of its effected character, i.e. of it being the outcome of processes of becoming, that the *diaphoron* person is a veritable agent capable of acting on the world with a great efficacy itself manifested in healing performances. In other words, it is only because it is an effect of processes of becoming that the *diaphoron* person can set other becomings in motion, such as those of helping others to become healthy. The persons healers are equipped with are therefore both effects of previous processes and quasi-causes of other becomings.

The processes of becoming-sacred entail two interrelated movements, one of descent, another of ascent. Descent is about the care and love Allah shows to the most esteemed of His creations, the human who knows both about temptation and repentance. Ascent is related to the religiously cultivated desire to seek intimacy with the creator and for dealing with the contingencies of suffering that press for immediate alleviation. The very point in which the trajectories of the two movements meet marks the zero point of temporary death and consequent rebirth. The space of zero is not empty, however, but full with the completeness of a relation, the human–divine intimacy.

The embodiment of divine grace in the form of the gift of a beam of light or a potent animal magnifies the composite nature of humanity which is said to consist of sets of four. Divine gifts are attached to what is already there as a given that is as a result of other sets of relationships; the relationships one is composed of due to past and future acts of procreation, the relationships of siblingship and the *kampong*. The persons healers are endowed with are extreme and excessive, characterized by surplus parts that have come about due to them entering into additional plateaus of sociality. Engagements with Allah and the beings populating *alam ghaib* create new relationships and additional exchanges. The parts with which healers are provided in these relationships amplify the composite character of their persons who in addition to the elements of the spirit body, the corporeal body, the four *nafsu* and the four plus one senses, are enhanced by non-human members.

In the following chapter, I turn my attention to a separate process of becoming that involves equally humans and non-humans engaged in complex relationships. In contrast to the processes of becoming-sacred which are devoted to enhancing life in the sense of promoting the well-being of others, processes of sorcery are aimed at the delivery of pain and death. Within the context of sorcery practices, the *diaphoron* person is instantiated as androgynous, made of both male and female attributes and capacities. This instantiation requires eliciting causes, guarantees specific effects and demands participation in particular exchanges. The intimacies achieved therein reverse the processes of becoming-kin we have seen so far as to in the unfolding of the *kampong* as a plateau of convivial sociality and manifest the still-hidden from our view process of becoming-enemy.

Chapter 6

THE MARITAL AND THE MARTIAL: GENDERING, KILLING, OSCILLATING

Cross-regional perspectives

'There is in truth no male, no female'[1]

In a recent interview, Didik Nini Thowok, the famous Javanese transvestite dancer, said of his performances:

> For me, I never think about who is behind the mask. I only see the character *in* the mask. … When a woman dances the male mask, she is transformed – it is mystical. And when a man dresses up as a woman, in *bedhaya*, we don't always recognise that the dancer is male – it is mystical. He, too, is transformed. I believe a better term [to transgender] is 'mystical gender'. I plan using this term. (Ross 2005, 226)

Didik refers here to his own work as male sexed dancer performing female roles, a practice that both continues and advances 'traditional' Javanese court dance practices, according to which the genders of the performer and the character being portrayed do not always coincide (see also Soedarsono 1969). Such cross-gender dances, as well as gender-crossing ones, in which the gender of the character changes in certain key episodes of the story, manifest an understanding of gender as unstable and always in motion. In the present chapter, I claim that this condition of mobility and mutability that Didik describes as 'mystical' is informed and facilitated by a concept of the person as androgynous. This androgyny is best exemplified by, but not necessarily limited to, Didik's status as a *banci* (Ind.), a transvestite, a plural combination of femininity and masculinity. In the context of dance performances, furthermore, both the wearing of a mask and the donning of a dress as objectifications of the gendered other are held as efficacious enough to induce an oscillatory movement from male to female, or female to male.

---

1 From *Suluk Lonthang*, an early nineteenth-century Sufi song from Java, as translated by Florida (1996, 208).

Didik's and other similar performances share a strong affinity with current Western academic efforts to get away from thinking in terms of fixed gendered categories. With respect to the latter, such an attempt has been marked by a proliferation of analytic modalities ranging from discourse analysis (Butler 1990) and queer and sexualities studies (Warner 2000; Boellstorff 2007) that emphasize the ways that individuals 'take up gendered subject positions through engagement with multiple discourses on gender' (Moore 1994, 56) and place a premium on the associated politics, to others such as that of Strathern (1988) that are embedded within the theoretical horizons of ethno-sociology and regional synthesis. Here I am particularly concerned with Strathern's dissociation of gendered subjects from gendered attributes and the introduction of the idea of personhood as a composite, androgynous 'entity'. Writing with respect to Melanesia, Strathern argues that 'being "male" or being "female" emerges as a holistic unitary state under particular circumstances … each male or female form may be regarded as containing within it a suppressed composite identity; it is activated as androgyny transformed' (1988, 14). To the extent that persons in Melanesia are thought of as a microcosm of social relations, they contain both male and female attributes. Such attributes allow persons to become gendered in a singular form, i.e. as male or as female, in specific contexts and as a result of entering into specific relations. Strathern puts it thus: 'a dividual androgyne is rendered an individual in relation to a counterpart individual. An internal duality is externalized or elicited in the presence of a partner; what was "half" a person becomes "one" of a pair' (1988, 15). In her scheme of things that are Melanesian, the eliciting cause is always the presence and actions of a social other, while the mechanism through which this elicitation is achieved and gender is made temporarily visible rests on exchanges, including those of valuables as well as those of substance.

Strathern's conceptualization of the Melanesian person as androgynous and her concern with the forces which give this person's singular form as alternately masculine and feminine invite us to posit difference as the ontological ground of the self. In other words, Strathern along with Deleuze (1994) sees difference at the heart of the person: androgynous, the person is pure difference, characterized by an internal difference and made up of both masculine and feminine attributes. Strathern also shares with Deleuze an emphasis on becoming as the singular forms the person takes – male or female – are always the effect of activities performed by others in the course of social praxis. Strathern talk of elicitations undertaken in the course of exchange practices echoes Deleuze's emphasis on the processes of deterritorialization and reterritorialization through which exact and distinct forms emerge from a plane of immanence and identity is given.

In the present chapter, I take inspiration from Strathern's approach to gender and gift-giving played out in Melanesia to explore sorcery practices in

East Java as involving exchange. I argue that such exchanges are underlined by an indigenous understanding of the person as *diaphoron*, i.e. constituted in and by means of difference, and as always already involved in processes of becoming. Thus, I claim that a consideration of sorcery exchanges provides a productive way of exploring the immanent presence of masculinity and femininity in the *diaphoron* person my friends and informants in Java are endowed with.

The cross-regional analysis I am attempting here rests on an experiment conducted with other experiments in mind; however, that should not blind us to an important difference and a change of direction. Firstly, gender does not operate in Java as the dominant aesthetic in the organization of social relations that Strathern (1988) claims for Melanesia. Secondly, positing one type of difference as pre-eminent is deeply problematic and the analytical move towards privileging one difference – be it gender, caste, class or honour – over others has haunted regional studies, fostering a tendency towards reduction. In this respect, I follow more closely Strathern's subsequent work (1999, 2005) which has done much to address and recalibrate this tendency through the invention and deployment of more sophisticated methods of comparison.

To return to my main argument, I claim that in East Java sorcery is a form of exchange that requires particular flows of substances and effects among the parties involved. Sorcery is also a specific technology that, as well as being perceived to induce death, is key for the elicitation of gender. I claim that sorcery, as it is envisaged in Java, seeks to en-gender the person first in masculine and then in feminine form in order to achieve its desired outcome, i.e. to bring about misfortune, illness and often death of a victim. The gendering process itself rests on a series of exchanges involving two sets of actors: the sorcerer and his client, and the victim and the sorcerer's spirit familiar. The gender of these actors takes alternate forms, while the exchanges instigated by sorcery rest on the evocation of marriage transactions. In this regard, Didik's comments of a 'mystical gender' in operation during masked performances acquire particular relevance. In the place of the mask, the sorcerer induces gender becomings through the employment of a set of macabre paraphernalia that includes effigies, spells and sacrifices. The anticipated effects, as in Didik's case, are possible only because of an indigenous understanding of the person as androgynous.

My treatment of sorcery is not limited to concerns regarding gender only, but extends to those of sociality. Although I do not see sociality in East Java as necessarily or by definition gendered, the deadly presencing of the other in oneself in sorcery carries certain implications for anthropological renditions of Javanese sociality as predicated on convivial harmony. Colonial and postcolonial descriptions of Javanese village life as orderly, peaceful and equalitarian, as unpacked by Newberry (2007) and Pemberton (1994), share an affinity with a long tradition of anthropological description; with a few notable exceptions, they all emphasize an aesthetics and ethics of convivial intimacy, mutual dependence, and solidarity. Clifford Geertz, for example, while noting the presence of divisive social forces in 1950s Java, highlighted the 'two points making for a moderation of religious conflict – tolerance based on "contextual relativism" and the growth of social mechanisms for a pluralistic non-syncretic form of social integration' (1960, 373). Despite the massacres of the 1960s, this one-sided picture of Javanese life has continued to permeate both indigenous and subsequent Western accounts. In his encompassing *Javanese Culture*, native anthropologist Koentjaraningrat (1989) describes the ritual of *slametan* as the ceremonial expression of the *gotong royong* (Ind., mutual assistance) ethic that serves to build and instil a sense of solidarity and equality among the ceremony's participants. More recently, Andrew Beatty has shown how Geertz's 'contextual relativism' is founded on the ritual promotion of an ethos stressing common humanity over and above difference (1999) and on a cognitive and affective scheme of 'changing places' and adopting the other's point of view (2002).

I do not make claims that this is a false representation of Javanese society; quite the contrary. In Chapters 1, 3 and 4, I myself showed how in Probolinggo 'the moral economy of intimacy', to borrow a term from Amazonian ethnography (see Overring and Passes 2000; Santos-Granero 2007), has been integral to the makings of mixed persons and duly emphasized the processes of becoming-siblings actualized in the exchange of children as spouses and the circulation of prayers, food and ancestors among neighbours in the *kampong*. However, the truth remains that this picture is one-sided and that anthropological descriptions of convivial harmony need to be complemented by research into the symbolic economy of predation. The excursion into sorcery practices here serves the purpose of making apparent the dark side of exchange and the violence that permeates sociality. However, it must be noted that I do not claim either that at the heart of Javanese sociality lay a dilemma between conviviality and predation. As Viveiros de Castro (1996) observes for Amazonia, the two modes do not refer to exclusive and formally opposed styles of sociality and/or frames of analysis. Rather, the two modes constantly invoke and presuppose one another in the same way that masculinity is revealed by the eclipsing of femininity in the androgynous person. After all, when in time of need, the people I interviewed look for support and comfort to their kin, neighbours, friends and colleagues. It is these same people who are also blamed for casting a spell when misfortune strikes.

Agency and affect

Alas Niser comprises of people whose economic status ranges from those who are relatively wealthy to those who are poor. The former are mostly landowners possessing several hectares of irrigated rice fields, some of whom are also engaged in trading goods with the provincial and national capitals. Some of the wealthy demographic also happen to be members of the state bureaucracy and of the religious elite, the famous *kyai*. Members of the poorer households pursue livelihoods in both the formal and informal economy as agricultural workers, petty traders of a bewildering variety of goods and factory workers in multinational industries located further afield. Shop owners and professionals such as teachers and nurses occupy the middle level of affluence. As in other parts of rural and peri-urban Java, a sense of relative equality does, however, inform the conceptualization of social relations. People are eager to highlight the absence of extreme polarities of wealth, and to emphasize processes of close interaction and co-operation that culminate in an ethos of sharing.

Yet, in this community, violence or the threat of it is by no means absent. As I have noted elsewhere, violence in the form of sorcery is a pervasive presence intrinsically associated with uncertainty over the intentions and 'true' feelings of social others (Retsikas 2006). As Wikan observes with respect to neighbouring Bali, 'behind a surface of aestheticism, grace, and gaiety, we found social uneasiness, great concern with the individual thoughts and intentions of others, and ubiquitous fear. A coat of politesse, and of forced, almost obsessive conviviality lends to Balinese life an aura of poise ... [but] this façade of good feelings fosters fear in turn' (1987, 338).

Given this fear's ubiquity, the relative scarcity of ethnographic documentation on sorcery in Java and Bali may at first appear surprising. Roy Ellen (1993) notes the highly influential Africanist and Melanesianist literatures on sorcery and witchcraft, observing that in Southeast Asia similar studies have been few and far between. He attributes this absence to the fact that in this region such phenomena do not translate themselves into social problems as they do in Africa, for example, with the periodic rise of anti-witchcraft movements and public witch trials.[2] However, there is another reason that explains this scarcity. In Java, sorcery evokes shame and silence; it is not something people casually bring into conversations. Quite the contrary, the less it is spoken the better.

---

2 There are of course exemptions such as the witchcraft panics and the ninja assassinations that Siegel (2006) and I (2006) have discussed with respect to late 1990s Java. Both these works place emphasis on the history that informs accusations of sorcery and sorcery-associated violence. Siegel points out that the widespread fear of sorcerers was directly related to the collapse of the structures of recognition that the end of the New Order brought about, while I have emphasized the continuities that popular imagination established between the ninja attacks on alleged sorcerers and the communist purges of 1965–66. In the present chapter, however, I have decided for reasons of space to bracket concerns over history and national politics in favour of a novel path of analysis, showing instead the parallel operation of an altogether different logic.

This quality of invisibility is, moreover, intrinsic to sorcery in which rituals are both secretive and private, and its mode of violence supernatural. However, as the following cases demonstrate, its existence is doubted by none.

Case A: Three days after Ibu Surina's funeral, her nephew, a young unmarried man named Putro, confided in me that the family, saddened by her unexpected death, felt that something untoward was involved.

Ibu Surina was a 55-year-old widow with two married sons and three grandchildren. She had never suffered from any major illnesses, being economically active and 'strong as a man'. Yet, she fell sick and died within the space of four days. As in most cases of abrupt and torturous passing, everybody's mind focused on sorcery.

Putro explained that his aunt had been involved in a dispute with a neighbour about a small garden plot that stood between their respective houses. Ibu Surina had been cultivating the plot with vegetables to sell in the market for the past seven years, since the owner of the plot had left for Surabaya to take a post in the civil service there. The owner was a relatively well-off teacher, Hajja Mariam. The two women were said to be close to each other since childhood. It was out of 'sisterly love' and piety, Putro explained, that Hajja Mariam had offered the plot to Ibu Surina to cultivate to augment her income which had become desperately meagre since the death of her husband.

This generous gesture, however, had displeased Hajja Mariam's first cousin who was also Ibu Surina's next-door neighbour. Ibu Halima, the cousin in question, had been involved in an altercation with Ibu Surina a couple of months before the latter's death. The reason for this was that Ibu Halima had erected a makeshift fence around the garden during Ibu Surina's short-term absence. A public confrontation followed Ibu Surina's demands for an explanation. According to Putro, Ibu Halima had been trying to convince Hajja Mariam to sell the garden to her. She wanted to build a house there for one of her daughters who was about to get married. Hajja Mariam, however, had repeatedly declined to sell, considering the dire consequences Ibu Surina would face if she was deprived of her main source of income. 'Now,' Putro whispered, 'she can have it; she can build the house … my aunt is gone.'

Case B: A compound (*tanean*, Mad.) had achieved notoriety due to the involvement of its members, all close relatives, in a long-running conflict. The conflict had partly to do with the ownership of the *langgar* (small prayer house) and the inheritance of the right to offer Islamic instruction to neighbourhood kids. At the centre of the conflict were two specific families related through first-degree cousinship; the family of Ibu Darminah and her husband, Pak Sajuri, on the one side, and the family of her cousin, Haji Sayem, on the other.

Pak Sajuri, a newcomer to the village from Bondowoso and a part-time religious instructor, had recently passed away after suffering from diabetes for several years. According to his children, despite the best efforts of doctors, his condition had deteriorated sharply the last few months of his life and his body had failed to react appropriately to insulin supplementation and dietary treatment. This failure was attributed to the presence of alien, uncanny and biomedically untreatable 'substances' that added to his suffering a supernatural dimension.

The work of sorcery was directly related by Pak Sajuri's children to the jealousy and envy of Haji Sayem. More than a decade ago, Haji Sayem had seen the ownership of the *langgar* transferred to an outsider, while his own claim to it as a male, direct descendant of the *tanean*'s original founder had been bypassed. Haji Sayem's claim to the *langgar* had been supported by several members of the *tanean*, who had argued against the wishes of Ibu Dasminah's father (Haji Sayem's uncle) that Pak Sajuri would be his successor on the grounds of his piety and higher religious knowledge.

The year before Pak Sajuri's death, Haji Sayem had performed the pilgrimage to Mecca. This had raised his status as a learned man. The children of the departed speculated that Haji Sayem had employed sorcery against their father to remove an obstacle and give himself another chance to local pre-eminence at a time when all the sons of Pak Sajuri were still in their teens and thus ineligible to act as religious officiates and instructors.

These sorcery accusations, although never publicly voiced, had created a deleterious atmosphere and had split the *tanean* into two opposing camps engaged in a temporary, uneasy truce. The houses supporting Haji Sayem hardly ever ventured outside through their front porches and kept all their doors and windows at the front, which faced the houses of their enemies, shut.

Case C: Pak Abdul Aziz was a deputy headteacher of a secondary school and a successful businessman who died suddenly at the age of 33 after a period of feeling unwell for reasons the doctors who had examined him failed to determine. His funeral was attended by a lot of people, several of whom were his colleagues and past students. All those attending described the departed as a loving teacher and generous employer.

About a month after his death, rumours began circulating in Probolinggo that Pak Aziz had been ensorcelled. According to the rumours, the widow of Pak Aziz had found several sharp objects hidden inside his favourite chair while cleaning the house. More items were also found throughout the house by the *dukun* (healer/sorcerer) that the widow subsequently hired. There were said to have been broken mirrors stored behind the toilet and rusty nails inside the bed pillows.

One of Pak Aziz's ex-employees confided that the widow suspected the school's headteacher of being behind all this, saying that the latter was envious of Pak Aziz's many accomplishments and afraid of losing his position to him. The fact that over the past few months head and deputy had been overheard arguing many times, by staff and students alike, over the school's running and expenses was adequate proof (*bukti*, Ind.) for the ex-employee to indicate of the evil intentions of the school's head.

I could provide several more such cases. The general point they all make is that in Java, accusations of sorcery always tend to focus on one's intimates, as sorcery is thought to be most commonly practiced against relatives, neighbours, friends and work colleagues (see Geertz 1960, 110; Weesing 1996). It is among people of these categories that elaborate forms of etiquette and deference are largely absent, as they are normally reserved for one's superiors and distant acquaintances and/or strangers. Relationships with one's equals and associates are marked by sociable mutuality in every day occasions, exemplified in relaxed conversing, informal visiting, playing, teasing, good humour and affective comfort, as well as by economic co-operation and ritual exchanges. The fact that sorcery is the flip side of the way that convivial intimacy is experienced in Java highlights the precarious and ambivalent nature of sociality and the fragility of the trust involved. Situated on the same 'plateau of intensity' (Deleuze and Guattari 2004, 22), conviviality harbours aggression; predation emerges out of the inherent risks and hazards of engagement with others. Unrequited love, rejection of a marriage proposal, adultery, betrayal of a friendship, failure of reciprocation, deterioration of an economic partnership, frustrations relating to inheritance imbalances – these are all phrased in terms of an offence delivered and an ensuing loss of face.[3] Resorting to sorcery empowers the offended party by taking command of the fortunes of those who have failed to behave according to expectations; thereby revenge is exacted and face regained.

Writing with respect to Sinhalese Buddhists, Kapferer (1997) notes that sorcery is a creative phenomenon that can play a constitutive role, as it furnishes people a means through which they can make and remake their lives. As such, sorcery has more than a merely expressive function. It is neither simply about the articulation of latent conflicts and contradictions in local political relations (Gluckman 1956) or the release of tensions (Turner 1957); nor is it solely about the vocalization of resistance to neoliberalism, globalization or the alienation

---

3 As Wiener (2007) shows, colonial encounters in Java were not exempt from similar risks and hazards. Fears of sorcery abound in the spaces animated by European men's desires for native women and by native women's desires for European men.

of labour under colonial and postcolonial regimes of value (Comaroff and Comaroff 1993). Kapferer (1997, 256) argues that, more generally, sorcery is about the 'contingency and magicality of human existence', about 'intentionality' and 'consciousness', 'highlighting the truly extraordinary capacity of humans to create and destroy the circumstances' they find themselves in. To the extent that sorcery is about agency, I would add that it is also about affectivity, the capacity for being sensitive and responsive mentally, bodily and emotionally to social relations. As I show later, vulnerability and susceptibility to sorcery stems largely from this condition of openness and receptivity.

The definition of sorcery as agency *and* affect is encapsulated in local conceptions of it as both a murder and an illness. As *penyaket alos* (Madurese), a refined or invisible illness, it is attributed to the intervention of a supernatural agent, most commonly an evil spirit, which acts under the orders of a sorcerer. Diagnosis is subsequent to the inefficacy of herbal and biomedical treatments to remedy a series of symptoms (Jordaan 1985). As a *rajha pate alos* (Madurese), a refined murder, sorcery is the invisible anger and rage of an offended party who, in its attempt to seek retribution, employs the services of a sorcerer. To construe sorcery as refined murder is to say that its force is qualitatively different from a slap in the face or an order shouted out loud, i.e. acts in which the identity of the agent is public. In sorcery, both the instigator and the sorcerer remain hidden, despite rumours and whispered accusations. Here, illness is a response to anger, affect the outcome of and a precondition for agency. In what follows, I discuss their gendered character.

Masculine and feminine bodies

It was Sunday afternoon, and Mas Bukhari and I were having a talk about his search for a wife. Mas Bukhari was an alumnus of the Islamic boarding school I was staying at and over time, we had come to form a close friendship. We were of similar age, both bachelors, and both in search of knowledge. Mas Bukhari, the son of farmer who had died when he was still a boy, had been the disciple of three Islamic scholars, all of whom had entrusted him not only with the basics of the faith, but also with the necessary knowledge (*ilmu*, Ind.) for facing misfortunes, his own and those of others. As an apprentice healer himself, he often liked talking in riddles and posing paradoxes, often laughing at the face of apparent contradictions that find no resolution.

'Having sex with a wife culminates in a "little" death (*kematian sementara*, Ind., temporary death),' he said looking at me seriously. Taken somewhat aback, I replied that it was Freud who had equated death with orgasm but Mas Bukhari insisted that these were the words of one of his teachers, preparing him for such an eventuality. 'The thing is,' he continued, directing attention to the real point he was trying to make before I interrupted him, 'how is it possible for the one who bears sharp weapons (*senjata tajam*, Ind., a common euphemism for the penis) to be killed, while the unarmed one to remain invulnerable (*kebal*, Ind.) and asking for more?' While the workings of female sexuality seem to have escaped this formulation, Mas Bukhari's observation nonetheless revealed one of the central paradoxes that, at least from a male perspective, surround femininity: namely, its inherent vulnerability due to being the penetrated rather than the penetrator, being coupled with a potency that defies (little) death. At the same time, this formulation portrayed masculinity as in danger of being overcome by both affective death and an insatiable femininity, a susceptibility normally suppressed in common designations of masculinity as being harder, more closed and better able to endure extreme conditions.

As Florida informs us, Mas Bukhari's statement is part of a long tradition of a 'treatment of sexuality which may be found in the Javanese classics' which uses a 'conventional martial imagery … to depict sexual relations between men and women' (1996, 209). This imagery was reiterated to me on countless occasions during fieldwork. Women, for example, would ask me teasingly whether I have had a 'sweet enemy' (*moso manes*, Mad.) meaning, a wife or a fiancé; herbal remedies for male fertility problems were referred to as 'filling up the bullets' (*mengisi peluru*, Ind.); the penis was euphemistically likened to *kris* (Ind.), the dragon-shaped dagger. In the wars of intimacy that lovers in Java are engaged in, men commonly occupy the role of the aggressor, while female genitalia is portrayed as a wound, the outcome of the insertion of daggers and a sign of the softness of female bodies and their innate vulnerability. These themes are confirmed by Niehof who observes that on the island of Madura, the bride, 'after her defloration, is supposed to faint', performing a death of sorts (1992, 175). Her unconscious body is then washed, has prayers recited over, and dressed in a new set of clothes, all acts that evoke the handling of corpses. However, parallel to the privileging of masculinity as endowed with a deadly erotic agency, in other contexts and situations, the powers of femininity are acknowledged and celebrated for being capable of both destruction and the generation of life. In this regard, Mas Bukhari's paradox was the result of the collapsing of the distinctiveness of contexts that elicited laughter as well as terror.

In Java, as in other parts of the world, knowledge about persons and social status are enshrined in cultural perceptions and experiences of the body. Gender, age, class and ethnicity manifest themselves in hierarchies between bodies (male over female, mature over immature, high over low, us over them) and within bodies (head and feet, the inner and the outer) (Osella and Osella 1999). Such hierarchies are, however, neither absolute nor complete. In their groundbreaking treatments of gender conceptualizations in island Southeast Asia, both Peletz (1996) and Brenner (1998) argue that according to 'hegemonic' or 'official representations' of gender, men are relatively superior because they are more successful in regulating their desires; this perspective coexists with 'counter-hegemonic' or 'practical representations' which invert the terms of the equation. What is even more important is that the contestable nature of the hierarchies involved is underwritten by both women and men, alternating in their evaluations of gender superiority according to context and the aims at hand. To make this picture of gender relations even more complicated, it is also necessary to add here that such hierarchies have been understood by anthropologists as embedded in a discourse that emphasizes the complementarity of men and women as husbands and wives, and brothers and sisters, highlighting the need for co-operation for the well-being of the household (Errington 1990; Ong 1989).

The question of the degree of control over the body's openness and closedness is of central importance in the articulation of sex wars and the conceptualization of hierarchies. In particular, the themes of achieving and/or being endowed with a high degree of bodily integrity, closure and impermeability inform Javanese understandings of power that Anderson's (1990) work discusses most eloquently. The interaction of the person with social others is deemed to be inherently dangerous and in need of careful regulation. The body's orifices mark these sensitive areas where exteriorizations and interiorizations take place, actions which can affect and alter one's sense of self. Potency (*kesaktian*, Ind.) and high status inheres in the mastery of such flows and interactions in the sense that through the disciplined observance of social norms and the performance of ascetic exercises – fasting, prayer and meditation, often carried out in isolation – one achieves and/or enhances one's control over one's own body. Mastery over one's own bodily integrity extends outwards and is equated with mastery over other people and the natural environment (Anderson 1990; Keeler 1987).

All the people I interviewed, men and women, high and low status, agreed that female bodies are more open and permeable than male ones, and that feminine persons are less capable of achieving control over their bodies. The concept of *nafsu* (Ind.; *nafs* in Arabic), and especially ideas and practices of menstruation were key resources in marking this difference. As noted in Chapter 5, *nafsu* is commonly translated as 'natural appetite', 'instinct', 'lust' or 'desire', primarily for food, sex and material possessions. It carries strong derogatory connotations, even though the satisfaction of such needs is acknowledged as being integral to maintaining well-being. What is signalled out for moral criticism is complacency, the absence of restraint and excessive indulgence, attributes which are strongly feminized. In this regard, my interlocutors would often refer to the deceitful character of Hawah (Eve), the wife of Adam. '*Nabi* Adam was created from clay,' a young female pupil informed me. 'Hawah was created from Adam's rib, and the rib is the most crooked [*paling cacat*, Ind.]

part of the body; if you try to make it straight, it will break; even broken, it still is crooked'. The fragility and lack of straightforwardness of the 'rib' is reinforced by Hawah's role in the Fall of mankind, i.e. the easiness with which she was deceived by Satan and the lead she took in persuading Adam to eat the forbidden fruit. Their subsequent exit from Paradise is commonly held by Muslims to have ushered in the possibility of both procreation and the menses. The same female informant explained the origins of menstruation in terms of a sacred physiology that was punishment for Hawah's role in corrupting Adam. 'Hawah was condemned to bleed for that once a month by Allah – since then, we all bleed,' she added.

Menstruating bodies are female bodies. Male bodies do not menstruate, having one less orifice, one less breach. Bodies that menstruate manifest an innate lack of control over bodily functions and integrity (see Hoskins 2002). Both this lack of agency and the dangers the transgression of bodily boundaries poses are connoted in the Quran by the term *adha* (*Al-Baqarah*, 2:222), which is variously translated as 'filth', 'hurt', 'pollution' and 'vulnerable condition'. In addition to the menses, both female and male involuntary sexual emissions during sleep are also referred to as *adha*. So is the voluntary exchange of fluids during sexual intercourse. All these cases call for the performance of *ghusl* (Arabic), a short cleansing ritual. In the case of the menses, however, a stricter regime of seclusion and enclosure is required. Menstruating women in Java, as in other Islamic societies, are thought of as particularly susceptible to evil spirit attacks which are attracted to the smell of blood. Their movements are carefully regulated, as much by this fear as by the fact that they can not enter spaces reserved for the performance of *solat* prayers. Restrictions regarding spousal intimacy include the prohibition of sex during menstruation. Any communication with the sacred is equally impeded by the proscription against touching the Quran, performing *solat*, fasting and circumambulation the Kaaba during the *hajj*.

Douglas explains the defilement of menstrual blood as a result of it being 'a person manqué' (1966, 96), a sign of infertility, or at least, the failure to conceive, equivalent to an aborted foetus and thus, associated with death. Male interviewees made similar associations, arguing that breaking the taboo against having sex with a menstruating woman results in the festering/ putrification (*busso*, Mad.) of the penis and thus male impotency, which could become permanent if the taboo is broken with regularity. The death by contagion connoted here is, however, different from death in the erotic battlefield of socially and religiously sanctioned sexual encounters to which Mas Bukhari's comments alluded. To better understand the latter, we need to see both menstruation and femininity as ambivalent. On the one hand, menstruation and femininity index *nafsu* as rapaciousness and insatiability, a condition pertaining to all humans irrespective of their gender; on the other hand, they connote openness, receptivity and affective capacities for the generation of life in the sense that bearing a child implies, and indeed requires, menstruation. Childbearing itself rests on forms of agency that male bodies lack; the production of new life is a female capacity. Mas Bukhari, when prompted, likened erotic death to 'having one's hot *kris* cooled down (*menjadi tenang kembali*, Ind.) by the vagina'; others associated women with *sawah* (Ind., irrigated rice fields) saying that the man provided the seed and the woman the soil. The association of women with land is not a metaphor; in matrifocal Alas Niser both houses and *sawah* are usually inherited by daughters. One particular man linked the origin of bull races to the practice of parading bulls over rice fields during the dry season to trigger earth fertility. This could not, however, be completed until the rains came and the fields were saturated with water, he added. In Java, coolness is a positive value as it is associated with the sensations of inner calmness and outward tranquillity that control over the *nafsu* generates. Coolness is closely associated with water with the latter indexing purity. For the people I spoke to, both men and women, the purity of femininity stems from the capacity for bearing children.

As Djajadiningrat-Nieuwenhuis observes, from the late nineteenth century onwards, a combination of Dutch bourgeois and 'traditional' Javanese values, further promoted by the New Order state, led to formation of the cult of *ibu* – the mother. *Ibu*-ism, which Islam also supports and promotes, 'sanctions any action [undertaken by a woman] provided it is taken as a mother who is looking after her family, a group, a class, a company or the state' (1992, 44). The image is of a woman who acts for the benefit of a collective, willing to sacrifice her body, labour and time for the benefit of those intimate others she is a part of, most notably her children. Femininity as motherhood is conceived as active. The transformation of semen and uterine blood in the womb into a foetus, and its growth there, manifest unique forms of agency which find their postnatal equivalent in the transformation of money, which women almost singlehandedly perform, into food, clothes, household possessions, property, etc. (Carsten 1997). Such agentive capacities are also manifested in what Newberry (2006) and Sullivan (1994) describe as *réwang* (to help, Jav.) networks, i.e. networks of reciprocal labour exchanges that connect neighbouring households. In Alas Niser, such activities are said to stem from *sepat niser* (Mad.), the charitable and merciful 'nature' of femininity.

Androgyny

The metonymic relations pertaining to femininity, blood and affective openness, on the one hand, and masculinity, semen and disciplined closed-ness, on the other, speak of the closely associated forms of being and acting. Both agency and affectivity are present in male and female forms, albeit with distinct emphases and implications. For example, female persons achieve agency in motherhood through being receptive and responsive to masculine activity; male persons are acted upon in sexual encounters through being 'swallowed' by their wives and made to emit semen, rather than blood, thus becoming in turn open and vulnerable and dirty. The two forms of being exist as transformations of each other, with masculinity inhering in femininity, and femininity subsisting in masculinity, a mode of relation that Deleuze and Guattari (2004) refer to as 'reciprocal presupposition'. Reciprocal presupposition is a relation characterized by intensity and mutual implication. As such, it differs in significant ways from complementarity as commonly understood in the literature on gender in Southeast Asia. Reciprocal presupposition negates the dialectical or Hegelian connotations of a harmonious combination of entities endowed with pre-determined and stable identities and emphasizes intensity, instability and becoming. Such becoming is predicated on movement, shifting forms and disjunctive synthesis. More generally, it characterizes an understanding of persons as self-differing, i.e. containing *within* heterogeneous elements that are never integrated or synthesized into a superior unity.

The reciprocal presupposition of gendered forms is also conveyed in Strathern's (1988) concept of androgyny. Androgyny affirms difference and corresponds to the shape that the *diaphoron* person takes in Java in terms of gender concerns. The *diaphoron* person is androgynous; it consists of both male and female parts with his/her singular gender form emerging contextually and situationally. More precisely, such emergence demands social interaction and the presence of others that act to achieve the eclipsing of one part and the elicitation of the other in the very persons with whom they exchange. In Java, androgyny is partly grounded on ideas of conception, the transfiguration of substances, and ideas and practices of siblingship. The elicitation of singularity out of composite androgyny is carried out in a multitude of contexts. Here, I concentrate only on circumcision and sorcery.[4]

As I discussed in Chapter 3, children in Java are considered to be made out of the combined role played by both genders in the production of human beings. The body of the foetus is a composite of 'male liquid' (sperm) and 'female liquid' (uterine blood). Blood and semen's identities are not, however, fixed; in certain

---

4 Institutionalized gender-switching as in certain dance performances and practices of transvestism such as those of *waria* (male transvestites) and *warok* performers (see Oetomo 1996; Boellstorff 2004; Wilson 2007) reminds us of the limits of this elicitation to take effect, with the excess that androgyny instantiates successfully resisting the powers of 'extraction' other persons exercise.

contexts, people admit to semen being a kind of blood. Some male interviewees argued that semen is a kind of blood that comes out white because it passes through the kidneys. Others claimed that semen is actually bone marrow, and the penis is an extension of the spine. For the latter, bone marrow was a kind of thicker, cooler, white or yellowish blood. Similarly, traditional midwives in Alas Niser construe breast milk as blood and give a specific herbal medicine (*jamo pejjeen*, Mad.) to mothers to consume that has the capacity to turn the blood located in their breasts into white baby food. Thus, semen, blood and breast milk correspond to multiple transfigurations of a single life substance. This life substance is immanent in all human beings and assumes differential forms according to the relations human beings engage with one another, i.e. as men in relation to women, or mothers in relation to infants.

The composition of human beings by female and male substances, given in acts of procreation, means that persons are considered as internally gender plural. They are so though in other ways as well. In distinct Southeast Asian fashion, persons are conceptualized as parts of a sibling set (see Chapter 3 and 4). The quintessential sibling set is that of brother and sister or alternatively the husband and the wife – who address each other as 'older brother/younger sister' until their first offspring is born – who together perform the ritual and social duties of house production and reproduction. As Howell observes for the Lio of Flores in Eastern Indonesia, 'in those contexts where they act as a cross-sex sibling couple, [persons] can be interpreted as androgynous beings' (1995, 258). According to some versions, Alas Niser was founded by a set of siblings who arrived from Madura early in the nineteenth century, cleared the forest and established the first human community. The androgynous origin of the community is replicated in key community events such as the famous ritual rice meals. In Alas Niser, as elsewhere in Java, rice meals dedicated to the promotion of life (*slametan*) are commonly female affairs, with women acting as representatives of their respective households, while funeral rice meals (*tahlilan*, Ind.) are predominately male. Small prayer houses located within residential compounds are predominately male spaces where men perform their afternoon and evening prayers, and engage in relaxed conversations about day-to-day life, often sleeping there too. Such men are related to each other through their wives, who are siblings of various degrees; the houses that compounds consist of are inherited by women, and are thus marked as female spaces. Furthermore, in rice agriculture, ploughing is performed by men only, while the planting of rice seedlings is carried out by women. The latter are also in charge of harvesting, while transportation is done mainly by men.

Perhaps the most telling instance of androgyny is to be found in male circumcision festivities. In cases where several 'male' children are to be circumcised together, a hopping horse (*jaran kenca*, Mad.) performance is

Figure 9. The gender uniform newlyweds

Figure 10. Parading androgyny

held during the day, if their parents are willing to go into great financial expense. These 'male' children along with 'female' ones, the latter being the sisters, cousins or neighbours of the former, are all made up and dressed in indistinguishable costumes that makes it extremely hard to tell 'male' from 'female' apart (Figure 9). All the children are then paraded around the locality on top of extravagantly decorated horses which stop in front of houses and hop in the tune of music (see Figure 10). The children are referred to collectively as *kemanten* (Jav.), newlyweds, with the word being gender neutral in the sense that it connotes as much the bridegroom as the bride.

The choice of circumcision for the parading of androgyny is no mere coincidence: circumcision evinces both masculine and feminine bodies. As Boddy observes, 'circumcision accomplishes the social definition of a child's sex [*sic*] by removing physical characteristics deemed appropriate to his or her opposite' (1982, 688). In the case of Alas Niser boys, this relates to the prepuce of the penis which covers the *hasyafah* (Arabic; *glans penis*, Lat.) and in the case of girls, to the soft scratching rather than the actual removal of the prepuce of the clitoris (*jelik*, Madurese) with or without bleeding (see also Ida 2005). The purpose of scratching the clitoris, an act performed without much ceremony and when the girls are still 7–40 days old, is to ensure they will menstruate later; it is supposed to render them fertile and thus capable of marriage. The presence of girls in the hopping horse performance anticipates these events and calls forth for the literal uncovering of masculinity. This was best put when a 15-year-old girl asked whether I was circumcised or not. She noted that 'the banana tastes better when peeled' (*makan pisang lebih enak jika dibuka kulitnya*, Ind.).

'Chronicle of a death foretold'

Circumcision is carried out most usually by *dukun*, although nurses and physicians do occasionally feature, especially among educated, upper-class people. In general, *dukun* are persons with sacred abilities to heal; such persons are often suspected of having additional, potentially harmful powers, and of dabbling in sorcery. In the case of circumcision, *dukun* have the capacity of educing gender singularity through the 'removal' of androgynous features. In the case of sorcery, I suggest, *dukun* transform the always-present androgyny into masculinity first and then, into femininity. The mystical rendering of the victim's body as open and vulnerable is central in the *dukun*'s capacity to inflict pain and death onto others. This series of gender transformations are the intended effect of these secret rituals which employ a variety of objects and techniques to create relations of affinity and enforce marriage upon the victim. In this context, death is the outcome of involuntary sex with non-human beings.

Given firstly, the general reluctance of people in Java to talk openly and publicly about sorcery and secondly, that people who are suspected of being sorcerers are normally ostracized and occasionally killed by their neighbours, it is no wonder that in my 18 months of fieldwork, I have never heard anyone admitting to being a sorcerer. Similarly, I have never met anyone who endorsed hiring one as a moral course of action for avenging insults. In addition, given the secrecy of the act, I have never witnessed the casting of a sorcerer's spell. What I present here is information I gathered quite late in my fieldwork through talking to *dukun* who perform healing and counter-sorcery rituals. These were *dukun* whose moral credentials were the least contested, given their observance of Islamic stipulations in their everyday lives and their generosity to kin and neighbours. Their descriptions of what might pertain to sorcery sessions were obtained after having spent a considerable amount of time in their houses, observing them treat sick people, often accompanied by Mas Bukhari who was instrumental in introducing me to them and discussing with me at great length the often enigmatic and piecemeal information offered. The descriptions, allusions and hints I am working with here refer to imagined activities rather than actual rites performed by sorcerers and observed by me. Yet to qualify them as imagined does not make them any less real, concrete or significant for our understanding of the conceptual universe of the peoples of East Java.

In Alas Niser, as in Malaysia (Peletz 1993) and South India (Nabokov 2000), it is widely assumed that the performance of sorcery involves four parties: the sorcerer, the knowledge/power/evil spirit (*ilmu*, Ind.) he commands, the sorcerer's client, i.e. the person who has ordered the casting of the spell, and the victim. What is quite particular in the Javanese case is that, during the course of the sorcery rite, the relations between these four actors are defined and redefined in an precise manner. The sorcerer and the client are made to stand as *bhesan* (Mad.) to each other, a reciprocal term of address used by parents whose children are married to each other. Moreover, the gender of this first pair of actors is defined as masculine throughout the rite. This is in agreement with the gender of persons who are eligible to act as *wali* (guardian, legal representative) in Islamic marriage law. At the same time, the gender of the victim and the *ilmu*, i.e. our marriage candidates, are transformed in the course of the rite; these two occupy alternate gender positions. In contrast to Thailand where sorcery rites draw extensively upon funerals (Rajah 2005), in East Java sorcery rites evoke and invert weddings.

The sorcerer (*dukun sihir, dukun santet*, Ind., or *dhukon kemudhung*, Mad.) achieves a self capable of deliberately destroying others through becoming-hyper-masculine. In the first instance, *dukun* suspected of being sorcerers are usually male, although female *dukun* are not excluded by definition from such suspicions. These people are reputed to have acquired the necessary knowledge/power (*ilmu*) through apprenticeship. The apprenticeship involves the undertaking of ascetic exercises (*tirakat*, Ind.), such as fasting, long periods of isolation in a forest or a sacred place such a tomb of a potent person, accompanied by repeated recitations of magic formulas in Arabic, Javanese or Madurese, under the guidance of a senior sorcerer. *Tirakat* are commonly undertaken by all aspiring *dukun* and those in search of benevolent knowledge, such as Sufi mystics, as the primary means of achieving control over *nafsu* (Keeler 1987). In the case of sorcery, *tirakat* is thought to be integral to bringing the apprentice into contact with malevolent or at least, morally ambiguous spirits. I was told that *tirakat* is usually performed by aspiring sorcerers in cemeteries on Thursday nights or during the first night of the Javanese month of Sura, times when the frustrated spirits of murdered people are extremely active. Alternatively, *tirakat* may attract a *setan* or a non-Muslim *jinn*, entities that are the sworn enemies of humankind's struggle to obey Allah's commandments. Such encounters are extremely dangerous as the spirits assume the forms of fearful animals such as tigers and serpents, ready to prey on the apprentice. Running away out of fear results in the apprentice going mad. The motif of disempowerment and the loss of the natural ability to command oneself is also highlighted in the case of locals attributing failure in *tirakat* to the apprentice being seduced by a spirit which has taken the form of a beautiful woman. To abandon *tirakat* due to giving in the erotic *nafsu* is considered analogous to being overtaken by fear: both result in the apprentice becoming the spirit's slave (*khadam*, Ind.). In contrast, successful completion of the trials ends with the spirit becoming the apprentice's slave and willing to perform whatever tasks assigned to it by its master. However, this power relation is said to be inverted after the sorcerer's death whereupon he will find himself as the spirit's servant in the afterlife domain of Hell.

The hyper-masculinity of sorcerers is manifested by their seeking continually to increase their levels of self-control, to detach themselves from other human beings through pursuing isolation and discipline routines, to withstand madness and avert possible possession in their dealings with non-human agents, building hard and impenetrable bodies that can withstand the challenges they are presented with by malevolent spirits. However, I should stress at this point that the hyper-masculinity of sorcerers is a relational and thus unfixed attribute that is sought after and solidified only in relation to other human beings and malevolent supernatural agents. As *tirakat* is generally employed in the larger context of Javanese spiritual practices that aim to bring humans in contact with a diverse array of spirits, angels and Allah Himself, the gender of the person undertaking such practices can equally be constituted from another perspective and with regards to another set of relations as female.

Both Sufi and *kejawen* discourses lay emphasis on the knowledge-seeker becoming the receptacle of otherworldly power (Anderson 1972; Woodward 1989) and I have repeatedly heard healers and Sufi mystics in Probolinggo construing their acquisition of special capacities as the result of their voluntary penetration by benevolent spirits and the divine itself (see Chapter 5). The fundamental indeterminacy of the gender of *ilmu*-seekers lends further support to my overall argument regarding the androgyny of persons and the relational character of the assumption of gender singularity. In this respect, the gender of *ilmu*-seekers is dependant on the kinds of agents with whom they interact, the latter's place in the overall cosmological hierarchy and the mode of their interaction, i.e. voluntary penetration, involuntary possession, contractual bondage, etc. In addition, the gender of *ilmu*-seekers shifts contextually with regard to whether relations with supernatural agents or with other human beings are the primary concern. So while a healer might be female in relation to a spirit or an angel, that same healer is masculine in relation to the patient as he is the repository of knowledge that endows him with extraordinary capacities.

As far as sorcerers and their relations to humans are concerned, their hyper-masculinity is manifested in them being construed as full of agency and devoid of affectivity: *dukun santet* do not hesitate in sacrificing a close relative or neighbour to the insatiable demands of the evil spirit for victims. The *ilmu* is commonly construed as making periodic demands upon the *dukun* and the continuity of its services is dependant upon the latter meeting them. If there is a shortage of victims due to the absence of clients, the evil spirit might turn against its master and 'eat' him. In these circumstances, the *dukun* has to offer a substitute to save himself. Such a substitute is often thought to come from the *dukun*'s own family or his neighbours.

If the sorcerer is hyper-masculine, what about the gender of the other actors in the sorcery drama? The gendering of the evil spirit as female is accomplished both by its intimate association with the insatiability of *nafsu* and the deadly desire for victims, as well as by its portrayal as a positionally ambivalent slave, an ambivalence which draws upon a general ambivalence that surrounds menstruation. Furthermore, the elicitation of the spirit's femininity is accomplished through the denotation of the fee the client has to pay the sorcerer as *mahar*. *Mahar* (*mahr* in Arabic; also referred to as *mas kawin*) is an essential part of the contract (*akad*) of marriage (*nikah*), according both to the *syariah* and its interpretation in the Indonesian Marriage Law of 1984. *Mahar* is usually construed as a bridal gift rather than as purchase money, and is the property of the bride (see Spies 2007). In Alas Niser, it is given either during the *akad nikah* ceremony by the groom or his *wali* to the *wali* of the bride, an act witnessed by an all-male congregation, or by the groom directly to the bride in their first meeting after the *akad nikah* has been completed. In all Islamic societies, the payment of *mahar* is of central importance for it validates and legalizes the union.

The designation of the fee as *mahar* alludes to sorcery as a kind of marriage, albeit an inverted one since it is aimed not in the regeneration of life but in its destruction. In addition, its payment defines the two parties, the sorcerer and his client as both males and *bhesan*, i.e. persons related through the marriage of their children. The client, as well as the sorcerer might well be female but, from the perspective of the exchanges in which they are engaged, they stand as *wali* to each other and thus male; the exchange of gifts engenders them in masculine form. In turn, the potential victim, who might be either male or female, is from this same perspective elicited as male: it is construed as the bridegroom. And finally, the evil spirit is configured as female. What follows has largely to do with the emasculation of the bridegroom and his turning into the bride.

Sorcery is said to be performed only at night in a windowless room, with the sorcerer summoning the spirit through incense burning and the presentation of offerings. Several people gave diverse descriptions of offerings, but all insisted that these are determined by the spirit and might include clothes, sweets or perfumes. They all insisted that flowers, roses, jasmine and cananga, had to be spread in the middle of the room. These flowers also appear at different stages of the marriage ceremony; they are used to purify the bride and to adorn the newlyweds' bedroom. Their choice is intimately related to their colour (red, white and green, respectively), which index the three elements of which human beings consist, namely the mother's uterine blood, father's sperm, and *roh*, the animating principle that comes from Allah. According to some people, summoning the spirit also demands the sorcerer urinate on the Quran or copulate on it with his wife.

The most potent forms of sorcery, i.e. those aimed at inflicting death, involve the use of effigies as the embodiment of the groom-victim (see also Koentjaraningrat 1989, 419; Wessing 1996, 27). While my informants confessed ignorance as to the materials used to make these effigies, they all agreed to the importance of using soil taken from the grave of an embryo to rub the effigy with. In Alas Niser, foetuses older than four months old are accorded quasi-funerals since they are wrapped in the same white cotton shroud used for full persons. However, their burial is unmarked by the usual ceremonies surrounding death. Dead embryos are considered extremely potent and are sometimes buried at the very centre of blighted rice fields or close to the water gate with the expectation that they will aid the plants' recovery. It is possible that the rubbing of the effigy with soil taken from dead embryo's grave serves to animate it, activating it with its latent life-force.

The presencing of the bridegroom-victim is also achieved by means of the inclusion of objects and substances which are in sympathetic relation to him. The client has to supply the sorcerer with some of the intended victim's clothes and/or soil on which he has stepped barefooted, i.e. objects that contain his sweat. Of the highest value are the victim's fingernails and hair, substances that once belonged to his body and thus, partake of his identity. A photograph might also be used, especially when the aim of the ritual is to make the victim fall in love with the client.

According to the people I interviewed, these personal objects are wrapped together in a bundle that contains other sharp and rusty objects such as needles, nails, parts of broken mirrors and iron chains, the instruments of pain and torture. The bundle is then either placed near the effigy or wrapped around it; most seemed to think the second was the case. These consecutive wrappings contain unequivocal references to the enclosing of corpses in white cotton shrouds. While reciting a specific *duwene* (Mad., spell), the sorcerer will immerse the effigy in a large bowl containing the blood of a *polos* (Ind., preferably of one colour; *molos*, Mad.) chicken, that the client has provided. The *polos* quality of the sacrificial animal is of central importance here. According to the Indonesian dictionary, *polos* also means 'smooth', 'plain', 'straightforward', 'without guile' (Echols and Shadily 1989). Wikan notes that in Balinese, a language which is related both to Javanese and Madurese, *polos* is used extensively to connote socially praiseworthy behaviour in the sense that a *polos* person observes the intricate code of etiquette and is capable of controlling one's negative feelings towards others, acting in a self-effacing and considerate way or being polite and helpful (1987, 345). The sacrifice of a *polos* chicken by the sorcerer heralds the annulment of the contractual masculinity of the groom-victim by violently removing the agency that male persons should display in their every day dealings. In other words, the slaying of a *polos* chicken cancels the control that the groom-victim exercises over his conduct, a control which is, as we have seen already, a highly masculine attribute.

If my interpretation thus far is correct, the annihilation of the groom's masculinity must be accompanied by the evincing of its femininity. Indeed, the immersion of the effigy in the bowl seems to me to be imitating and inverting the purification ritual bath called *siraman* (Jav.) that the bride undergoes the day before her marriage (Figure 11). This ritual bath is performed by the bride's parents and other senior female relatives at the back of the bride's parents' house, using water mixed with the petals of the three kinds of flowers described above.

The bath is accompanied by the bestowal of blessings (*doa restu*) carried over by the water onto the bride's body (Koentjaraningrat 1989, 128–9). The sorcerer's spell is equivalent to these blessings, while the substitution of water for blood achieves the instantiation and spread of pollution. The transformation

Figure 11. Purifying the bride

of the victim's masculinity into femininity is therefore evinced through the effigy's forced menstruation, an act that follows upon the cancelling of its control over its body functions.

Next, the sorcerer supposedly unties the bundle with the sharp and rusty objects and inserts (*masok*, Mad.) them into the effigy. The latter's sharpness qualifies them as death instruments, a power that is augmented by the presence of blood and the spell.[5] Due to being penetrated violently, the effigy's femininity is further manifested. The effigy's body is made open, and vulnerable, affective and responsive to outside influences. Many people pointed out that the sorcerer is particularly intent on penetrating the effigy's navel (*bujhel*, Mad.). The navel sits at the centre of *tabu'* (Mad.) that stretches from the stomach to the genitals, inclusive of the womb and the *hati* (heart/liver). The *hati* is the most important of the human organs for it is the centre of cognition and emotion, as well as of the production (as liver) of blood (see Chapter 5). Newborn babies have their umbilical cord tied with a thread and their navel wrapped in a cotton shroud that contains a mixture of kitchen ashes, salt and tamarind. When ill, people are particularly attentive to their navel which is always treated, whatever the specific symptoms of the illness might be, by rubbing it with kerosene.

The insertion of the sharp objects untie the navel, achieving the regression of the victim into the state of a newborn baby, a state of immense vulnerability and

5 All of my *dukun* informants denied possessing sorcery spells.

lack of agency. Alternatively, the penetration of the effigy might be construed as an instruction given to the evil spirit of what is expected to do (see Endicott 1970, 174). If the manipulation of the effigy by the sorcerer was sufficiently efficacious by itself, there would be no reason to summon an evil spirit and induce it to marry the victim. The insertion of the instruments of pain and death must be, therefore, a call to the spirit to perform an act of imitation, and aggressively seek to penetrate the bride, acting as the 'groom'. This interpretation is supported by common talk about sorcery that describes it as an arrow made of fire often seen crossing the night sky over villages. In this regard, the sharp objects and the arrow intent as it is on finding its target are equivalent to the spirit's penis which is set to violate the bride, impregnating her with her own death.

The difference between blessed marriages and sorcery-induced ones does not rest on any qualitative difference between the sexual acts that consummate both types; in either case, sex involves death. However, in the case of the former, death is deemed essential to the reproduction of life; in the latter, it signals its abrupt end. It is no coincidence that both consummations are socially marked by overgrown bellies, for among the most common symptoms of sorcery affliction is a swollen *tabu'*, as well as blood spitting and mud vomiting. The swollen belly is commonly attributed to the placement of sharp and rusty objects into the victim's *hati* by the evil spirit, something that causes the *hati* to malfunction because of the spread of pollution and deadly words. Counter-sorcery rituals (*kalocotan*, Mad., meaning release, separation, freedom), which I have observed, focus on locating such objects in the victim's body. In this context, healing consists of attempts at either dissolving such objects through an application of counter-spells and herbal remedies, or extracting them violently with the *dukun* often presenting material proof to those witnessing the ritual. In the latter case, such proof – nails, broken mirrors and rusty chains – can be and is sometimes returned to the sender.

Alternatively, penetration involves the placement of polluting objects not in the victim's body but in or next to the victim's house. It is often the case that *dukun* recover nails, broken mirrors and rusty chains from inside pillows, mattresses or chairs, underneath kitchen hearths and inside house walls. These are the places that the sorcery arrow has hit. While death is unlikely to occur from this kind of contagion, serious illness is considered a certainty as the intended victim comes into contact with pollution when it is at its most vulnerable, i.e. when sleeping, relaxing, digesting food, etc.

Becoming-gendered

Substantial or essential gender forms have been critiqued in a variety of ways. Butler's critique proposes the concept of performativity that accounts for gender as tenuously accomplished through 'a stylized repetition of acts' (1990, 140) themselves undertaken within the confines of regulatory discourses concerning the natural and the morally appropriate. In this scheme of analysis, gendered subjects are self-effected and formed out of the undertaking of discursively sanctioned routine and habitual activities with repetition taken by Butler as ensuring the attainment of stability, continuity and identity.

The ethnographic material presented in this chapter speaks of different sorts of becoming-gendered. This becoming does not render stable subjects; emphasis is placed not on subject formation but on transformation, oscillation and reversibility. The becoming-gendered privileged in our case is premised on persons assuming alternate gender forms: what is masculine in certain contexts does in certain others appear feminine, what is masculine now manifests itself as feminine later, and vice versa. Furthermore, what the material underscores is that the motor of becoming-gendered is veritably the social other with subjects understood as other, rather than self-effected. The other is recognized and given primacy as the cause of the singular gendered forms the person assumes. The completion achieved in ever specific relations is wholly contingent on the role the other plays in making the person 'whole', i.e. rendering it part of a pair or a set.

In previous chapters, such pairs were configured as husband and wife, brother and sister with completion eventuated by the actions of the parents as in-laws and origin points. The present chapter adds the pairs of the sorcerer and his spirit familiar, and that of the victim and the *ilmu*. The latter pair is explicitly construed as husband and wife due to the activities of the sorcerer and his client who stand as *bhesan* to each other. The singular gendered forms that the parts making up the pair of victim and evil spirit assume are reversible and interchangeable. While in the beginning of the rite, the payment of the bridal gift fabricates the victim as masculine and the evil spirit as feminine, the force of sorcery works to reverse the positions that the parts occupy while keeping their relation intact. Sorcery forces the husband to become the wife and the wife to become the husband with the marital implicating the martial and sexual intimacy eventuating unreciprocal death.

The effects that sorcery produces reveal male and female, neither as essences transcendentally given nor as subjects who are constituted by means of repetition. Male and female are better understood as attributes and capacities inhabiting the person. Such capacities are manifested contextually, drawn out in the course of relationships. Relationships have a constitutive effect on the momentary actualizations of gender, which is always shifting and changing. The unstable and tense combination of male and female attributes renders the person androgynous; androgyny captures the contours of the *diaphoron* person in the intersections of kinship, gender and sorcery. In terms of gender, the *diaphoron* person partakes in a double articulation. In the first instance, it is made of male and female parts. This constitutive difference is given by means of procreation, the passing of semen and blood, which is realized in sets of social relations of which the person is derivative. The *diaphoron* person is also constituted as androgynous in other senses as well. As a pair or set of siblings (see Chapter 3), the *diaphoron* person is founded on the internal difference that the gendering of its parts as male and female ensures. The *diaphoron* person is thus a paradoxical entity that has two sides/parts, with masculinity and femininity comprising the assemblage it is. The second articulation relates to the subsequent relationships that the *diaphoron* person enters into and the relation of the two sides to each other. What the actions of others effect is the manifestation of the person as either male or female, eliciting one side and eclipsing the other, making the person assume a singular gendered form. Such actions rearrange and redistribute the parts of which the person is made, backstaging one part and foregrounding the other, with all the effort put towards the establishment of new pairs or sets that the singularly gendered person participates in as a part. In such a way, a person becomes alternately male and female depending on the social relations that it is made to enter into and the part it is demanded of it to fill.

The *diaphoron* person is also made present in the material covered in this chapter in yet another way, which in turn relates to the status of the neighbourhood as a House. As already mentioned, sorcery in Java is practiced against one's close associates. In marked contrast to other places in the world where it is usually outsiders who are suspected of instigating attacks through sorcery, in Java it is relatives, friends and neighbours who are normally thought to be responsible when misfortune, illness and death strikes. As far as the neighbourhood is concerned, sorcery attacks work so as to undo the similarity between neighbours that the incessant sharing of ancestors, potent speech and food has produced. This accomplishment, which was discussed in Chapter 4 as provisional, is subject to reverse processes that the symbolic economy of predation sets in motion.

The neighbourhood as a House is permeated both by a sociality of convivial intimacy and a sociality of intense enmity. The House that the neighbourhood instantiates, therefore, can be productively thought of as another instance of the *diaphoron* person in the sense of being constituted in and by means of difference with conviviality and predation subsisting and inhering in the relations actualizing the *kampong*. While the conviviality achieves the rendering of neighbours as siblings whose relations are regulated by equal claims to a pool of ancestors and food, predation foregrounds hierarchy, difference and competition, exposing the dark side of becoming-siblings with neighbours attacking and preying on each other. Sorcery effects the differentiation of what has been previously rendered as indistinguishable, deterritorializing the identity achieved by neighbours and reterritorializing their relations on a plane in which consistency is animated by an intense drive towards separation. The move towards separation is aptly captured in the deployment of sorcery as there is no categorical distinction more complete than that which exists between the living and the ensorcelled, destined to be dead. It is also conveyed by the transformations that the victim undergoes in the hands of the sorcerer and his client who force it to turn from masculine into feminine. The turning female of the victim effects the separation of peoples who had previously been produced as identical.

EPILOGUE

How does one close a thought experiment that revolves around becoming? What kind of full stop requires inventing for becoming not to be foreclosed and locked down? What sort of epilogue does becoming demand as its proper due, so that the differences on which it thrives are not betrayed? In the introduction, I suggested that becoming is betrayed every time we attempt to pin it down to a few fundamentals or principles that purport to explain the phenomenon under consideration; whether this is kinship, the state, religion, the person, etc., in this or that part of the world makes very little difference. The attempts that betray becoming do so for they ultimately explain it away, conflating the provision of explanation with what still demands our full attention. If, on the contrary, knowledge is to be taken as provisional and forever deferred, this is because there is always something that remains, something that never gets absolutely solved, something that cannot be subsumed by the categories and the measures we have invented for the world. This ever-unfolding and ever-circulating 'something' is definitely not, my argument has been, a fundamental or an essence but an excessive and elusive figure that assumes many shapes and forms, passing through all of them.

In the thirteen years I have known the inhabitants of Alas Niser and Probolinggo, many things have undeniably changed. Yet things have also remained recognisably familiar: a habituated pattern of present expectations and future anticipations interspersed with few surprises and innovations. For one, the post-*reformasi* era in Indonesia and the economic crisis it entailed have presented dire challenges to the city's inhabitants, who in the course of events seem to have effectively addressed many of them. After several years' hiatus, a new economic dynamism now permeates the area with new factories and new port facilities spurring things onwards. Added to these is a booming retail industry, with several new shopping malls and supermarkets having made their appearance in the city centre, as well as a resurrected tourist industry that owes its continued relevance to the city's proximity to Mount Bromo, one of Java's key destinations. Of course, some people have fared better than others and still many manage only to scrape a living. Yet, during my latest visit in the summer of 2010, there was marked optimism in the air and a conviction that the worst was over. The streets have been beautified, the creation of a new museum is under way, the central mosque has been revamped and the square adjacent to it now witnesses thousands of teenagers that flock to it every Saturday night to hang out in the many roadside restaurants that now sprawl in the vicinity.

Nevertheless, certain recognisable patterns from the past are still at work. Despite a marked preference among young couples for having fewer children, due to the expense their bringing up entails, there is still the same striking emphasis on marriage as bringing to fruition the destiny of both men and women alike. As a self-proclaimed *jender aktivis* put it in a public conversation over reproductive health in Alas Niser, 'gender equality does not mean that women are now free to behave in sexually promiscuous ways like feminists allow for in the West. … Marriage is where the struggle for equal rights and obligations is conducted [in Indonesia]. Islam encourages men and women to be husbands and wives. This is just. [And turning to me] So are you married yet?'

So too is the case that newlywed couples continue to address each other as elder brother/younger sister; so too that neighbourhood feasts are dedicated to the production of vitality for the living and of merit for the dead. With the possible exception that the latter seems to involve more than ever before office or factory mates and friends as neighbours, i.e. people drawn from beyond the *kampong*, the active making of siblingship as an expansive relationship through the distribution and dispersion of detachable parts of one's self is very much preserved and cared for. And just as conviviality and well-being are promoted, so too are fears of symbolic predation and mystical attacks which maintain their pervasiveness. In the aftermath of policies towards administrative and fiscal decentralization enacted and supported by a series of post-*reformasi* governments, a new base for the formation of local elites has been created in Probolinggo, as elsewhere in the country, that combines participation in party politics, demands successive victories in local elections and presupposes considerable financial resources and social capital. The competitive streak of democratic politics, together with increased levels of prosperity and consumption levels that are differentially distributed among and enjoyed by the city's population, have provided a new element to the fears regarding the intentions and innermost feelings of social intimates.

Decentralized democracy and the impetus towards finding new sources for local prosperity go hand in hand. In Probolinggo, this synergy is about to profoundly affect the ways in which the category *orang campuran* is deployed and understood, as the municipal administration becomes a major stakeholder in the representation of 'mixed people'. Through its support, it has led to the establishment and operation of the local museum for the purpose of boosting tourism. The museum is housed in an imposing white-washed and spacious colonial building at the heart of the city. Although it is yet to be inaugurated, it aims to narrate the social history of the area through photographs borrowed from collections in the Netherlands, as well as local artefacts which together will present, as one of the curators put it, the *adat campuran* (Ind.), the mixed customs, of Probolinggo in their temporal register, to new audiences. While in the past the creation and deployment of mixed identity was located outside the orbit of attention and influence of the state and local administration, its future seems bound to be articulated in relation to new concerns and emerging power constellations, the outcome and implication of which are currently in the making.

What lies ahead for the people of Alas Niser and Probolinggo will furnish new plateaus for becoming to pass through and new arenas for the *diaphoron* person as an unstable assemblage of heterogeneous elements to be manifested. The future will undeniably create new combinations and arrangements of the materials this ethnographic has dealt with and carry them onwards to unanticipated directions. The ethnographic present this book has attempted to capture is the temporary conduit for such materials to pass through on their way to future crystallizations. Yet it is the very unpredictable and unforeseeable character of the future that makes the present into an inexhaustible source of perplexity and aporia.

BIBLIOGRAPHY

Adas, Michael. 1981. 'From Avoidance to Confrontation: Peasant Protest in Precolonial and Colonial Southeast Asia'. *Society for Comparative Study of Society and History* 23 (2): 217–47.

Adelaar, Alexander. 1997. 'An Exploration of Directional Systems in West Indonesia and Madagascar'. In *Referring to Space: Studies in Austronesian and Papauan Languages*, ed. G. Senft. Oxford: Clarendon Press.

Altorki, Soraya. 1980. 'Milk-Kinship in Arab Society: An Unexplored Problem in the Ethnography of Marriage'. *Ethnology* 19 (2): 233–4.

Anderson, Benedict. 1990. 'The Idea of Power in Javanese Culture'. In *Language and Power: Exploring Political Cultures in Indonesia*. Ithaca, NY: Cornell University Press.

Astuti, Rita. 1995. '"The Vezo are not a Kind of People": Identity, Difference, and "Ethnicity" among a Fishing People of Western Madagascar.' *American Ethnologist* 22 (3): 464–82.

Austin, John. 1962. *How to Do Things with Words: The William James Lectures Delivered at Harvard University in 1955*, ed. J. O. Urmson and M. Sbisà. New York: Oxford University Press.

Banks, David. J. 1983. *Malay Kinship*. Philadelphia: Institute for the study of Human Issues.

Barth, Fredrik. 1969. 'Introduction'. In *Ethnic Groups and Boundaries: The Social Organisation of Culture Difference*, ed. Fredrik Barth. Oslo: Universitets Forlaget.

Basso, Keith. 1996. 'Wisdom Sits in Places. Notes on a Western Apache Landscape'. In *Senses of Place*, ed. S. Feld and K. Basso. Santa Fe: School of American Research Press.

Bastin, John. 1954. 'The Chinese Estates in East Java during the British Administration'. *Indonesie* 7 (5): 433–9.

Baumann, Gerd. 2004. 'Grammars of Identity/Alterity'. In *Grammars of Identity/Alterity: A Structural Approach*, ed. G. Baumann and A. Gingrich. New York: Berghahn Books.

Beatty, Andrew. 1999. *Varieties of Javanese Religion*. Cambridge: Cambridge University Press.

———. 2002. 'Changing Places: Relatives and Relativism in Java'. *Journal of the Royal Anthropological Institute* n.s. 8 (3): 469–91.

———. 2005. 'Feeling Your Way in Java: An Essay on Society and Emotion'. *Ethnos* 70 (1): 53–78.

Bell, Jeffrey. 1998. *The Problem of Difference: Phenomenology and Poststructuralism*. Toronto: University of Toronto Press.

———. 2006. *Philosophy at the Edge of Chaos: Gilles Deleuze and the Philosophy of Difference*. Toronto: University of Toronto Press.

Benda, Harry. 1958. *The Crescent and the Rising Sun: Indonesian Islam under the Japanese Occupation, 1942–1945*. The Hague: W. von Hoeve.

Bertrand, Jacques. 2003. *Nationalism and Ethnic Conflict in Indonesia*. Cambridge: Cambridge University Press.

Bloch, Maurice. 1978. 'Marriage amongst Equals: An Analysis of the Marriage Ceremony of the Merina of Madagascar'. *Man* n.s. 13 (1): 21–33.

Blust, Robert. 1997. 'Semantic Changes and the Conceptualization of Spatial Relationships in Austronesian Languages'. In *Referring to Space: Studies in Austronesian and Papauan Languages*, ed. G. Senft. Oxford: Clarendon Press.

Boddy, Janice. 1982. 'Womb as Oasis: The Symbolic Context of Pharaonic Circumcision in Rural Northern Sudan'. *American Ethnologist* 9 (4): 682–98.

Boellstorff, Tom. 2004. 'Playing Back the Nation: *Waria*, Indonesian Transvestites'. *Cultural Anthropology* 19 (2): 159–95.

———. 2007. *A Coincidence of Desires: Anthropology, Queer Studies, Indonesia*. Durham, NC: Duke University Press.

Boomgaard, Peter. 1989a. *Between Sovereign Domain and Servile Tenure: The Development of Rights to Land in Java, 1780–1870*. Amsterdam: Free University Press.

———. 1989b. *Children of the Colonial State: Population Growth and Economic Development in Java*. Amsterdam: Free University Press.

Boow, Justine. 1988. *Symbol and Status in Javanese Batik*. Nedlands: University of Western Australia.

Borthwick, Fiona. 2000. 'Olfaction and Taste: Odours and Disappearing Objects (Critical essay)'. *Australian Journal of Anthropology* 11 (2): 127–39.

Bousfield, Jonathan. 1983. 'Islamic Philosophy in South-East Asia'. In *Islam in South-East Asia*, ed. M. Hooker. Leiden: E. J. Brill.

Bouvier, Hélène. 1995a. *La Matière des Emotions: Les Arts du Temps at du Spectacle dans la Société Madouraise, Indonésie*. Paris: Ecole Francaise d'Extrême-Orient.

———. 1995b. 'Diversity, Strategy, and Function in East Madurese Performing Arts'. In *Across the Madura Straits: The Dynamics of an Insular Society*, ed. K. van Dijk, H. de Jonge and E. Touwen-Bouwsma. Leiden: KITLV Press.

Bowen, John. 1993. *Muslims Through Discourse*. Princeton: Princeton University Press.

———. 1995. 'The Forms that Culture Takes: A State-of-the-Field Essay on the Anthropology of Southeast Asia'. *Journal of Asian Studies* 54 (4): 1047–78.

Brakel-Papenhuysen, Clara. 1995. *Classical Javanese Dance: The Surakarta Tradition and its Terminology*. Leiden: KITLV Press.

Brenner, Susanne. 1998. *The Domestication of Desire: Women, Wealth, and Modernity in Java*. Princeton: Princeton University Press.

Busby, Cecilia. 2000. *The Performance of Gender. An Anthropology of Everyday Life in a South Indian Fishing Village*. London: Athlone Press.

Butler, Judith. 1990. *Gender Trouble: Feminism and the Subversion of Identity*. London: Routledge.

Canessa, Andrew. 1998. 'Procreation, Personhood and Ethnic Difference in Highland Bolivia'. *Ethnos* 63 (2): 227–47.

Carrey, Peter. 1986. 'Waiting for the "Just King": The Agrarian World of South-Central Java from Giyanti (1755) to the Java War'. *Modern Asian Studies* 20 (1): 59–137.

Carroll, Lewis. 2006. *Alice's Adventures in Wonderland*. London: Penguin Books.

Carsten, Janet. 1995. 'The Politics of Forgetting: Migration, Kinship and Memory on the Periphery of the Southeast Asian State'. *Journal of the Royal Anthropological Institute* n.s. 1 (2): 317–35.

———. 1997. *The Heat of the Hearth: The Process of Kinship in a Malay Fishing Community*. Oxford: Clarendon Press.

Carsten, Janet and Steven Hugh-Jones, eds. 1995. *About the House: Lévi-Strauss and Beyond*. Cambridge: Cambridge University Press.

Casey, Edward. 1996. 'How to Get from Space to Place in a Fairly Short Stretch of Time: Phenomenological Prolegomena'. In *Senses of Place*, ed. S. Feld and K. Basso. Santa Fe: School of American Research Press.

Cedercreutz, S. 1999. 'Every Infant is Born with its "Younger Sibling"': Childbirth and Care among Amurang Fishermen'. In *Conceiving Persons. Ethnographies of Procreation, Fertility and Growth*, ed. P. Loizos and P. Heady. London: Athlone Press.

Chittick, William C. 1995. 'Sufi Thought and Practice'. In *The Oxford Encyclopedia of the Modern Islamic World*, ed. J. Esposito, vol. 4. New York: Oxford University Press.

Christie, Anthony. 1978. 'Natural Symbols in Java'. In *Natural Symbols in South East Asia*, ed. G. B. Milner. London: School of Oriental and African Studies, University of London.

Colebrook, Claire. 1999. 'A Grammar of Becoming: Strategy, Subjectivism, and Style'. In *Becomings: Explorations in Time, Memory, and Futures*, ed. E. Grosz. Ithaca, NY: Cornell University Press.

Comaroff, Jean and John. Comaroff. 1993. 'Introduction'. In *Modernity and its Malcontents: Ritual and Power in Postcolonial Africa*, ed. J. Comaroff and J. Comaroff. Chicago: Chicago University Press.

Crossley, Nick. 1995. 'Merleau-Ponty, the Elusive Body and Carnal Sociology'. *Body and Society* 1 (1): 43–63.

Daniels, Timothy. 2009. *Islamic Spectrum in Java*. Surrey: Ashgate.

Delaney, Carol. 1991. *The Seed and the Soil*. Berkeley: University of California Press.

Deleuze, Gilles. 1994. *Difference and Repetition*. New York: Columbia University Press.

———. 2001. *The Logic of Sense*. London: Continuum.

Deleuze, Gilles and Félix Guattari. 1977. *Anti-Oedipus*. New York: Viking Press.

———. 2004. *A Thousand Plateaus: Capitalism and Schizophrenia*. London: Continuum.

Djajadiningrat-Nieuwenhuis, M. 1992. 'Ibuism and Priyayization: Path to Power?' In *Indonesian Women in Focus: Past and Present Notions*, ed. A. Locher-Scholten and A. Niehof. Leiden: KITLV Press.

de Jonge, Huub. 1982. 'State Formation by Contract: The Madurese Regency of Sumenep, the VOC and the Netherlands East Indies, 1680–1883'. *Review of Indonesian and Malayan Affairs* 16 (1): 37–58.

———. 1986. 'Heyday and Demise of the Apanage System in Sumenep (Madura)'. In *Papers of the Fourth Indonesian-Dutch History Conference: Volume 1: Agrarian History*, ed. S. Katrodirdjo. Yogyakarta: Gadjah Mada University Press.

———. 1989. *Madura Dalam Empat Zaman*. Jakarta: Gramedia.

———. 1995. 'Stereotypes of the Madurese'. In *Across the Madura Straits: The Dynamics of an Insular Society*, ed. K. van Dijk, H. de Jonge and E. Touwen-Bouwsma. Leiden: KITLV Press.

Dhofier, Zamakhsyari. 1980. 'Islamic Education and Traditional Ideology on Java'. In *Indonesia: The Making of a Culture*, ed. J. Fox. Canberra: Research School of Pacific Studies, Austalian National University.

———. 1982. *Tradisi Pesantren: Studi tentang Pandangan Kyai*. Jakarta: LP3ES.

Douglas, Mary. 1966. *Purity and Danger: An Analysis of Concepts of Pollution and Taboo*. London: Routledge & Kegan Paul.

Drake, Christine. 1989. *National Integration in Indonesia*. Honolulu: University of Hawaii Press.

Dumont, Louis. 1986. *Essays on Individualism*. Chicago: University of Chicago Press.

———. 1998. *Homo Hierarchicus: The Caste System and its Implications*. Delhi: Oxford University Press.

Echols, John and Hassan Shadily. 1989. *An Indonesian-English Dictionary*. Ithaca, NY: Cornell University Press.

Eickelman, Christine. 1984. *Women and Community in Oman*. New York: New York University Press.

Elkaisy-Friemuth, Maha. 2006. *God and Humans in Islamic Thought*. London: Routledge.

Ellen, Roy. 1993. 'Introduction'. In *Understanding Witchcraft and Sorcery in Southeast Asia*, ed. C. W. Watson and R. Ellen. Honolulu: University of Hawaii Press.

Elson, Robert. 1984. *Javanese Peasants and the Colonial Sugar Industry: Impact and Change in an East Java Residency, 1830–1940*. Singapore: Oxford University Press.

———. 2005. 'Constructing the Nation: Ethnicity, Race, Modernity and Citizenship in Early Indonesian Thought'. *Asian Ethnicity* 6 (3): 145–60.

Embree, John F. 1950. 'Thailand: A Loosely Structured System'. *American Anthropologist* 52 (2): 181–93.

Endicott, Kirk M. 1970. *An Analysis of Malay Magic*. Kuala Lumpur: Oxford University Press.

Errington, Joseph. 1984. 'Self and Self-Conduct among the Javanese "Priyayi" Elite'. *American Ethnologist* 11 (2): 275–90.

———. 1988. *Structure and Style in Javanese: A Semiotic View of Linguistic Etiquette*. Philadelphia: University of Pennsylvania Press.

Errington, Shelly. 1987. 'Incestuous Twins and the House Societies of Insular Southeast Asia'. *Cultural Anthropology* 2 (4): 403–44.

———. 1989. *Meaning and Power in a Southeast Asian Realm*. Princeton: Princeton University Press.

———. 1990. 'Recasting Sex, Gender, and Power: A Theoretical and Regional Overview'. In *Power and Difference: Gender in Island Southeast Asia*, ed. J. M. Atkinson and S. Errington. Stanford: Stanford University Press.

Ernst, Carl W. 1997. *The Shambhala Guide to Sufism. An Essential Introduction to the Philosophy and Practice of the Mystical Tradition of Islam*. Boston: Shambhala.

Evans-Prichard, Edward. 1969. *The Nuer: A Description of the Modes of Livelihood and Political Institutions of a Nilotic People*. Oxford: Oxford University Press.

Evers, Hans-Dieter. 1980a. 'Ethnic and Class Conflict in Urban South-East Asia'. In *Sociology of South-East Asia: Readings of Social Change and Development*, ed. H. D. Evers. Kuala Lumpur: Oxford University Press.

———, ed. 1980b. *Sociology of South-East Asia: Readings on Social Change and Development*. Kuala Lumpur: Oxford University Press.

Eves, Richard. 1995. 'Shamanism, Sorcery and Cannibalism: The Incorporation of Power in the Magical Cult of Buai'. *Oceania* 65 (3): 212–33.

Fajans, Jane. 1988. 'The Transformative Value of Food: A Review Essay'. *Food and Foodways* 3: 143–66.

Feher, Michel. 1989. 'Introduction'. In *Fragments for a History of the Human Body*, part 1, ed. M. Feher, R. Naddaff and N. Tazi. New York: Zone.

Fischler, Claude. 1988. 'Food, Self, and Identity'. *Social Science Information* 27 (2): 275–92.

Florida, Nancy. 1996. 'Sex Wars: Writing Gender Relations in Nineteenth-Century Java'. In *Fantasizing the Feminine in Indonesia*, ed. L. J. Spears. Durham, NC: Duke University Press.

Fortier, Corinne. 2007. 'Blood, Sperm and the Embryo in Sunni Islam and in Mauritania: Milk Kinship, Descent, and Medically Assisted Procreation'. *Body & Society* 13 (3): 15–36.

Foster, Robert. 1990. 'Value without Equivalence: Exchange and Replacement in a Melanesian Society'. *Man* n.s. 25 (1): 54–6.

Foucault, Michel. 1973. *The Birth of the Clinic: An Archaeology of Medical Perception*. London: Tavistock Publications.

———. 1979. *Discipline and Punish: The Birth of the Prison*. Harmondsworth: Penguin Books.

Fox, James. 1971. 'Sister's Child as Plant: Metaphors in an Idiom of Consanguinity'. In *Rethinking Kinship and Marriage*, ed. R. Needham. London: Tavistock.

———. 1997. 'Place and Landscape in Comparative Austonesian Perspective'. In *The Poetic Power of Place: Comparative Perspectives on Austronesian Ideas of Locality*, ed. J. Fox. Canberra: Research School of Pacific and Asian Studies, Australian National University.

Freeman, Jonathan. 1960. 'The Iban of Western Borneo'. In *Social Structure in Southeast Asia*, ed. G. P. Murdoch. Chicago: Quadrangle Books.

———. 1970. *Report on the Iban*. London: Athlone Press.

Geertz, Clifford. 1960. *The Religion of Java*. Chicago: University of Chicago Press.

———. 1962. 'The Rotating Credit Association: A "Middle Rung" in Development'. *Economic Development and Cultural Change* 10 (3): 241–63.

———. 1963. *Agricultural Involution: The Process of Ecological Change in Indonesia*. Berkeley: University of California Press.

———. 1965. *The Social History of an Indonesian Town*. Cambridge, MA: MIT Press.

———. 1993. '"From the Native's Point of View": On the Nature of Anthropological Understanding'. In *Local Knowledge: Further Essays in Interpretative Anthropology*, ed. C. Geertz. London: HarperCollins.

Geertz, Hildred. 1961. *The Javanese Family. A Study of Kinship and Socialization*. New York: Free Press of Glencoe.

Geertz, Hildred and Clifford Geertz. 1964. 'Teknonymy in Bali: Parenthood, Age-Grading and Genealogical Amnesia'. *Journal of the Royal Anthropological Institute* 94 (2): 94–108.

Giambelli, Rodolfo. 1999. 'Working the Land. *Babad* as Forest Clearing and the Analogy between Land and Human Fertility in Nusa Penida (Bali)'. *Bijdragen tot de Taal-, Land- en Volkenkunde* 155 (4): 493–516.

Gibson, Thomas. 1985. 'The Sharing of Substance versus the Sharing of Activity among the Buid'. *Man* n.s. 20 (3): 391–411.

———. 1986. *Sacrifice and Sharing in the Philippine Highlands*. London: Athlone Press.

———. 1995. 'Having Your House and Eating It: Houses and Siblings in Ara, South Sulawesi'. In *About the House: Lévi-Strauss and Beyond*, ed. J. Carsten and S. Hugh-Jones. Cambridge: Cambridge University Press.

Gluckman, Max. 1956. *Custom and Conflict in Africa*. Oxford: Basil Blackwell.

Gonda, Jan. 1973. *Sanskrit in Indonesia*. New Delhi: International Academy of Indian Culture.

Gooszen, Hans. 1999. *A Demographic History of the Indonesian Archipelago, 1880–1942*. Leiden: KITLV Press.

Gow, Peter. 1991. *Of Mixed Blood. History and Kinship in Peruvian Amazonia*. Oxford: Oxford University Press.

Guinness, Patrick. 2009. *Kampung, Islam and State in Urban Java*. Singapore: Asian Association of Australia in association with NUS Press.

Haraway, Donna. 1991. *Simians, Cyborgs, and Women: The Reinvention of Nature*. London: Free Association.

———. 2003. *The Companion Species Manifesto: Dogs, People, and Significant Otherness*. Chicago: Prickly Paradigm Press.

———. 2008. *When Species Meet*. Minneapolis: University of Minnesota Press.

Hatley, Ron. 1984. 'Mapping Cultural Regions of Java'. In *Other Javas away from the Kraton*, ed. R. Hatley. Clayton: Monash University.

Headley, Stephen. 1997. 'The Islamization of Central Java: The Role of Muslim Lineages in Kalioso'. *Studia Islamika* 4 (2): 52–82.

———. 2004. *Durga's Mosque: Cosmology, Conversion, and Community in Central Javanese Islam*. Singapore: Institute of Southeast Asian Studies.

Hefner, R. 1985. *Hindu Javanese*. Princeton: Princeton University Press.

———. 1987. 'Islamizing Java? Religion and Politics in Rural East Java'. *Journal of Asian Studies* 46 (3): 533–54.

———. 1990. *The Political Economy of Mountain Java*. Berkeley: University of California Press.

———. 2000. *Civil Islam: Muslims and Democratization in Indonesia*. Princeton: Princeton University Press.

Heringa, Rens. 1997. 'Dewi Sri in Village Garb: Fertility, Myth, and Ritual in Northeast Java'. *Asian Folklore Studies* 56 (2): 355–77.

Hobsbawm, Eric and Terence Ranger, eds. 1992. *The Invention of Tradition*. Cambridge: Cambridge University Press.

Hooykaas, Christiaan. 1974. *Cosmogony and Creation in Balinese Tradition*. The Hague: M. Nijhoff.

Horne, Elinor. 1974. *Javanese-English Dictionary*. New Haven: Yale University Press.

Hoskins, Janet. 2002. 'The Menstrual Hat and the Witch's Lair in Two Eastern Indonesian Societies'. *Ethnology* 41 (4): 317–33.

Houseman, Micheal. 1988. 'Toward a Complex Model of Parenthood: Two African Tales'. *American Ethnologist* 15 (4): 658–77.

Howell, Julia D. 2001. 'Sufism and the Indonesian Islamic Revival'. *Journal of Asian Studies* 60 (3): 701–29.

———. 2005. 'Muslims, the New Age, and Marginal Religions in Indonesia: Changing Meanings of Religious Pluralism'. *Social Compass* 52 (4): 473–93.

———. 2010. 'Indonesia's Salafist Sufis'. *Modern Asian Studies* 44 (5): 1029–51.

Howell, Signe. 1995. 'Many Contexts, Many Meanings: Gendered Values Among the Northern Lio of Flores, Indonesia'. *Journal of the Royal Anthropological Institute* n.s. 2 (2): 253–69.

Hughes-Freeland, Felicia. 1997. 'Art and Politics: From Javanese Court Dance to Indonesian Art'. *Journal of the Royal Anthropological Institute* 3 (3): 473–95.

Hugo, Greame. 1982. 'Circular Migration in Indonesia'. *Population and Development Review* 8 (1): 59–83.

Husson, Laurence. 1990. 'Madura et le Carok: Violence Coutumière et Monde Moderne'. *Archipel* 40: 29–39.

———. 1995. *La Migration Madurese vers l'Est de Java*. Paris: L' Harmattan.

————. 1997. 'Eight Centuries of Madurese Migration to East Java'. *Asian and Pacific Migration Journal* 6 (1): 77–102.

Ida, Rachmah. 2005. *Sunat, Belenggu Adat Perempuan Madura*. Yogyakarta: Universitas Gadjah Mada.

Imron, Zawawi D. 1993. *Cerita Rakyat dari Madura*. Jakarta: Grasindo.

Ingold, Tim. 1991. 'Becoming Persons: Consciousness and Sociality in Human Evolution'. *Cultural Dynamics* 4 (3): 335–78.

————. 2000. *The Perception of the Environment*. London: Routledge.

————. 2009. 'Against Space: Place, Movement, Knowledge'. In *Boundless Worlds: An Anthropological Approach to Movement*, ed. P. Kirby. New York: Berghahn Books.

Jackson, Michael. 1983. 'Thinking Through the Body: An Essay on Understanding Metaphor'. *Social Analysis* 14 (1): 127–48.

Jaques, Kevin. 2006. 'Sejarah Leluhur: Hindu Cosmology and the Construction of Javanese Muslims Genealogical Authority'. *Journal of Islamic Studies* 17 (2): 129–57.

Jay, Robert. 1969. *Javanese Villagers: Social Relations in Rural Modjokuto*. Cambridge, MA: MIT Press.

Jellinek, Lea. 1978. 'Circular Migration and the Pondok Dwelling System: A Case Study of Ice-Cream Traders in Jakarta'. In *Food, Shelter and Transport in Southeast Asia and the Pacific*, ed. P. J. Rimmer, D. W. Drakakis-Smith and T. G. McGee. Canberra: Australian University Press.

Jordaan, Roy. 1985. 'Folk Medicine in Madura (Indonesia)'. PhD thesis, University of Leiden.

Jordaan, Roy and Anke Niehof. 1980. 'Aspects of Fishing in Patondu, a Village on the North Coast of Madura'. *Review of Indonesian and Malayan Affairs* 14 (1): 81–111.

Kammerer, Cornelia Ann. 1990. 'Customs and Christian Conversion among the Akha Highlanders of Burma and Thailand'. *American Ethnologist* 17 (2): 277–91.

Kano, Hiroyoshi. 1981. 'Employment Structure and Labour Migration in Rural Central Java: A Preliminary Observation'. *Developing Economies* 19 (4): 348–66.

Kapferer, Bruce. 1997. *The Feast of the Sorcerer: Practices of Consciousness and Power*. Chicago: University of Chicago Press.

Keane, Webb. 1994. 'The Value of Words and the Meaning of Things in Eastern Indonesian Exchange'. *Man* n.s. 29 (3): 605–29.

Keeler, Ward. 1987. *Javanese Shadow Plays, Javanese Selves*. Princeton: Princeton University Press.

————. 1990. 'Speaking of Gender in Java'. In *Power and Difference. Gender in Island Southeast Asia*, ed. J. M. Atkinson and S. Errington. Stanford: Stanford University Press.

Kipp, Rita Smith. 1986. 'Terms of Endearment: Karo Batak Lovers as Siblings'. *American Ethnologist* 13 (4): 632–45.

Koentjaraningrat, R. M. 1960. 'The Javanese of South Central Java'. In *Social Structure in Southeast Asia*, ed. G. P. Murcock. Chicago: Quadrangle Books.

————. 1989. *Javanese Culture*. Oxford, New York, Singapore: Oxford University Press.

Kumar, Ann. 1976. *Surapati: Man and Legend*. Leiden: E. J. Brill.

————. 1979. 'Javanese Historiography in and of the "Colonial Period": A Case Study'. In *Perceptions of the Past in Southeast Asia*, ed. A. Reid and D. Marr. Singapore: Heinemann Educational Books.

————. 1997. *Java and Modern Europe: Ambiguous Encounters*. Richmond: Curzon Press.

Kuntowijoyo. 1981. 'Social Change in an Agrarian Society: Madura, 1850–1940'. PhD thesis. Ann Arbor, MI: University Microfilms International.

————. 1986. 'The Noble and the Rich: The Decline of the Tributary Fiscal System of Madura in the Nineteenth Century'. In *Papers of the Fourth Indonesian-Dutch History Conference: Volume 1: Agrarian History*, ed. S. Katrodirdjo. Yogyakarta: Gadjah Mada University Press.

Kusnadi. 2001. *Pangamba' Kaum Perempuan Fenomenal: Pelopor dan Penggerak Perekonomian Masyarakat Nelayan*. Bandung: Humaniara Utama Press.

Kwee, Hui Kian. 2006. *The Political Economy of Java's North East Coast, c. 1740–1800: Elite Synergy*. Leiden: Brill.

Nabokov, Isabelle. 2000. 'Deadly Power: A Funeral to Counter Sorcery in South India'. *American Ethnologist* 27 (1): 147–68.

Newberry, Jan. 2006. *Back Door Java: State Formation and the Domestic in Working Class Java*. Peterborough, ON: Broadview Press.

————. 2007. 'Rituals of Rule in the Administered Community: Javanese Slametan Reconsidered'. *Modern Asian Studies* 41 (6): 1295–1329.

Lakoff, George and Mark Johnson. 1980. 'Conceptual Metaphor in Everyday Language'. *Journal of Philosophy* 77 (8): 453–86.

Latour, Bruno. 1993. *We Have Never Been Modern*. Cambridge, MA: Harvard University Press.

Leach, Edmund. 1970. *Political Systems of Highland Burma: A Study of Kachin Social Structure*. London: Athlone Press.

Lévi-Strauss, Claude. 1988. *The Way of the Masks*. Seattle: University of Washington Press.

Li, Tanya Murray. 1998. 'Working Separately but Eating Together: Personhood, Property, and Power in Conjugal Relations'. *American Ethnologist* 25 (4): 675–94.

Liddle, William. 1988. *Politics and Culture in Indonesia*. Ann Arbor: University of Michigan Press.

Lindsey, Tim. 2005. 'Reconstituting the Ethnic Chinese in Post-Suharto Indonesia: Law, Racial Discrimination, and Reform'. In *Chinese Indonesians: Remembering, Distorting, Forgetting*, ed. T. Lindsey and H. Pausacker. Singapore: Institute of Southeast Asian Studies.

Lombard, Denys. 1972. 'Les Nécropoles Princières de l'île de Madura'. *Bulletin de l' École Française d'Extrême-Orient* 59: 257–84.

McKinley, Robert. 1981. 'Cain and Abel on the Malay Penisula'. In *Siblingship in Oceania. Studies in the Meaning of Kin Relations*, ed. M. Marshall. ASAO Monographs. Lanham, MD: University Press of America.

Mansurnoor, Iik. 1990. *Islam in an Indonesian World: Ulama in Madura*. Yogyakarta: Gadjah Mada University Press.

Mauss, Marcel. 1970. *The Gift: Forms and Functions of Exchange in Archaic Societies*. London: Cohen & West.

————. 1985. 'A Category of the Human Mind: The Notion of Person; The Notion of Self'. In *The Category of the Person: Anthropology, Philosophy, History*, ed. M. Carrithers. Cambridge: Cambridge University Press.

Merleau-Ponty, Maurice. 1962. *Phenomenology of Perception*. London: Routledge & Kegan Paul.

————. 1968. *The Visible and the Invisible*. Evaston, IL: Northwestern University Press.

Möller, André. 2005. *Ramadan in Java: The Joy and Jihad of Ritual Fasting*. Lund: Department of History and Anthropology of Religions, Lund University.

Moore, Henrietta. 1994. *A Passion for Difference: Essays on Anthropology and Gender*. London: Polity Press.

Newberry, Jan. 2006. *Back Door Java: State Formation and the Domestic in Working Class Java*. Peterborough, ON: Broadview Press.

Niehof, Anke. 1982. 'The Island of Madura: A Deceptive Unity'. In *Focus on the Region in Asia*, ed. O. van den Muijzenberg, R. Streefland and W. Wolters. Rotterdam: Erasmus University Rotterdam Press.

————. 1985. *Women and Fertility in Madura*. PhD thesis, University of Leiden.

————. 1992. 'Madurese Women as Brides and Wives'. In *Indonesian Women in Focus: Past and Present Notions*, ed. A. Locher-Scholten and A. Niehof. Leiden: KITLV Press.

Nietzsche, Friedrich Wilhelm. 1967. *On the Genealogy of Morals*. New York: Vintage.

————. 1969. *Thus Spoke Zarathustra*. Harmondsworth: Penguin Books.

Nourse, Jennifer. 1999. *Conceiving Spirits: Birth Rituals and Contested Identities among Laujé of Indonesia*. Washington, DC: Smithsonian Institution Press.

Oetomo, Dede. 1996. 'Gender and Sexual Orientation in Indonesia'. In *Fantasizing the Feminine in Indonesia*, ed. L. J. Spears. Durham, NC: Duke University Press.

Ong, Aihwa. 1989. 'Center, Periphery and Hierarchy: Gender in Southeast Asia'. In *Gender and Anthropology: Critical Reviews for Research and Teaching*, ed. S. Morgen. Washington, DC: American Anthropological Association.

Osella, Caroline and Filippo Osella. 1999. 'Seepage of Divinised Power through Social, Spiritual and Bodily Boundaries'. *Purusartha – La Possession en Asie du Sud: Parole Corps Territoire* 21: 183–210.

Overring, Joanna and Alan Passes. 2000. 'Introduction: Convivial Intimacy and the Opening up of Amazonian Anthropology'. In *The Anthropology of Love and Anger: The Aesthetics of Conviviality in Native Amazonia*, ed. J. Overring and A. Passes. London: Routledge.

Parkes, Peter. 2005. 'Milk Kinship in Islam: Substance, Structure, History'. *Social Anthropology* 13 (3): 307–29.

Peletz, Michael. 1993. 'Knowledge, Power, and Personal Misfortune in a Malay Context'. In *Understanding Witchcraft and Sorcery in Southeast Asia*, ed. R. Ellen and C. W. Watson. Honolulu: University of Hawaii Press.

————. 1996. *Reason and Passion: Representations of Gender in a Malay Society*. Berkeley: University of California Press.

Pemberton, John. 1994. *On the Subject of 'Java'*. Ithaca, NY: Cornell University Press.

Peper, Bram. 1970. 'Population Growth in Java in the Nineteenth Century: A New Interpretation'. *Population Studies* 24 (1): 71–84.

Peluso, Nancy. 1992. *Rich Forests, Poor People: Resource Control and Resistance in Java*. Berkeley: University of California Press.

Peluso, Nancy and Emily Harwell. 2001. 'Territory, Custom, and the Cultural Politics of Ethnic War in West Kalimantan Indonesia'. In *Violent Environments*, ed. N. L. Peluso and M. Watts. Ithaca, NY: Cornell University Press.

Pigeaud, Theodore. 1960–63. *Java in the Fourteenth Century: A Study in Cultural History*, 5 vols. The Hague: Martinus Nijhoff.

————. 1967. *Literature of Java. Catalogue Raisonné of Javanese Manuscripts in the Library of the University of Leiden and other Public Collections in the Netherlands*, vol.1. The Hague: Martinus Nijhoff.

Pinard, Sylvain. 1991. 'A Taste of India: On the Role of Gestation in the Hindu Sensorium'. In *The Varieties of Sensory Experience: A Sourcebook in the Anthropology of the Senses*, ed. D. Howes. Toronto: University of Toronto Press.

Priest, Stephen. 1998. *Merleau-Ponty*. London: Routledge.

Raffles, Thomas Stamford. 1830. *The History of Java*, vol. 2. London: John Murray.

Rajah, Ananda. 2005. 'Political Assassination by Other Means: Public Protest, Sorcery, and Morality in Thailand'. *Journal of Southeast Asian Studies* 36 (1): 111–29.

Rasanayagam, Johan. 2006. 'Healing with Spirits and the Formation of Muslim Selfhood in Post-Soviet Uzbekistan'. *Journal of the Royal Anthropological Institute* n.s. 12 (2): 377–93.

Retsikas, Konstantinos. 2006. 'The Semiotics of Violence: Ninja, Sorcerers, and State Terror in Post-Soeharto Indonesia'. *Bijdragen tot de Taal-, Land- en Volkenkunde* 162 (1): 56–94.

———. 2007a. 'Being and Place: Movement, Ancestors, and Personhood in East Java, Indonesia'. *Journal of the Royal Anthropological Institute* 13(4): 969–86.

———. 2007b. 'The Power of the Senses: Ethnicity, History, and Embodiment in East Java. Indonesia'. *Indonesia and the Malay World* 35 (102): 183–210.

———. 2008. 'Knowledge from the Body: Fieldwork, Power, and the Acquisition of a New Self'. In *Knowing How to Know: Fieldwork and the Ethnographic Present*, ed. N. Halstead, E. Hirsch and J. Okely. Oxford: Berghahn.

———. 2010a. 'Unconscious Culture and Conscious Nature: Exploring East Javanese Conceptions of the Person through Bourdieu's Lenses'. *Journal of the Royal Anthropological Institute* 16 (1): s140–s157.

———. 2010b. 'The Sorcery of Gender: Sex, Death, and Difference in East Java, Indonesia'. *South East Asia Research* 18 (3): 471–502.

Ricklefs, Merle Calvin. 1981. *A History of Modern Indonesia: c. 1300 to the Present*. Bloomington: Indiana University Press.

———. 2007. *Polarizing Javanese Society: Islamic, and Other Visions, 1830–1930*. Honolulu: University of Hawaii Press.

Rao, Aparna. 2000. 'Blood, Milk, and Mountains: Marriage Practice and Concepts of Predictability among the Bakkarwal of Jammu and Kashmir'. In *Culture, Creation and Procreation. Concepts of Kinship in South Asian Practice*, ed. M. Bock and A. Rao. New York: Berghahn Books.

Robson, Stuart. 1987. 'The Terminology of Javanese Kinship'. *Bijdragen tot de Taal-, Land- en Volkenkunde* 143 (4): 507–18.

Ross, Laurie. 2005. 'Mask, Gender, and Performance in Indonesia: An Interview with Didik Nini Thowok'. *Asian Theatre Journal* 22 (2): 214–26.

Sahlins, Marshall. 1972. *Stone Age Economics*. New York: Aldine De Gruyter.

Sairin, Sjafri. 1982. *Javanese Trah: Kin-Based Social Organisation*. Yogyakarta: Gadja Mada University Press.

Santos-Granero, Fernando. 2007. 'Of Fear and Friendship: Amazonian Sociality beyond Kinship and Affinity'. *Journal of the Royal Anthropological Institute* n.s. 13 (1): 1–18.

Schulte Nordholt, Henk, ed. 1997. *Outward Appearances: Dressing State and Society in Indonesia*. Leiden: KITLV Press.

Schimmel, Annemarie. 1975. *Mystical Dimensions of Islam*. Chapel Hill: North Carolina University Press.

———. 1994. *Deciphering the Signs of God: A Phenomenological Approach to Islam*. Edinburgh: Edinburgh University Press.

Schrauwers, Albert. 2000. 'Three Weddings and a Performance: Marriage, Households, and Development in the Highlands of Central Sulawesi, Indonesia'. *American Ethnologist*. 27 (4): 855–76.

———. 2004. 'H(h)ouses, E(e)states, and Class: On the Importance of Capitals in Central Sulawesi'. *Bijdragen tot de Taal-, Land- en Volkenkunde* 160 (1): 72–94.

Siegel, James. 2001. 'Thoughts on the Violence of May 13 and 14, 1998, in Jakarta'. In *Violence and the State in Suharto's Indonesia*, ed. B. Anderson. Ithaca, NY: South-East Asia Program Publications, Cornell University.

————. 2005. *Naming the Witch*. Stanford: Stanford University Press.

Slaney, Frances. 1997. 'Double Baptism: Personhood and Ethnicity in the Sierra Tarahumara of Mexico'. *American Ethnologist* 24 (2): 279–310.

Smith, Jane. 1980. 'Concourse Between the Living and the Dead in Islamic Eschatological Literature'. *History of Religions* 19 (3): 224–36.

Smith, Jane and Yvonne Yazbeck Haddad. 1981. *The Islamic Understanding of Death and Resurrection*. Albany: State University of New York Press.

Smith-Henfer, Nancy. 1989. 'A Social History of Language Change in Highland East Java'. *Journal of Asian Studies* 48 (2): 257–71.

Speare, Alden Jr and John Harris. 1986. 'Education, Earnings and Migration in Indonesia'. *Economic Development and Cultural Change* 34 (2): 223–44.

Spies, Otoo. 2007. 'Mahr'. In *Encyclopaedia of Islam*, ed. P. Bearman, T. Bianquis, C. E. Bosworth, E. van Donzel and W. P. Heinrichs. Brill Online (subscription required). http://www.brillonline.nl/subscriber/entry?entry=islam_SIM-4806 (accessed 19 July 2007).

Soedarsono. 1969. 'Classical Javanese Dance: History and Characterisation'. *Ethnomusicology* 13 (3): 498–506.

Stange, Paul. 1984. 'The Logic of Rasa in Java'. *Indonesia* 38: 113–34.

Stoller, Paul. 1984. 'Sound in Songhay Cultural Experience'. *American Ethnologist* 11 (3): 559–70.

Strathern, Andrew and Micheal Lambek. 1998. 'Introduction. Embodying Sociality: Africanist-Melanesianist Comparisons'. In *Bodies and Persons: Comparative Perspectives from Africa and Melanesia*, ed. A. Strathern and M. Lambek. Cambridge: Cambridge University Press.

Strathern, Marilyn. 1988. *The Gender of the Gift. Problems with Women and Problems with Society in Melanesia*. Berkeley: University of California Press.

————. 1991. *Partial Connections*. Maryland: Rowman & Littlefield.

————. 1992. 'Parts and Wholes: Refiguring Relationships in a Post-Plural World'. In *Conceptualizing Society*, ed. A. Kuper. London: Routledge.

————. 1995. *The Relation: Issues in Complexity and Scale*. Cambridge: Prickly Pear Press.

————. 1999. *Property, Substance and Effect: Anthropological Essays on Persons and Things*. London: Athlone Press.

————. 2005. *Kinship, Law and the Unexpected: Relatives are Always a Surprise*. Cambridge: Cambridge University Press.

Sullivan, Norma. 1994. *Masters and Managers: A Study of Gender Relations in Urban Java*. Sydney: Allen & Unwin.

Suryadinata, Leo. 1992. *Pribumi Indonesians, the Chinese Minority, and China*. Singapore: Heinemann Asia.

Sutherland, Heather. 1979. *The Making of a Bureaucratic Elite: The Colonial Transformation of the Javanese Priyayi*. Singapore: Heinemann Educational Books.

Sviri, Sara. 2002. 'The Self and its Transformation in Sufism'. In *Self and Self-Transformation in the History of Religions*, ed. D. Shulman and G. Stroumsa. Oxford: Oxford University Press.

Taylor, Jean Gelman. 1997. 'Costume and Gender in Colonial Java, 1800–1940'. In *Outward Appearances: Dressing State and Society in Indonesia*, ed. H. Schulte Nordholt. Leiden: KITLV Press.

Telle, Kari. 2000. 'Feeding the Dead: Reformulating Sasak Mortuary Practices'. *Bijdragen tot de Taal-, Land- en Volkenkunde* 156 (4): 771–805.

Tjiptoatmodjo, Sutjipto. 1983. 'Kota-kota Pantai di sekitar Selat Madura (Abad 17 sampai Medio Abad 19)'. PhD thesis, Universitas Gadjah Mada, Yogyakarta.

Tooker, Deborah. 1992. 'Identity Systems of Highland Burma: "Belief", Akha Zah, and a Critique of Interiorized Notions of Ethno-religious Identity'. *Man* n.s. 27 (4): 799–819.

Tsintjilonis, Dimitri. 1997. 'Embodied Difference: The "Body-Person" of the Sa'dan Toraja'. *Bijdragen tot de Taal-, Land- en Volkenkunde* 153 (2): 243–72.

Tsuchiya, Kenji. 1990. 'Javanology and the Age of Ranggawarsita: An Introduction to Nineteenth-century Javanese Culture'. In *Reading Southeast Asia: Translation of Contemporary Japanese Scholarship on Southeast Asia*, ed. T. Shiraishi. Ithaca, NY: Cornell University Press.

Turner, Victor. 1957. *Schism and Continuity in an African Society.* Manchester: Manchester University Press.

Ullmann, Manfred. 1978. *Islamic Medicine.* Edinburgh: Edinburgh University Press.

Van Bruinessen, Martin. 1994. *Tarekat Naqsyabandiyah di Indonesia: Survei Historis, Geographis, dan Sosiologis.* Bandung: Mizan.

———. 1995. 'Tarekat and Tarekat Teachers in Madurese Society'. In *Across the Madura Straits: The Dynamics of an Insular Society*, ed. K. van Dijk, H. de Jonge and E. Touwen-Bouwsma. Leiden: KITLV Press.

Van Dijk, Kees, Huub de Jonge and Elly Touwen-Bouwsma. 1995. 'Introduction'. In *Across Madura Strait: The Dynamics of an Insular Society*, ed. K. van Dijk, H. de Jonge and E. Touwen-Bouwsma. Leiden: KITLV Press.

Van Niel, Robert. 2005. *Java's Northeast Coast, 1740–1840: A Study in Colonial Encroachment and Dominance.* Leiden: CNWS Publications.

Viveiros de Castro, Eduardo. 1996. 'Images of Nature and Society in Amazonian Ethnology'. *Annual Review of Anthropology* 25: 179–200.

———. 1998. 'Cosmological Deixis and Amerindian Perspectivism'. *Journal of the Royal Anthropological Institute* n.s. 4 (3): 469–88.

———. 2007. 'Transversal Shamanism: Form and Force in Amazonian Cosmopolitics'. Lecture delivered at Cambridge University, 31 October.

———. 2009. 'The Gift and the Given: Three Nano-Essays on Kinship and Magic'. In *Kinship and Beyond: The Genealogical Model Reconsidered*, ed. S. Bamford and J. Leach. Oxford: Berghahn Books.

———. 2010. 'Intensive Filiation and Demonic Alliance'. In *Deleuzian Intersections in Science, Technology and Anthropology*, ed. K. Rodje and C. B. Jensen. Oxford: Berghahn.

Warner, Micheal. 2000. *The Trouble with Normal.* Cambridge, MA: Harvard University Press.

Warsito, Pak. 1994. 'Sejarah Nama Desa dan Upacara Bersih Desa'. Unpublished report. Departemen Pendidikan dan Kebudayaan, Kodya Probolinggo.

Waterson, Roxanne. 1990. *The Living House: An Anthropology of Architecture in South-East Asia.* Kuala Lumpur: Oxford University Press.

Werbner, Pnina. 2003. *Pilgrims of Love: The Anthropology of a Global Sufi Cult.* London: Hurst & Company.

Werbner, Pnina and Helene Basu. 1998. 'The Embodiment of Charisma'. In *Embodying Charisma: Modernity, Locality, and the Performance of Emotion in Sufi Cults*, ed. P. Werbner and H. Basu. London: Routledge.

Wessing, Robert. 1995. 'The Last Tiger in East Java: Symbolic Continuity in Ecological Change'. *Asian Folklore Studies* 54 (2): 191–218.

———. 1996. 'Rumours of Sorcery at an Indonesian University'. *Journal of Southeast Asian Studies* 27 (2): 261–79.

Wiener, Margaret. 2007. 'Dangerous Liaisons and other Tales from the Twilight Zone: Sex, Race, and Sorcery in Colonial Java'. *Comparative Studies in Society and History* 49 (3): 495–526.

Wikan, Unni. 1987. 'Public Grace and Private Fears: Gaiety, Offence, and Sorcery in Northern Bali'. *Ethos* 15 (4): 337–65.

Wilson, Ian. 2007. 'Reog Ponorogo: Spirituality, Sexuality, and Power in a Javanese Performance Tradition'. In *Intersections: Gender, History, and Culture in the Asian Context* 2 (electronic journal). http://wwwsshe.murdoch.edu.au/intersections/issue2/Warok.html (accessed 3 July 2007).

White, Benjamin. 1976. 'Population, Involution and Employment in Rural Java'. *Development and Change* 7 (2): 267–90.

Woodward, Mark. 1988. 'The *Slametan*: Textual Knowledge and Ritual Performance in Central Javanese Islam'. *History of Religions* 28 (1): 54–89.

———. 1989. *Islam in Java: Normative Piety and Mysticism in the Sultanate of Yogyakarta*. Tucson: University of Arizona Press.

Zoetmulder, Petrus. 1995. *Pantheism and Monism in Javanese Suluk Literature*. Leiden: KITLV Press.

INDEX

Page numbers in boldface refer to figures.

www.ingramcontent.com/pod-product-compliance
Lightning Source LLC
Chambersburg PA
CBHW030836300326
41935CB00036B/172